AF540274

# Mac OS and Programming

# Mac OS and Programming

Pinkesh Anand

CENTRUM PRESS
NEW DELHI-110002 (INDIA)

**CENTRUM PRESS**
**H.O.:** 4360/4, Ansari Road, Daryaganj,
New Delhi-110002 (India)
Tel: 23278000, 23261597, 23255577, 23286875
**B.O.:** No. 1015, Ist Main Road, BSK IIIrd Stage,
IIIrd Phase, IIIrd Block, Bangalore-560085 (INDIA)
Tel: 080-41723429
*Email:* centrumpress@gmail.com
*Visit us at:* www.centrumpress.com

*Mac OS and Programming*



First Edition, 2011

PRINTED IN INDIA

---

*Printed at* Tarun Offset Printers, Delhi-110053

# Contents

*Preface* *vii*

1. Origins 1

2. Remote OS Detection 24

3. XCG Programing 72

4. Cocoa Programming 110

5. Mac Printing 126

6. Xnu Kernel 141

7. OSX Memory 155

8. Interprocess Communication 198

9. Building and Debugging Kernels 220

10. Performance 239

*Bibliography* 267

*Index* 269

# Preface

Modern operating systems have become so large and complex that it is impossible to reasonably describe an entire system in a book. This book is somewhat ambitious in that it attempts to cover Mac OS X in substantial breadth and depth. The most important contributors to the book's depth are the carefully selected programming examples.

With the arrival of Mac OS X, Apple recommends that all new applications be written using Cocoa. Cocoa is a powerful collection of tools and libraries that will make writing new programs a much faster process.

The reader is not expected to have any experience with Mac programming. It is a hands-on book and assumes that the reader has access to Mac OS X and the developer tools. As a programmer, a solid understanding of system internals is immensely useful in design, development, and debugging.

The purpose of this book is to deconstruct and demystify Mac OS X by describing it from a system-design perspective. It takes an implementation-oriented approach to understanding the system. Consider the example of Interprocess Communication (IPC) Rather than just showing how to use these mechanisms, the book explains the design and implementation of the most fundamental mechanism (Mach IPC), and then discusses how the other mechanisms are layered on top of one another.

Application programmers can gain a deeper understanding of how their applications interact with the system. System programmers can use the book as a reference and to construct a better picture of how the core system works.

*Author*

# 1

# Origins

## RUNNING ORIGIN/ORIGINPRO ON AN MAC

Did you know you can run Origin/OriginPro on a Mac? Using a virtualization software, you can easily install and run Origin and OriginPro on a Macintosh computer from Apple. This page outlines what you will need and shows you how easy it is to get started.

*Installing the Origin and OriginPro software on a Mac computer requires the following:*

- *An Intel-based Mac*: MacBook, MacBook Pro, iMac, Mac Pro, Mac Mini.
- *Virtualization software*: VMWare Fusion or Parallels Desktop.
- *Microsoft Windows*: 2000, XP, Microsoft Vista, or Windows 7.
- Origin or OriginPro.
- Install the virtualization software on your Mac computer.
- Using the virtualization software, create a new virtual computer and install Windows on the virtual computer.
- Run the virtual computer on which Windows is installed. When Windows is ready, install Origin.

## USING THE VIRTUALIZATION SOFTWARE, YOU CAN

Seamlessly run Origin as an application on your Mac desktop. Drag-and-drop an OPJ from a Mac folder onto the

Origin workspace. Export graphs and other output from Origin to a folder in the Windows partition, and then drag-and-drop the exported file onto Mac applications

## TIPS FOR RUNNING ORIGIN ON MAC

### What License Types are Supported Using This Configuration

ALL license types have been found to run successfully on an Intel-based Mac using virtualization software. This includes node-locked, dongle-managed, and concurrent licenses.

### Why Can't I Paste the Licence Text from the Web Page Onto the Origin Dialog

Note that the shortcut keys for copy and paste are different for Mac (cmd+c and cmd+v) and for Windows (ctrl+c and ctrl+v). If you copied the licence text from browser running on Mac OS using cmd+c, you should use ctrl+v to paste the text onto the Origin dialog.

### Can I Paste an Origin Graph to Word as an OLE Embedded Object

If you are runnin g Word for Mac, then the pasted object is treated only as an image and you cannot double-click the image to open the Origin project. If, on the other hand, you are running Word on the Windows partition, then you can OLE-paste your graph from Origin onto Word.

### How Do I Exchange Files Between Mac and Windows

Just drag-and-drop the file between the Mac and Windows partitions! The virtual machine creates a copy when a file is dragged and dropped in either direction.

You could thus easily open an OPJ by dragging and dropping the file from a Mac folder right onto the Origin workspace.

Similarly, you can export a graph from Origin to a folder in the Windows partition and then drag-and-drop the exported file to a Mac application for publication purposes.

## A BRIEF HISTORY OF MAC OS X

The goal of this document is not to trace the history of Mac OS X in great detail, so this section would be brief. A more extensive history of Apple's operating systems is covered in *A History of Apple's Operating Systems.*

All of Steve Jobs' operational responsibilities at Apple were "taken away" on May 31, 1985. Soon (within weeks), Jobs had come up with an idea for a startup for which he pulled in five other Apple employees. The idea was to create the *perfect* research computer (for Universities and research labs). Jobs had earlier met up with Nobel laureate biochemist Paul Berg, who had jumped at Jobs' suggestion of using a computer for various simulations. Although Apple *was* interested in investing in Jobs' startup, they were outraged (and*sued* Jobs) when they learnt about the five Apple employees joining Jobs. Apple dropped the suit later after some subsequent mutual agreements. The startup was NeXT Computer, Inc.

Jobs unveiled the first NeXT Computer (running NEXTSTEP 0.8) on October 12, 1988, in San Francisco, although a mature release of the operating system took another year. The name "NEXTSTEP" has gone through a number of capitalization permutations, so we shall simply use "NEXTSTEP". NEXTSTEP 1.0 shipped on September 18, 1989, over two years later than what Jobs had first predicted and hoped for. NEXTSTEP was based on Mach 2.5 and 4.3BSD, and had an advanced GUI system based on Postscript. It used Objective-C as its native programming language, and included the NeXT Interface Builder.

In the fall of 1990, the first web browser (offering WYSIWYG browsing *and* authoring) was created at CERN by Tim Berners-Lee on a NeXT computer. Tim's collaborator, Robert Cailliau, later went on to say that "*... Tim's prototype implementation on NeXTStep is made in the space of a few months, thanks to the qualities of the NeXTStep software development system...*"

NEXTSTEP 2.0 was released exactly a year later on September 18, 1990 (with support for CD-ROMs, colour monitors, NFS, on-the-fly spell checking, dynamically loadable device drivers...). 2.1 followed on March 25, 1991, and 3.0 in September, 1992.

In the 1992 NeXTWORLD Expo, NEXTSTEP 486, a version (costing $995) for the PC was announced. Versions 3.1 and 3.2 were released in May and October, 1993, respectively. The last version of NEXTSTEP, 3.3, was released in February, 1995. A bit earlier, in 1994, NeXT and Sun had jointly released specifications for OpenStep, an open platform (comprised of several APIs and frameworks) that anybody could use to create their own implementation of *STEP. NeXT's implementation was named OPENSTEP, the successor to the NEXTSTEP operating system. Three versions of OPENSTEP were ever released: 4.0 (July 22, 1996), 4.1 (December, 1996), and 4.2 (January, 1997). SunOS, HP-UX, and even Windows NT had implementations at a point. The GNUstep Project still exists. Even though *STEP ran on many architectures (multi-architecture "fat binaries" were introduced by NeXT), by 1996, things were not looking good for them, and NeXT was giving more importance to *WebObjects*, a development tool for the Web.

Meanwhile, Apple had been desperately seeking to create an operating system that could compete with the onslaught from Microsoft. They actually wanted to beat Windows 95 to market, but failed. Apple suffered a setback when *Pink OS*, a joint venture between IBM and Apple, was killed in 1995. Apple eventually started work on an advanced operating system codenamed *Copland*, which was first announced to the public in 1994. The first beta of Copland went out in November, 1995, but a 1996 release (as planned and hoped) did not seem feasible. Soon afterwards, Apple announced that they would start shipping "pieces of Copland technology" beginning with System 7.6. Copland turned out to be a damp squib.

At this point Apple became interested in buying Be, a company that was becoming popular as the maker of the BeBox, running the BeOS. The deal between Apple's Gil Amelio and Be's Gassée never materialized-it has been often reported that Apple offered $125 million while Be wanted an "outrageous" $200 million plus. The total investment in Be at that time was estimated to be only $20 million! Apple then considered Windows NT, Solaris and even Pink OS. Then, Steve Jobs called Amelio, and advised him that Be was not a good fit for Apple's OS roadmap. NeXT contacted Apple to discuss possibilities of licensing OPENSTEP, which, unlike BeOS, had at least been proven in the market. Jobs pitched NeXT technology very strongly to Apple, and asserted that OPENSTEP was many years ahead of its time. All this worked out, and Apple acquired NeXT in February, 1997, for $427 million. Amelio later quipped that *"We choose Plan A instead of Plan Be."*

Apple named its upcoming NeXT-based system *Rhapsody*, while it continued to improve the existing Mac OS, often with technology that was supposed to go into Copland. Rhapsody saw two developer releases, in September, 1997, and May, 1998.

Jobs became the interim CEO of Apple on September 16, 1997. Mac OS X was first mentioned in Apple's OS strategy announcement at the 1998 WWDC. Jobs said that OS X would ship in the fall of 1999, and would inherit from both Mac OS and Rhapsody. Moreover, backward compatibility would be maintained to ease customers into the transition.

## ARCHITECTURE OF MAC OS X

Mac OS X did come out in 1999, as Mac OS X Server 1.0 (March 16, 1999), a developer preview of the desktop version, and as Darwin 0.1. Mac OS X beta was released on September 13, 2000. At the time of this writing, Mac OS X has seen four major releases: 10.0 ("Cheetah", March 24, 2001), 10.1 ("Puma", September 29, 2001), 10.2 ("Jaguar", August 13, 2002), and 10.3 ("Panther", October 24, 2003). It would be an understatement to say that OS X is derived from NEXTSTEP and OPENSTEP. In many respects, it's not just similar, it's the *same*. One can think of it as OpenStep 5 or 6, say. This is not a bad thing at all-rather than create an operating system from scratch, Apple tried to do the *smart* thing, and used what they already had to a great extent. However, the similarities should not mislead you: Mac OS X is evolved enough that what you can do with it is far above and beyond NEXTSTEP/OPENSTEP. While unrelated to Mac OS X, Apple came out with their version of UNIX, called A/UX, in 1988. A/UX was a POSIX compliant system based on AT&T UNIX System V (various releases) and BSD4.2/4.3, with a wide spectrum of features (STREAMS, TCP/IP, FFS, job control, NFS with YP, SCCS, printing, X Window System, compatibility with SYSV and BSD in addition to POSIX, and so on). More importantly, A/UX*combined* various features of the Macintosh with Unix-A/UX 3.x was a combination of the above mentioned Unix features with System 7 for the Macintosh, with the Finder and other Mac applications running under A/UX. The last version of A/UX, 3.1.1, was released in 1995. A/UX was regarded as the*holy grail* of Unices by some people.

## ARCHITECTURE OF MAC OS X

This page briefly describes the architecture of Mac OS X and the Mac's firmware. Description of an operating system in reasonable detail would take up one or more books, which this page is not. Consider it as a high-level description of some low-level details, if you will. As mentioned in A Brief History of Mac OS X, Mac OS X is a descendent of NEXTSTEP. We shall not point out any further similarities or differences between Mac OS X and these earlier systems.

## DARWIN

The first version of Darwin, 0.1, was released on March 16, 1999 as a fork of a developer release of Rhapsody. Although Darwin is an operating system in itself, it can be best understood as a collection of technologies that have been integrated by Apple to form a major, central part of Mac OS X. Critical application environments of Mac OS X, such as Cocoa and Carbon, are not part of Darwin. So isn't Aqua, the overall GUI of Mac OS X (including the Windowing System), and several other components.

## CONTENTS

Darwin 7.0.x (corresponding to Mac OS X 10.3.x) consists

of over 250 packages. Many of these are Apple packages (including the Mac OS X kernel and various drivers), while the others originate from *BSD, GNU, etc. Apple has leveraged a lot of existing open source software by integrating it well (usually) with their system: apache, bind, binutils, cvs, gcc, gdb, gimp_print, kerberos, mysql, openssh, openssl, pam, perl, postfix, ppp, python, rsync, samba, and many more BSD/GNU/ other packages... are all part of Darwin. In many cases, Apple has made important modifications to open source code to optimize/adapt it to their platform (consider gcc and gdb). Moreover, even though one can always configure and control such software "as usual" (editing their configuration file in vi or emacs, say), Apple provides simplified user interfaces that work well for at least the not-so-contrived cases.

An indicator of how well Apple has made use of existing open source software is the large number of sources Darwin draws from: *BSD, GNU, Mach... and even Linux./usr/sbin/ pcsd is a daemon used to dynamically allocate/deallocate Smart Card reader drivers at runtime and manage connection to the readers. This, and related tools, are taken from the MUSCLE (Movement for the Use of Smart Cards in a Linux Environment) Project. The much advertised "Secure Trash Deletion" is a simple adaptation of the open source srm utility (it has been extended to support named forks, for example). Such eclecticism in ingesting technology from various sources and wrapping/integrating it to create a uniform effect is one of the great strengths of Mac OS X.

## PORTABILITY

Darwin runs on the PowerPC and x86 platforms. What's more, it is even possible to build a "fat" kernel, containing both platform executables in a single file.

## LICENSING

Darwin packages that are originally from Apple are usually covered under the Apple Public Source License (APSL). The current version (2.0) of APSL qualifies as a free software license, although it is not compatible with the GPL.

The Free Software Foundation offers its views on APSL on their web site. The GNU-Darwin Project aims to leverage the combination of Darwin and GNU. OpenDarwin is an Apple co-founded effort for fostering cooperative Darwin development. You can download bootable Darwin CD images for both the PowerPC and x86 platforms from these projects' web sites.

## LAYERS

The pieces of software that constitute Mac OS X can be grouped into logical layers as shown below:

## FIRMWARE

The Mac firmware and the Mac OS X bootloader are described in the section Booting Mac OS X.

## XNU: THE KERNEL

XNU, the Mac OS X kernel, is described in XNU: The Kernel. The kernel and its extensions make up the Kernel Environment, the lowest (most fundamental) layer of Mac OS X (the firmware and the bootloader are not technically parts of Mac OS X).

## HIGHER LEVEL SERVICES AND ENVIRONMENTS

Still higher layers of Mac OS X are described in the section Above the Kernel.

## HIGHER LEVEL SYSTEM STARTUP

Mac OS X System Startup describes the user-level sequence of events that happen when Mac OS X boots.

## BOOTING MAC OS X

This page contains a brief description of the Mac's firmware (analogous to the PC BIOS in many respects), the bootloader, and the typical Mac OS X boot up sequence. There are significant differences between how older (68k, "Old World" PowerMacs) and newer (everything currently, but essentially "New World" machines with Open Firmware 3.x that *load* ROM from a file) boot. The discussion here applies to the newer systems. The firmware is not part of Mac OS X, but it plays an important role in the operation of the machine, and is useful in debugging. Hence, we discuss it here.

## OPEN FIRMWARE

### Background

Open Firmware (*IEEE-1275 Standard for Boot Firmware: Core Requirements and Practices*) is a non-proprietary, platform (CPU and system) independent boot firmware. Similar to a PC's BIOS, Open Firmware is stored in ROM and is the first stored program to be executed upon power-up.

An Open Firmware implementation is based on the Forth programming language, in particular, the FCode dialect (FCode is an ANS Forth compliant dialect that supports compilation of FCode source to bytecode). Apple and Sun are two prominent computer system makers that use implementations of Open Firmware in their systems (Sun's trademark is called *OpenBoot*). The Open Firmware Working Group's home page is hosted at various places, including Apple and Sun.

Thus, the firmware is implemented in Forth, and stored in the ROM as FCode bytecode. Device drivers that are required during system startup are also implemented similarly. Such drivers usually exist in the expansion ROM of expansion cards that are needed before the operating system has loaded.

### Interaction

Enter Open Firmware by pressing the key combination cmd-opt-O-F just as you power on a Macintosh. The cmd key is the one with the Apple logo, and the opt (option) key is the same as the alt key. You should see a welcome message and some other verbiage, and should be dropped into a prompt like the following:

```
ok
0 >
```

You can continue booting the machine by typing mac-boot, or shut it down by typing shut-down. Even though this Forth "shell" supports reasonable (for a BIOS) command line editing (you can use ctrl-ato go to the beginning of a line, ctrl-e to go to the end, ctrl-u to erase a line, the up-arrow key for history, etc.), you would find it more convenient (particularly if you are trying to *write* any code in the firmware) to access a Mac's Open Firmware from another (arbitrary) computer, over the network.

Here is the command sequence to do this (everything is typed at the Open Firmware prompt, unless stated otherwise):

```
0 > dev/packages/telnet
```

Note that upon success, Open Firmware prints the string "ok" on the *same line* as you press <return>. In the examples on this page, if you see ok, remember that it is printed by Open Firmware and you are not supposed to type it in (it's not a valid Open Firmware word anyway).

*If your Mac's Open Firmware includes the telnet package, you would see:*

```
0 > dev/packages/telnet ok
```

If you do get an ok, you can run a TELNET server on it:

```
" enet:telnet,10.0.0.1" io
```

This would run a TELNET server on the machine with IP address 10.0.0.1 (you can and should choose any appropriate address). Thereafter, you can connect to Open Firmware on this machine using a TELNET client-say, from a Windows machine.

For a programming example. Note that current (at least G4 and above) Apple computers come with Ethernet ports that are auto-sensing and self-configuring, so you do *not* need a cross-over cable to connect it directly to another computer (no hub is required, etc.).

### *Examples*

- *The following command prints the device tree:*

```
0 > dev/ls
ff880d90:/cpus
ff881068:/PowerPC,750@0
ff881488:/l2-cache
ff882148:/chosen
ff882388:/memory@0
ff882650:/openprom
ff882828:/client-services
...
More[<space>,<cr>,q,a]? _
```

- *The following command gives you information about installed RAM:*

```
0 > dev/memory.properties ok
name            memory
device_type     memory
reg             00000000 10000000
                10000000 10000000
                slot-names 00000003
                SODIMM0/J25LOWER
                SODIMM1/J25UPPER
...
dimm-types      DDR SDRAM
                DDR SDRAM
dimm-speeds     PC2700U-25330
                PC2700U-25330
...
```

The machine in the above command (a PowerBook G4 15, although that is not relevant) has two PC2700 DDR SDRAM chips installed. The two pairs of numbers against reg are specify the starting address and size of the chips. Thus, the first RAM chip starts at address 0x0000000 and has a size 0x10000000 (which is 256 MB). The second chip starts at 0x1000000 (256 MB) and has a size 256 MB. The total RAM is thus 512 MB.

If you need to *reduce* the installed RAM size (as seen by Mac OS X) for any reason, without actually having to remove a RAM stick (or you want to simulate an arbitrary size that's less than the total installed RAM), you can actually *delete* the reg entry using the delete-property command, and specify your own reg.

Referring to the previous example of the 512 MB PowerBook, the following command essentially *disables*the second RAM stick (note that this change is *not* written to NVRAM-it is transient-once you reboot, the other chip will be detected and used as before):

```
0 > " reg" delete-property ok
0 > 0 encode-int 10000000 encode-int encode+ "
reg" property ok
```

It must be kept in mind though that the reg properties can change from machine to machine, or more likely with architectural changes (for example, the format changed with the PowerMac G5).

A less adventurous and more appropriate way to limit visible RAM is to use the maxmem boot argument, such as at the shell prompt:

```
# nvram boot-args="maxmem=128"
```

- The following command sequence shows you various information on the machine's CPU(s):

```
0 > dev/ok
0 > dev/cpus ok
0 > ls
ff886d58:     /PowerPC,G4@0
ff8871f8:     /l2-cache
ok
0 > dev PowerPC,G4@0 ok
0 >.properties
name              cpu
reg               00000000
cpu-version       80020101
state             running
clock-frequency   4a817c7b
bus-frequency     09ef21aa
...
```

The rest of the output contains various cache sizes, the

processor's graphics capabilities (Altivec, support for certain instructions...), and so on. You can think of this as analogous to/proc/cpuinfo on Linux.

- The following command lists files in the root directory of the disk (partition) referred to by the "alias" hd

```
0 > dir hd:\
Size/GMT                          File/Dir
bytes    date         time          Name
6148     12/25/3     4:25:25      .DS_Store
156       9/12/3     20:41:59     .hidden
589824  12/25/3     6:45: 6      .hotfiles.btree
...
```

- The following command expands the alias hd, and gives you the complete path of the device in the tree (type devalias by itself to see a list of current aliases, along with what they refer to):

```
0 > devalias hd/pci@f4000000/ata-6@d/disk@0 ok
```

- You can load a file (kernel) using the load command, and boot it using the boot command. As stated earlier, mac-boot and shut-down are predefined to boot the machine normally, or shut it down, respectively. You can get and set variables (options) using the printenv and setenv commands. These variables are stored in the non-volatile memory (NVRAM) of Open Firmware. For example, if you want your e-mail address to be used as the "OEM banner", you should do the following:

```
0 > setenv oem-banner you@your.e-mail.address
0 > setenv oem-banner? true
```

You do not actually need to drop into Open Firmware to set the NVRAM variables. You can access (get and set) these from within Mac OS X via the nvram command line utility. To sum up, Open Firmware is a powerful tool for controlling, debugging, and exploring the computer.

### Operation

When an Open Firmware equipped Macintosh (all current

Apple systems at the time of this writing) is powered on, hardware is diagnosed (by some POST code) and initialized. The first entity to control the CPU thereafter is the firmware. Open Firmware (which runs with interrupts disabled) builds a device tree, probes slots for devices, queries PCI devices and assigns them address space appropriately, and then looks for the default boot device (unless one was specified explicitly). The following "snag" keys let the user specify a boot device as the system is powered on:

```
C device referred to by the 'cd' alias, a CD-ROM
      drive
D device referred to by the 'hd' alias, a hard
      disk drive
N device referred to by the 'enet' alias, a network
      card
Z device referred to by the 'zip' alias, a ZIP
      drive
```

It is worth noting that pressing T while your Mac powers on would boot it into what's called the *FireWire Target Disk Mode*. Essentially, your Mac becomes a fancy external FireWire disk drive. You can also specify the complete pathname of a device, or have the machine boot over the network using TFTP:

```
boot enet:<server IP>,<file>,<my IP>;<subnet>,;<gateway IP>
```

If Open Firmware fails to find a boot device, a *blinking folder* is displayed. Open Firmware then loads a file of type tbxi (ToolBox ROM Image, for historical reasons) from the system partition. Note that this would have been the file called "Mac OS ROM" in the System Folder on Mac OS 9, while OS X loads/System/Library/CoreServices/BootX, which is the bootloader as well. BootX is then executed and Control is then passed to it. Note that Open Firmware can directly load ELF, XCOFF and "bootinfo" (any supported format with an XML header) binaries, but not Mach-O, the native executable format on Mac OS X. BootX can load Mach-O binaries.

## BOOTLOADER

BootX (/System/Library/CoreServices/BootX) is the

**default bootloader on Mac OS X.**

BootX is also the name of an open source bootloader (different from Apple's BootX) that allows dual-booting Mac OS and Linux on "Old World" machines. BootX can load kernels from various filesystems: HFS+, HFS, UFS, ext2, and TFTP (network, abstracted to look like a filesystem). In addition to Mach-O, BootX can also load ELF kernels, although Mac OS X does not use this feature. To reiterate, BootX can load ELF kernels from an ext2 partition!

The X "Old World" Macs had various issues with the implementation of Open Firmware, which in turn caused many booting problems for Apple engineers, and even more problems for the PowerPC Linux port. Now, Apple had access to the firmware's source.

They solved most of the problems either via NVRAM patches, or by integrating required changes into BootX itself (in the instances where the changes could not be implemented as patches). As BootX matured, Apple added support for ext2 and ELF with the goal of making the platform more amenable to PowerPC Linux.

*The sequence of events when BootX starts executing (after being handed control by Open Firmware) is described below:*

- BootX first initializes the Open Firmware client interface (that it would use to talk to the firmware), and retrieves the firmware version.
- It then creates a pseudo-device called sl_words ('sl' implies *secondary loader*) in the firmware, and defines various FORTH words in it (it is here that code for the spinning cursor is set up).
- BootX looks up the options device in the firmware, which contains various variables (that you can see and set using the printenv and setenv commands in Open Firmware).

```
0 > dev/options.properties
name                options
little-endian?      false
real-mode?          false
auto-boot?          true
```

```
diag-switch?      false
...
boot-command      mac-boot
...
```

BootX looks up the chosen device, which contains handles for entities such as the boot input/output devices, memory, the MMU, the PMU, the CPU, the PIC, etc. For example, the following command at the Open Firmware prompt shows you the contents of chosen:

```
0 > dev/chosen ok
0 >.properties
name        chosen
stdin       ffbc6e40
stdout      ffbc6600
memory      ffbdd600
mmu...
...
```

- BootX initializes handles to the MMU and memory using chosen.
- BootX initializes handles to the boot display and the keyboard (if present).
- BootX checks if the "security mode" is "none", or
- BootX checks if the "verbose" (cmd-v) or "single user" (cmd-s) flags were specified, and sets the "output level" accordingly.
- BootX checks if the system is booting in "Safe Mode".
- BootX claims memory for various purposes.
- BootX finds all displays and sets them up. It does this by searching for nodes of type "display" in the device tree. The primary display is referred to by the screen alias. For example, you can try this at the Open Firmware prompt:

```
0 > dev screen ok
0 >.properties
name              ATY,Bee_A
compatible        ATY,Bee
width             00000400
height            00000300
```

```
linebytes          00000400
depth              00000008
display-type       4c434400
device_type        display
character-set      ISO859-1
...
```

- While opening the display(s), BootX also sets the screen colour to the familiar whitish gray.
- BootX looks up the boot device, boot arguments, etc., and determines where to get the kernel from (via a network device, from a block device, etc.), whence the path to the kernel file (mach_kernel) is constructed. If booting from a block device (which is the usual case), the path to the kext cache (seekextcache(8)) is calculated, along with the extensions directory (usually/System/Library/ Extensions).
- Mac OS X uses a few kinds of "kext" (kernel extension) caches to speed up loading of kexts. Kernel caches are kept in the directory/System/Library/ Caches/com.apple.kernelcaches. The cache files are named kernelcache.XXXXXXXX, where the suffix is a 32-bit adler checksum (the same algorithm as used by Gzip).
- At this point, BootX draws the Apple logo splash screen, and starts the spinning cursor. If booting from a network device, a spinning globe is drawn instead.
- Depending on various conditions, BootX tries to retrieve and load the kernel cache file.
- The next step is to "decode" the kernel. If the kernel header indicates a compressed kernel, BootX tries to decompress it (typical LZSS compression is used, as you compress this kind of data once but expand it many times). Since the kernel binary can potentially be a "fat" binary (code for multiple architectures residing in the same binary), BootX checks if it indeed is (fat), and if so, "thins" it (figures out the PowerPC code).

- BootX attempts to decode the file (possibly "thinned") as a Mach-O binary. If this fails, BootX also tries to decode it as ELF.
- If the above fails, BootX gives up, draws the failed boot picture, and goes into an infinite loop.
- If BootX is successful so far, it saves filesystem cache hits, misses and evicts, sets up various boot arguments and values (such as whether this is a graphical or verbose boot, whether there are some flags to be passed to the kernel, the size of installed RAM), and also calls a recursive function to flatten the device tree.
- Finally, BootX "calls" the kernel, immediately before which it "quiesces" Open Firmware, an operation as a result of which any asynchronous tasks in the firmware, timers, or DMA get stopped, etc.

## SYSTEM STARTUP

Mac OS X user level startup is neither pure BSD style, nor SYSV style, although the presence of/etc/rcindicates a BSD heritage. In fact, various things are unsurprisingly similar to NEXTSTEP. The next section, *XNU: The Kernel,* describes some of the things the kernel does as it comes up. *Mac OS X System Startup* continues with a description of (mostly) user-level startup.

### BootCache

Mac OS X uses a boot-time optimization (effectively a smart readahead) called "BootCache" that monitors the pattern of incoming read requests to a block device (the boot disk), and sorts the pattern into a "playlist" (it also measures the cache hit rate and stores the request pattern into a "history list" for being adaptive in future). The loadable (sorted) read pattern is stored in/var/db/BootCache.playlist. Once this is loaded, the cache comes into effect. Note that this feature requires *at least* 128 MB of physical RAM before it is enabled (automatically).

/System/Library/Extensions/BootCache.kext is the location

of the kernel extension implementing the cache while Contents/ Resources/BootCacheControl within that directory is the user-level control utility (it lets you load the playlist, among other things). The effectiveness of BootCache can be gauged from the following: in a recent update to "Panther", a reference to BootCacheControl was broken. BootCache is started (via the control utility) in/etc/rc, and a prefetch tag is inserted (unless the system is booting in safe mode)./etc/rc looks for BootCacheControl in the "kext" directory, as well as in/usr/ sbin, and finds it in the former (it doesn't exist in the latter). However, another program (possibly loginwindow.app) accesses/usr/sbin/BootCacheControl directly, and does not find it. For what it's worth, makingBootCacheControl available in/ usr/sbin, say via a symlink, reduces the boot time (measured from clicking on the "Restart" confirmation button to the point where *absolutely* everything has shown up on the system menu) from 135 seconds to 60 seconds on one of my machines!

## THE ROOTS OF MACOSX

Steve was drawing things out, as he is wont to do. We'd seen demonstrations by Adobe, we got to see the iBook's new larger look, he'd prattled on and on about the virtues of iPhoto, we were getting restless. We wanted to see IT. Whatever Steve Jobs had up the sleeve of that black mock-neck we wanted to see it. In all fairness those of us that are rabid weblog addicts had already seen it. Slashdot had broken the news the night before when 'Time Canada' plastered it all over their website. It was the new iMac, and inside the 'reality distortion field' that Steve Jobs projects at every MacWorld keynote, it was insanely great.

- *Editorial notice:* All opinions are those of the author and not necessarily those of osnews.com

The introduction of the new iMac was a huge event for Apple. After all, at its heart Apple is a hardware company, focused on selling cool boxes of silicon to comsumers. The introduction of Apple's new operating system, Mac OS X, in many ways will have a more lasting impression on the computing world's landscape. When IT people look at their landscape they don't see the huge lamp-shaped shrine to the new iMac, they see the past, transmuted into a stylish, Jobsian vision of the future.

OS X began to trickle out to the public in 2000. Officially that's pronounced OS ten, but as you'll see that X has more connotations than the roman numeral. OS X was touted as being based on UNIX, and inheriting some of the technology acquired from the NeXT buyout. In reality, it's a fair assessment to call it NEXTSTEP 5. As if caught in some freak transporter accident where two entities are fused into one it appeared that the old, archaic Mac OS and NeXT had fused to become Mac OS X.

Steve Jobs was forced out of Apple in the late 1980s when his managerial style clashed with that of then CEO John Sculley and others in Apple's management. It was a bitter departure, with Jobs quickly founding NeXT Inc. Hoping to repeat his success with the Macintosh Jobs brought the NeXT Cube to the world, but the world wasn't listening. NeXT was perhaps ahead of its time. The object oriented programing paradigm was different from Mac to be sure, and the adoption of UNIX at its core appealed to the monkish UNIX crowd, but it was lost on the Mac faithful that Jobs knew how to market to. NeXT was also overpriced, costing more than twice that of a decent PC or Mac at the time. NeXT floundered, eventually dropping its hardware component and became a purely software company.

The computing world had all but written off NeXT when Apple bought it in 1996. Apple was in trouble. It had been attempting to update the Mac OS for years, with a string of code name projects, such as Copland and Rhapsody, all of which were stillborn. In the meantime Microsoft had managed to catch, and then surpass Mac in the OS race with Windows 95 and NT. Apple needed to acquire the technology that it had been unable to produce on its own or it would diminish into a bit player, and eventually into the computer platform graveyard with Amiga and Commodore. Enter NeXT.

NeXT, and by inheritance Mac OS X, is at its base almost as old as the original Mac OS. Indeed, with its UNIX roots it can be argued that OS X is actually older than MacOS Classic. OS X can trace its roots back through FreeBSD, through BSD UNIX, and eventually back to Bell Labs and the birth of UNIX. Something important had changed though since Steve Jobs tried to market NeXT in the late eighties, UNIX had gotten hip, thanks to a computer science student in Finland, Linus Torvalds.

The '90s saw the birth, growth, and then explosion of Linux, the operating system that Torvalds created and set free onto the unsuspecting Internet. A new generation of geeks and compsci students flocked to the idea of owning their very own UNIX system, tweaking, playing, creating. The quickly evolving Internet enabled gaggles of programmers to collaborate on the new operating system. Linux evolved from a study project into a fully-featured operating system at an unprecedented rate. Suddenly the cool place to be was running Linux.

However, Linux was pretty much a niche OS for use by knowledgeable digerati. It excelled in running the servers that were needed to quench the hunger of the exponential growth of the World Wide Web. As desktop system for average users however it was clunky and intimidati ng. Linux, and UNIX, was powerful, that much at least had filtered through to the public via the media. It was in front of the back drop of the Internet revolution, the heady days of the late '90s, when every computer dweeb worth his salt claimed to be running Linux at home that Apple and Steve Jobs announced Mac OS X.

Jobs had primed the pump with success such as the iMac and a departure from the beige boxes that plagued Apple in his absence. Apple was hip again, out of Wal-Mart and into The Sharper Image. Now Jobs combined great hardware with great new software that, amazingly had the same roots as the golden child of the moment, Linux. Linux on an iMac, what could be more insanely great than that?

Mac OS X can still run applications written for the older Mac OS in what is called 'Classic Mode'. This is little more than a very slick Mac OS Emulator written inside OS X. When you start the Classic Environment you even see the old Mac

OS startup screen, with the ever familiar smiley face. Apple has also provided libraries that allow specially modified programs to run natively in Mac OS X. The process, called Carbonizing, after the name of the supporting libraries, is only an interim solution though. What Apple really wants is for developers to use their 'new' Cocoa environment.

The funny thing though is that at its base the Cocoa environment is, you guessed it, NeXT. Even the library names give the charade away. NSDocument, a base library in Cocoa, stands for NEXTSTEP Document. Cocoa is a pretty slick environment to work in. It's possible to whip up a simple text editor in minutes and the proliferation of developers out there adopting Cocoa and creating applications for the 'new' Operating System is growing quickly. One only need look at software announcement websites, such as www.versiontracker.com, to see this.

At its heart Mac OS X is a descendant of FreeBSD. The Apple engineers used FreeBSD as a blueprint for OS X, however there are differences at the heart of the OS. At the very heart, the OS X kernel is based on the Mach project at Carnegie Mellon University. However where most UNIX people interact with the system, at the shell, Mac OS X greatly resembles a BSD-based UNIX, albeit with a few Apple twists.

Within weeks of the release of the OS X Public Beta people began to port applications to the new OS. Because of Apple's shaky relationship with the GNU folks Mac OS X ships with almost no GPL code, though the developer tools do have the GNU C Compiler at their core. Most UNIX users make use of at least a few GNU tools, and work porting these apps began quickly. To be fair to Apple, many tools could be compiled as is, without any tweaking of the code required. The porting initiative has bloomed in the wake of OS X, sprouting such projects as Fink, which is porting many many UNIX and Linux apps to OS X, and MacGIMP, a port of the popular free Photoshop-grade graphics tool.

By the time Apple released Mac OS X 10.1 in August 2001 there was a quiet buzz taking off in the UNIX and Linux community about Apple's new/old OS. Apple did a very smart thing when it released the 10.1 update, they gave it away. What may have otherwise been an upgrade, such as Windows 98SE, Apple gave away to anyone who stopped by an Apple retailer. 10.1 was a major upgrade in performance. With 10.1 many people started using OS X as their primary OS, and interestingly it began to gain converts in the UNIX world.

UNIX System Administrators and programmers are monkish curmudgeons more often resembling Ted Kaczynski than the hip designers and artists that have been Apple's core clientele. However as the buzz around OS X took wing UNIX people quickly snatched up PowerBooks, iBooks, anything to be able to communicate with the business world while keeping their familiar UNIX.

This is where some of Apple's future lies. To be sure Apple will continue as a consumer computer manufacturer. It has spent the last two years preparing the Mac faithful for the conversion away from their old trusty OS and will most likely continue to bottle-feed the newly converted for the next two years as well. However if Apple is to grow into markets beyond their core they need to capture mindshare in those other markets. The UNIX and Linux market just happen to be an easy sell for Apple.

# 2

# Remote OS Detection

## INTRODUCTION

When exploring a network for security auditing or inventory/administration, you usually want to know more than the bare IP addresses of identified machines. Your reaction to discovering a printer may be very different than to finding a router, wireless access point, telephone PBX, game console, Windows desktop, or Unix server. Finer grained detection (such as distinguishing Mac OS X 10.4 from 10.3) is useful for determining vulnerability to specific flaws and for tailoring effective exploits for those vulnerabilities.

In part due to its value to attackers, many systems are tight-lipped about their exact nature and operating system configuration.

Fortunately, Nmap includes a huge database of heuristics for identifying thousands of different systems based on how they respond to a selection of TCP/IP probes. Another system (part of version detection) interrogates open TCP or UDP ports to determine device type and OS details. Results of these two systems are reported independently so that you can identify combinations such as a Checkpoint firewall forwarding port 80 to a Windows IIS server. While Nmap has supported OS detection since 1998, this chapter describes the 2nd generation system released in 2006.

## REASONS FOR OS DETECTION

While some benefits of discovering the underlying OS and device types on a network are obvious, others are more obscure. This section lists the top reasons I hear for discovering this extra information.

## DETERMINING VULNERABILITY OF TARGET HOSTS

It is sometimes very difficult to determine remotely whether an available service is susceptible or patched for a certain vulnerability. Even obtaining the application version number doesn't always help, since OS distributors often back-port security fixes without changing the version number. The surest way to verify that a vulnerability is real is to exploit it, but that risks crashing the service and can lead to wasted hours or even days of frustrating exploitation efforts if the service turns out to be patched.

OS detection can help reduce these false positives. For example, the Rwho daemon on unpatched Sun Solaris 7 through 9 may be remotely exploitable (Sun alert #57659). Remotely determining vulnerability is difficult, but you can rule it out by finding that a target system is running Solaris 10. Taking this from the perspective of a systems administrator rather than a pen-tester, imagine you run a large Sun shop when alert #57659 comes out. Scan your whole network with OS detection to find machines which need patching before the bad guys do.

## TAILORING EXPLOITS

Even after you discover a vulnerability in a target system, OS detection can be helpful in exploiting it. Buffer overflows, format-string exploits, and many other vulnerabilities often require custom-tailored shellcode with offsets and assembly payloads generated to match the target OS and hardware architecture. In some cases, you only get one try because the service crashes if you get the shellcode wrong. Use OS detection first or you may end up sending Linux shellcode to a FreeBSD server.

## NETWORK INVENTORY AND SUPPORT

While it isn't as exciting as busting root through a specially crafted format string exploit, there are many administrative reasons to keep track of what is running on your network. Before you renew that IRIX support contract for another year, scan to see if anyone still uses such machines. An inventory can also be useful for IT budgeting and ensuring that all company equipment is accounted for.

## DETECTING UNAUTHORIZED AND DANGEROUS DEVICES

With the ubiquity of mobile devices and cheap commodity networking equipment, companies are increasingly finding that employees are extending their networks in undesirable ways. They may install a $20 wireless access point (WAP) in their cubicle without realizing (or caring) that they just opened up the protected corporate network to potential attackers in the parking lot or nearby buildings. WAPs can be so dangerous that Nmap has a special category for detecting them. Users may also cause sysadmins grief by connecting insecure and/or worm-infected laptops to the corporate network. Regular scanning can detect unauthorized devices for investigation and containment.

## SOCIAL ENGINEERING

Another possible use is social engineering. Lets say that you are scanning a target company and Nmap reports a "Datavoice TxPORT PRISM 3000 T1 CSU/DSU 6.22/2.06". You could call up the target pretending to be Datavoice support and discuss some issues with their PRISM 3000. Tell them you are about to announce a big security hole, but are first providing the patch to valued customers. Some naive administrators might assume that only an authorized engineer from Datavoice would know so much about their CSU/DSU. Of course the patch you send them is a Trojan horse that gives you remote access to sniff and traipse through their network. Be sure to read the rest of this chapter for detection accuracy and verification advice before trying this. If you guess the target system wrong and they call the police, that will be an embarrassing story to tell your cellmates.

## USAGE AND EXAMPLES

### DEVICE TYPE

All fingerprints are classified with one or more high-level device types, such as router, printer, firewall, or (as in this case)general purpose. These are further described in the section called "Device and OS classification (Class lines)". Several device types may be shown, in which case they will be separated with the pipe symbol as in "Device Type: router|firewall".

### RUNNING

This field is also related to the OS classification scheme described in the section called "Device and OS classification (Class lines)". It shows the OS Family (Linux in this case) and OS generation (2.6.X) if available. If there are multiple OS families, they are separated by commas. When Nmap can't narrow down OS generations to one specific choice, options are separated by the pipe symbol ('|') Examples include OpenBSD 3.X, NetBSD 3.X|4.X and Linux 2.4.X|2.5.X|2.6.X.

If Nmap finds too many OS families to print concisely, it will omit this line. When there are no perfect matches, Nmap changes the field to Running (JUST GUESSING) and adds an accuracy percentage (100% is a perfect match) in parentheses after each candidate family name. If no fingerprints are close matches, the line is omitted.

### OS DETAILS

This line gives the detailed description for each fingerprint that matches. While the Device type and Running lines are from predefined enumerated lists that are easy to parse by a computer, the OS details line contains free-form data which is useful to a human reading the report. This can include more exact version numbers, device models, and architectures specific to a given fingerprint. In this example, the only matching fingerprint was Linux 2.6.20-1 (Fedora Core 5). When there are multiple exact matches, they are comma-separated. If there aren't any perfect matches, but some close guesses, the field is renamed Aggressive OS guesses and fingerprints are shown followed by a percentage in parentheses which specifies how close each match was.

## UPTIME GUESS

As part of OS detection, Nmap receives several SYN/ACK TCP packets in a row and checks the headers for a timestamp option. Many operating systems use a simple counter for this which starts at zero at boot time then increments at a constant rate such as twice per second. By looking at several responses, Nmap can determine the current values and rate of increase. Simple linear extrapolation determines boot time. The timestamp algorithm is used for OS detection too since the increment rate on different systems varies from 2 Hz to 1,000 Hz.

The uptime guess is labeled a "guess" because various factors can make it completely inaccurate. Some operating systems do not start the timestamp counter at zero, but initialize it with a random value, making extrapolation to zero meaningless. Even on systems using a simple counter starting at zero, the counter eventually overflows and wraps around. With a 1,000 Hz counter increment rate, the counter resets to zero roughly every 50 days. So a host that has been up for 102 days will appear to have been up only two days. Even with these caveats, the uptime guess is accurate much of the time for most operating systems, so it is printed when available, but only in verbose mode. The uptime guess is omitted if the target gives zeros or no timestamp options in its SYN/ACK packets, or if it does not reply at all. The line is also omitted if Nmap cannot discern the timestamp increment rate or it seems suspicious (like a 30-year uptime).

## NETWORK DISTANCE

A side effect of one of the OS detection tests allows Nmap to compute how many routers are between it and a target host. The distance is zero when you are scanning localhost, and one for a machine on the same network segment. Each additional router on the path adds one to the hop count. The Network

Distance line is not printed in this example, since Nmap omits the line when it cannot be computed (no reply to the relevant probe).

## TCP SEQUENCE PREDICTION

Systems with poor TCP initial sequence number generation are vulnerable to blind TCP spoofing attacks. In other words, you can make a full connection to those systems and send (but not receive) data while spoofing a different IP address. The target's logs will show the spoofed IP, and you can take advantage of any trust relationship between them. This attack was all the rage in the mid-nineties when people commonly used rlogin to allow logins to their account without any password from trusted IP addresses. Kevin Mitnick is alleged to have used this attack to break into Tsutomu Shimomura's computers in December 1994.

The good news is that hardly anyone uses rlogin anymore, and many operating systems have been fixed to use unpredictable initial sequence numbers as proposed by RFC 1948. For these reasons, this line is only printed in verbose mode. Sadly, many vendors still ship vulnerable operating systems and devices. Even the fixed ones often vary in implementation, which leaves them valuable for OS detection purposes. The class describes the ISN generation algorithm used by the target, and difficulty is a rough estimate of how hard the system makes blind IP spoofing (0 is the easiest). The parenthesized comment is based on the difficulty index and ranges fromTrivial joke to Easy, Medium, Formidable, Worthy challenge, and finally Good luck! Further details about sequence tests are provided in the section called "TCP ISN greatest common divisor (GCD)".

While the rlogin family is mostly a relic of the past, clever attackers can still find effective uses for blind TCP spoofing. For example, it allows for spoofed HTTP requests. You don't see the results, but just the URL (POST or GET request) can have dramatic side effects. The spoofing allows attackers to hide their identity, frame someone else, or exploit IP address restrictions.

## TCP/IP FINGERPRINTING METHODS SUPPORTED BY NMAP

Nmap OS fingerprinting works by sending up to 16 TCP, UDP, and ICMP probes to known open and closed ports of the target machine. These probes are specially designed to exploit various ambiguities in the standard protocol RFCs. Then Nmap listens for responses. Dozens of attributes in those responses are analysed and combined to generate a fingerprint. Every probe packet is tracked and resent at least once if there is no response. All of the packets are IPv4 with a random IP ID value. Probes to an open TCP port are skipped if no such port has been found. For closed TCP or UDP ports, Nmap will first check if such a port has been found. If not, Nmap will just pick a port at random and hope for the best.

The following sections are highly technical and reveal the hidden workings of Nmap OS detection. Nmap can be used effectively without understanding this, though the material can help you better understand remote networks and also detect and explain certain anomalies. Plus, some of the techniques are pretty cool. Readers in a hurry may skip to the section called "Dealing with Misidentified and Unidentified Hosts". But for those of you who are ready for a journey through TCP explicit congestion notification, reserved UDP header bits, initial sequence numbers, bogus flags, and Christmas tree packets: read on! Even the best of us occasionally forget byte offsets for packet header fields and flags. For quick reference, the IPv4, TCP, UDP, and ICMP header layouts can be found in the section called "TCP/IP Reference". The layout for ICMP echo request and destination unreachable packets are shown in Figure and Figure.

### PROBES SENT

This section describes each IP probe sent by Nmap as part of TCP/IP fingerprinting. It refers to Nmap response tests and TCP options which are explained in the following section.

### SEQUENCE GENERATION (SEQ, OPS, WIN, AND T1)

A series of six TCP probes is sent to generate these four

test response lines. The probes are sent exactly 100 milliseconds apart so the total time taken is 500 ms. Exact timing is important as some of the sequence algorithms we detect (initial sequence numbers, IP IDs, and TCP timestamps) are time dependent. This timing value was chosen to take 500 ms so that we can reliably detect the common 2 Hz TCP timestamp sequences.

Each probe is a TCP SYN packet to a detected open port on the remote machine. The sequence and acknowledgment numbers are random (but saved so Nmap can differentiate responses). Detection accuracy requires probe consistency, so there is no data payload even if the user requested one with —data-length.

These packets vary in the TCP options they use and the TCP window field value. The following list provides the options and values for all six packets. The listed window field values do not reflect window scaling. EOL is the end-of-options-list option, which many sniffing tools don't show by default.

- *Packet #1*: Window scale (10), NOP, MSS (1460), timestamp (TSval: 0xFFFFFFFF; TSecr: 0), SACK permitted. The window field is 1.
- *Packet #2*: MSS (1400), window scale (0), SACK permitted, timestamp (TSval: 0xFFFFFFFF; TSecr: 0), EOL. The window field is 63.
- *Packet #3*: Timestamp (TSval: 0xFFFFFFFF; TSecr: 0), NOP, NOP, window scale (5), NOP, MSS (640). The window field is 4.
- *Packet #4*: SACK permitted, Timestamp (TSval: 0xFFFFFFFF; TSecr: 0), window scale (10), EOL. The window field is 4.
- *Packet #5*: MSS (536), SACK permitted, Timestamp (TSval: 0xFFFFFFFF; TSecr: 0), window scale (10), EOL. The window field is 16.
- *Packet #6*: MSS (265), SACK permitted, Timestamp (TSval: 0xFFFFFFFF; TSecr: 0). The window field is 512.

The results of these tests include four result category lines.

The first, SEQ, contains results based on sequence analysis of the probe packets. These test results are GCD, SP, ISR, TI, II, TS, and SS. The next line, OPS contains the TCP options received for each of the probes (the test names are O1 through 06). Similarly, the WIN line contains window sizes for the probe responses (named W1 through W6). The final line related to these probes, T1, contains various test values for packet #1. Those results are for the R, DF, T, TG, W, S, A, F, O, RD, and Q tests.These tests are only reported for the first probe since they are almost always the same for each probe.

## ICMP ECHO (IE)

The IE test involves sending two ICMP echo request packets to the target. The first one has the IP DF bit set, a type-of-service (TOS) byte value of zero, a code of nine (even though it should be zero), the sequence number 295, a random IP ID and ICMP request identifier, and 120 bytes of 0x00 for the data payload. The second ping query is similar, except a TOS of four (IP_TOS_RELIABILITY) is used, the code is zero, 150 bytes of data is sent, and the ICMP request ID and sequence numbers are incremented by one from the previous query values.

The results of both of these probes are combined into a IE line containing the R, DFI, T, TG, and CD tests. The R value is only true (Y) if both probes elicit responses. The T, and CD values are for the response to the first probe only, since they are highly unlikely to differ. DFI is a custom test for this special dual-probe ICMP case. These ICMP probes follow immediately after the TCP sequence probes to ensure valid results of the shared IP ID sequence number test.

## TCP EXPLICIT CONGESTION NOTIFICATION (ECN)

This probe tests for explicit congestion notification (ECN) support in the target TCP stack. ECN is a method for improving Internet performance by allowing routers to signal congestion problems before they start having to drop packets. It is documented in RFC 3168. Nmap tests this by sending a SYN packet which also has the ECN CWR and ECE congestion control flags set. For an unrelated (to ECN) test, the urgent field value of 0xF7F5 is used even though the urgent flag is not set.

The acknowledgment number is zero, sequence number is random, window size field is three, and the reserved bit which immediately precedes the CWR bit is set. TCP options are WScale (10), NOP, MSS (1460), SACK permitted, NOP, NOP. The probe is sent to an open port. If a response is received, the R, DF, T, TG, W, O, CC, and Q tests are performed and recorded.

**TCP (T2–T7)**

The six T2 through T7 tests each send one TCP probe packet. With one exception, the TCP options data in each case is (in hex)03030A0102040109080AFFFFFFFF000000000402. Those 20 bytes correspond to window scale (10), NOP, MSS (265), Timestamp (TSval: 0xFFFFFFFF; TSecr: 0), then SACK permitted. The exception is that T7 uses a Window scale value of 15 rather than 10.

*The variable characteristics of each probe are described below:*

- *T2:* Sends a TCP null (no flags set) packet with the IP DF bit set and a window field of 128 to an open port.
- *T3:* Sends a TCP packet with the SYN, FIN, URG, and PSH flags set and a window field of 256 to an open port. The IP DF bit is not set.
- *T4:* Sends a TCP ACK packet with IP DF and a window field of 1024 to an open port.
- *T5:* Sends a TCP SYN packet without IP DF and a window field of 31337 to a closed port.
- *T6:* Sends a TCP ACK packet with IP DF and a window field of 32768 to a closed port.
- *T7:* Sends a TCP packet with the FIN, PSH, and URG flags set and a window field of 65535 to a closed port. The IP DF bit is not set.

In each of these cases, a line is added to the fingerprint with results for the R, DF, T, TG, W, S, A, F, O, RD, and Q tests.

## UDP (U1)

This probe is a UDP packet sent to a closed port. The character 'C' (0x43) is repeated 300 times for the data field. The IP ID value is set to 0x1042 for operating systems which allow us to set this. If the port is truly closed and there is no firewall in place, Nmap expects to receive an ICMP port unreachable message in return. That response is then subjected to the R, DF, T, TG, IPL, UN, RIPL, RID, RIPCK,RUCK, and RUD tests.

## RESPONSE TESTS

The previous section describes probes sent by Nmap, and this one completes the puzzle by describing the barrage of tests performed on responses. The short names (such as DF, R, and RIPCK) are those used in the nmap-os-db fingerprint database to save space. All numerical test values are given in hexadecimal notation, without leading zeros, unless noted otherwise. The tests are documented in roughly the order they appear in fingerprints.

## TCP ISN GREATEST COMMON DIVISOR (GCD)

The SEQ test sends six TCP SYN packets to an open port of the target machine and collects SYN/ACK packets back. Each of these SYN/ACK packets contains a 32-bit initial sequence number (ISN). This test attempts to determine the smallest number by which the target host increments these values. For example, many hosts (especially old ones) always increment the ISN in multiples of 64,000.

The first step in calculating this is creating an array of differences between probe responses. The first element is the difference between the 1st and 2nd probe response ISNs. The second element is the difference between the 2nd and 3rd responses. There are five elements if Nmap receives responses to all six probes. Since the next couple of sections reference this array, we will call it diff1. If an ISN is lower than the previous one, Nmap looks at both the number of values it would have to subtract from the first value to obtain the second, and the number of values it would have to count up (including wrapping the 32-bit counter back to zero). The smaller of those two values is stored indiff1. So the difference between 0x20000 followed by 0x15000 is 0xB000. The difference between 0xFFFFFF00 and 0xC000 is 0xC0FF. This test value then records the greatest common divisor of all those elements. This GCD is also used for calculating the SP result.

## TCP ISN COUNTER RATE (ISR)

This value reports the average rate of increase for the returned TCP initial sequence number. Recall that a difference is taken between each two consecutive probe responses and stored in the previously discussed diff1 array. Those differences are each divided by the amount of time elapsed (in seconds—will generally be about 0.1) between sending the two probes which generated them. The result is an array, which we'll call seq_rates containing the rates of ISN counter increases per second. The array has one element for each diff1 value. An average is taken of the array values. If that average is less than one (*e.g.* a constant ISN is used), ISR is zero. Otherwise ISR is eight times the binary logarithm (log base-2) of that average value, rounded to the nearest integer.

## TCP ISN SEQUENCE PREDICTABILITY INDEX (SP)

While the ISR test measures the average rate of initial sequence number increments, this value measures the ISN variability. It roughly estimates how difficult it would be to predict the next ISN from the known sequence of six probe responses. The calculation uses the difference array (seq_rates) and GCD values discussed in the previous section. This test is only performed if at least four responses were seen. If the previously computed GCD value is greater than nine, the elements of the previously computed seq_rates array are divided by that value. We don't do the division for smaller GCD values because those are usually caused by chance. A standard deviation of the array of the resultant values is then taken. If the result is one or less, SP is zero. Otherwise the binary logarithm of the result is computed, then it is multiplied by eight, rounded to the nearest integer, and stored as SP.

Please keep in mind that this test is only done for OS detection purposes and is not a full-blown audit of the target ISN generator. There are many algorithm weaknesses that lead to easy predictability even with a high SP value.

## IP ID SEQUENCE GENERATION ALGORITHM (TI, CI, II)

There are three tests that examine the IP header ID field of responses. TI is based on responses to the TCP SEQ probes. CI is from the responses to the three TCP probes sent to a closed port: T5, T6, and T7. II comes from the ICMP responses to the two IE ping probes. For TI, at least three responses must be received for the test to be included; for CI, at least two responses are required; and for II, both ICMP responses must be received.

For each of these tests, the target's IP ID generation algorithm is classified based on the algorithm below. Minor differences between tests are noted. Note that difference values assume that the counter can wrap. So the difference between an IP ID of 65,100 followed by a value of 700 is 1,136. The difference between 2,000 followed by 1,100 is 64,636.

*Here are the calculation details:*

- If all of the ID numbers are zero, the value of the test is Z.
- If the IP ID sequence ever increases by at least 20,000, the value is RD (random). This result isn't possible for II because there are not enough samples to support it.
- If all of the IP IDs are identical, the test is set to that value in hex.
- If any of the differences between two consecutive IDs exceeds 1,000, and is not evenly divisible by 256, the test's value is RI(random positive increments). If the difference is evenly divisible by 256, it must be at least 256,000 to cause this RI result.
- If all of the differences are divisible by 256 and no greater than 5,120, the test is set to BI (broken increment). This happens on systems like Microsoft

Windows where the IP ID is sent in host byte order rather than network byte order. It works fine and isn't any sort of RFC violation, though it does give away host architecture details which can be useful to attackers.

- If all of the differences are less than ten, the value is I (incremental). We allow difference up to ten here (rather than requiring sequential ordering) because traffic from other hosts can cause sequence gaps.
- If none of the previous steps identify the generation algorithm, the test is omitted from the fingerprint.

## SHARED IP ID SEQUENCE BOOLEAN (SS)

This Boolean value records whether the target shares its IP ID sequence between the TCP and ICMP protocols. If our six TCP IP ID values are 117, 118, 119, 120, 121, and 122, then our ICMP results are 123 and 124, it is clear that not only are both sequences incremental, but they are both part of the same sequence. If, on the other hand, the TCP IP ID values are 117-122 but the ICMP values are 32,917 and 32,918, two different sequences are being used.

This test is only included if II is RI, BI, or I and TI is the same. If SS is included, the result is S if the sequence is shared and O (other) if it is not. That determination is made by the following algorithm:

Let avg be the final TCP sequence response IP ID minus the first TCP sequence response IP ID, divided by the difference in probe numbers. If probe #1 returns an IP ID of 10,000 and probe #6 returns 20,000, avg would be (20,000 ? 10,000)/(6 – 1), which equals 2,000. If the first ICMP echo response IP ID is less than the final TCP sequence response IP ID plus three times avg, the SS result is S. Otherwise it is O.

## TCP TIMESTAMP OPTION ALGORITHM (TS)

TS is another test which attempts to determine target OS characteristics based on how it generates a series of numbers. This one looks at the TCP timestamp option (if any) in responses to the SEQ probes. It examines the TSval (first four bytes of the option) rather than the echoed TSecr (last four bytes) value. It takes the difference between each consecutive TSval and divides that by the amount of time elapsed between Nmap sending the two probes which generated those responses. The resultant value gives a rate of timestamp increments per second.

*Nmap computes the average increments per second over all consecutive probes and then calculates the TS as follows:*

- If any of the responses have no timestamp option, TS is set to U (unsupported).
- If any of the timestamp values are zero, TS is set to 0.
- If the average increments per second falls within the ranges 0-5.66, 70-150, or 150-350, TS is set to 1, 7, or 8, respectively. These three ranges get special treatment because they correspond to the 2 Hz, 100 Hz, and 200 Hz frequencies used by many hosts.
- In all other cases, Nmap records the binary logarithm of the average increments per second, rounded to the nearest integer. Since most hosts use 1,000 Hz frequencies, A is a common result.

## TCP OPTIONS (O, O1–O6)

This test records the TCP header options in a packet. It preserves the original ordering and also provides some information about option values.

Because RFC 793 doesn't require any particular ordering, implementations often come up with unique orderings. Some platforms don't implement all options (they are, of course, optional).

When you combine all of those permutations with the number of different option values that implementations use, this test provides a veritable trove of information. The value for this test is a string of characters representing the options being used.

Several options take arguments that come immediately after the character. Supported options and arguments are all shown in Table.

**Table: O Test Values**

| Option Name | Character | Argument (if any) |
|---|---|---|
| End of Options List (EOL) | L | |
| No operation (NOP) | N | |
| Maximum Segment Size (MSS) | M | The value is appended. Many systems echothe value used in the corresponding probe. |
| Window Scale (WS) | W | The actual value is appended. |
| Timestamp (TS) | T | The T is followed by two binary characters representing the TSval and TSecr valuesrespectively.Thecharacters are 0 if the field is zero and 1otherwise. |
| Selective ACK permitted (SACK) | S | |

As an example, the string M5B4NW3NNT11 means the packet includes the MSS option (value 0x5B4) followed by a NOP. Next comes a window scale option with a value of three, then two more NOPs. The final option is a timestamp, and neither of its two fields were zero. If there are no TCP options in a response, the test will exist but the value string will be empty. If no probe was returned, the test is omitted.

While this test is generally named O, the six probes sent for sequence generation purposes are a special case. Those are inserted into the special OPS test line and take the names O1 through O6 to distinguish which probe packet they relate to. The "O" stands for "options". Despite the different names, each test O1 through O6 is processed exactly the same way as the other O tests.

## TCP INITIAL WINDOW SIZE (W, W1–W6)

This test simply records the 16-bit TCP window size of the received packet. It is quite effective, since there are more than 80 values that at least one OS is known to send. A down side is that some operating systems have more than a dozen possible values by themselves. This leads to false negative results until we collect all of the possible window sizes used by an operating system. While this test is generally named W, the six probes sent for sequence generation purposes are a special case.

Those are inserted into a special WIN test line and take the names W1 through W6. The window size is recorded for all of the sequence number probes because they differ in TCP MSS option values, which causes some operating systems to advertise a different window size. Despite the different names, each test is processed exactly the same way.

## RESPONSIVENESS (R)

This test simply records whether the target responded to a given probe. Possible values are Y and N. If there is no reply, remaining fields for the test are omitted.

A risk with this test involves probes that are dropped by a firewall. This leads to R=N in the subject fingerprint. Yet the reference fingerprint innmap-os-db may have R=Y if the target OS usually replies. Thus the firewall could prevent proper OS detection. To reduce this problem, reference fingerprints generally omit the R=Y test from the IE and U1 probes, which are the ones most likely to be dropped. In addition, if Nmap is missing a closed TCP port for a target, it will not set R=N for the T5, T6, or T7 tests even if the port it tries is non-responsive. After all, the lack of a closed port may be because they are all filtered.

## IP Don't Fragment Bit (DF)

The IP header contains a single bit which forbids routers from fragmenting a packet. If the packet is too large for routers to handle, they will just have to drop it (and ideally return a "destination unreachable, fragmentation needed" response). This test records Y if the bit is set, and Nif it isn't.

## DON'T FRAGMENT (ICMP) (DFI)

This is simply a modified version of the DF test that is used for the special IE probes. It compares results of the don't fragment bit for the two ICMP echo request probes sent. It has four possible values, which are enumerated in Table.

**Table: DFI Test Values**

| Value | Description |
|---|---|
| N | Neither of the ping responses have the DF bit set. |
| S | Both responses echo the DF value of the probe. |
| Y | Both of the response DF bits are set. |
| O | The one remaining other combination—both responses have the DF bit toggled. |

## IP INITIAL TIME-TO-LIVE (T)

IP packets contain a field named time-to-live (TTL) which is decremented every time they traverse a router. If the field reaches zero, the packet must be discarded. This prevents packets from looping endlessly.

Because operating systems differ on which TTL they start with, it can be used for OS detection. Nmap determines how many hops away it is from the target by examining the ICMP port unreachable response to the U1 probe.

That response includes the original IP packet, including the already-decremented TTL field, received by the target. By subtracting that value from our as-sent TTL, we learn how many hops away the machine is. Nmap then adds that hop distance to the probe response TTL to determine what the initial TTL was when that ICMP probe response packet was sent. That initial TTL value is stored in the fingerprint as the T result.

Even though an eight-bit field like TTL can never hold values greater than 0xFF, this test occasionally results in values of 0x100 or higher. This occurs when a system (could be the source, a target, or a system in between) corrupts or otherwise fails to correctly decrement the TTL. It can also occur due to asymmetric routes.

Nmap can also learn from the system interface and routing tables when the hop distance is zero (localhost scan) or one (on the same network segment). This value is used when Nmap prints the hop distance for the user, but it is not used for T result computation.

## IP INITIAL TIME-TO-LIVE GUESS (TG)

It is not uncommon for Nmap to receive no response to the U1 probe, which prevents Nmap from learning how many hops away a target is. Firewalls and NAT devices love to block unsolicited UDP packets. But since common TTL values are spread well apart and targets are rarely more than 20 hops away, Nmap can make a pretty good guess anyway. Most systems send packets with an initial TTL of 32, 60, 64, 128, or 255. So the TTL value received in the response is rounded up to the next value out of 32, 64, 128, or 255. 60 is not in that list because it cannot be reliably distinguished from 64. It is rarely seen anyway. The resulting guess is stored in the TG field. This TTL guess field is not printed in a subject fingerprint if the actual TTL (T) value was discovered.

## EXPLICIT CONGESTION NOTIFICATION (CC)

This test is only used for the ECN probe. That probe is a SYN packet which includes the CWR and ECE congestion control flags. When the response SYN/ACK is received, those flags are examined to set the CC (congestion control) test value as described in Table.

**Table: CC Test Values**

| Value | Description |
|---|---|
| Y | Only the ECE bit is set (not CWR). This host supports ECN. |
| N | Neither of these two bits is set. The target does not support ECN. |
| S | Both bits are set. The target does not support ECN, but it echoes back what it thinks is a reserved bit. |
| O | The one remaining combination of these two bits (other). |

## TCP MISCELLANEOUS QUIRKS (Q)

This tests for two quirks that a few implementations have in their TCP stack. The first is that the reserved field in the TCP header (right after the header length) is nonzero. This is particularly likely to happen in response to the ECN test as that one sets a reserved bit in the probe. If this is seen in a packet, an "R" is recorded in the Q string. The other quirk Nmap tests for is a nonzero urgent pointer field value when the URG flag is not set. This is also particularly likely to be seen in response to the ECN probe, which sets a non-zero urgent field. A "U" is appended to the Q string when this is seen. The Q string must always be generated in alphabetical order. If no quirks are present, the Q test is empty but still shown.

## TCP SEQUENCE NUMBER (S)

This test examines the 32-bit sequence number field in the TCP header. Rather than record the field value as some other tests do, this one examines how it compares to the TCP acknowledgment number from the probe that elicited the response. It then records the appropriate value as shown in Table.

**Table: S Test Values**

| Value | Description |
|---|---|
| Z | Sequence number is zero. |
| A | Sequence number is the same as the acknowledgment number in the probe. |
| A+ | Sequence number is the same as the acknowledgment number in the probe plus one. |
| O | Sequence number is something else (other). |

## TCP ACKNOWLEDGMENT NUMBER (A)

This test is the same as S except that it tests how the acknowledgment number in the response compares to the sequence number in the respective probe. The four possible values are given in Table.

**Table: A Test Values**

| Value | Description |
|---|---|
| Z | Acknowledgment number is zero. |
| S | Acknowledgment number is the same as the sequence number in the probe. |
| S+ | Acknowledgment number is the same as the sequence number in the probe plus one. |
| O | Acknowledgment number is something else (other). |

## TCP FLAGS (F)

This field records the TCP flags in the response. Each letter represents one flag, and they occur in the same order as in a TCP packet (from high-bit on the left, to the low ones). So the value AS represents the ACK and SYN bits set, while the value SA is illegal (wrong order). The possible flags are shown in Table.

**Table: F Test Values**

| Character | Flag name | Flag byte value |
|---|---|---|
| E | ECN Echo (ECE) | 64 |
| U | Urgent Data (URG) | 32 |
| A | Acknowledgment (ACK) | 16 |
| P | Push (PSH) | 8 |
| R | Reset (RST) | 4 |
| S | Synchronize (SYN) | 2 |
| F | Final (FIN) | 1 |

## TCP RST DATA CHECKSUM (RD)

Some operating systems return ASCII data such as error messages in reset packets. This is explicitly allowed by section 4.2.2.12 of RFC 1122. When Nmap encounters such data, it performs a CRC32 checksum and reports the results. When there is no data, RD is set to zero. Some of the few operating systems that may return data in their reset packets are HP-UX and versions of Mac OS prior to Mac OS X.

## IP TOTAL LENGTH (IPL)

This test records the total length (in octets) of an IP packet. It is only used for the port unreachable response elicited by the U1 test. That length varies by implementation because they are allowed to choose how much data from the original probe to include, as long as they meet the minimum RFC 792 requirement. That requirement is to include the original IP header and at least eight bytes of data.

## UNUSED PORT UNREACHABLE FIELD NONZERO (UN)

An ICMP port unreachable message header is eight bytes

long, but only the first four are used. RFC 792 states that the last four bytes must be zero. A few implementations (mostly ethernet switches and some specialized embedded devices) set it anyway. The value of those last four bytes is recorded in this field.

## RETURNED PROBE IP TOTAL LENGTH VALUE (RIPL)

ICMP port unreachable messages (as are sent in response to the U1 probe) are required to include the IP header which generated them. This header should be returned just as they received it, but some implementations send back a corrupted version due to changes they made during IP processing. This test simply records the returned IP total length value. If the correct value of 0 × 148 (328) is returned, the value G(for good) is stored instead of the actual value.

## RETURNED PROBE IP ID VALUE (RID)

The U1 probe has a static IP ID value of 0 × 1042. If that value is returned in the port unreachable message, the value G is stored for this test. Otherwise the exact value returned is stored. Some systems, such as Solaris, manipulate IP ID values for raw IP packets that Nmap sends. In such cases, this test is skipped. We have found that some systems, particularly HP and Xerox printers, flip the bytes and return 0x4210 instead.

## INTEGRITY OF RETURNED PROBE IP CHECKSUM VALUE (RIPCK)

The IP checksum is one value that we *don't* expect to remain the same when returned in a port unreachable message. After all, each network hop during transit changes the checksum as the TTL is decremented. However, the checksum we receive should match the enclosing IP packet. If it does, the value G (good) is stored for this test. If the returned value is zero, then Z is stored. Otherwise the result isI (invalid).

## INTEGRITY OF RETURNED PROBE UDP CHECKSUM (RUCK)

The UDP header checksum value should be returned

exactly as it was sent. If it is, G is recorded for this test. Otherwise the value actually returned is recorded.

## INTEGRITY OF RETURNED UDP DATA (RUD)

This test checks the integrity of the (possibly truncated) returned UDP payload. If all the payload bytes are the expected 'C' (0 × 43), or if the payload was truncated to zero length, G is recorded; otherwise, I (invalid) is recorded.

## ICMP RESPONSE CODE (CD)

The code value of an ICMP echo reply (type zero) packet is supposed to be zero. But some implementations wrongly send other values, particularly if the echo request has a nonzero code (as one of the IE tests does). The response code values for the two probes are combined into a CD value as described in Table.

**Table: CD Test Values**

| Value | Description |
|---|---|
| Z | Both code values are zero. |
| S | Both code values are the same as in the corresponding probe. |
| <NN> | When they both use the same non-zero number, it is shown here. |
| O | Any other combination. |

## FINGERPRINTING METHODS AVOIDED BY NMAP

Nmap supports many more OS detection techniques than any other program, and we are always interested in hearing about new ideas. Please send them to the Nmap development list (nmap-dev) for discussion. However there are some methods that just aren't a good fit. This section details some of the most interesting ones. While they aren't supported by Nmap, some are useful in combination with Nmap to verify findings or learn further details.

## PASSIVE FINGERPRINTING

Passive fingerprinting uses most of the same techniques

as the active fingerprinting performed by Nmap. The difference is that a passive system simply sniffs the network, opportunistically classifying hosts as it observes their traffic. This is more difficult than active fingerprinting, since you have to accept whatever communication happens rather than designing your own custom probes. It is a valuable technique, but doesn't belong in a fundamentally active tool such as Nmap. Fortunately, Michal Zalewski has written the excellent p0f passive OS fingerprinting tool. He also devised a couple of the current Nmap OS fingerprinting tests. Another option is SinFP by GomoR, which supports both active and passive fingerprinting.

## EXPLOIT CHRONOLOGY

TCP/IP fingerprinting works well for distinguishing different operating systems, but detecting different versions of the same operating system can be troublesome. The company must change their stack in some way we can differentiate. Fortunately, many OS vendors regularly update their systems to comply with the latest standards. But what about those who don't? Most of them at least get around to fixing exploitable stack bugs eventually. And those fixes are easy to detect remotely. First send the exploit payload, be it a land attack, teardrop, ping of death, SYN flood, or WinNuke. Send one attack at a time, then immediately try to contact the system again. If it is suddenly non-responsive, you have narrowed down the OS to versions which didn't ship with the fix.

- *Warning:* If you use denial of service (DoS) exploits as part of your OS detection suite, remember to perform those tests last.

## RETRANSMISSION TIMES

TCP implementations have significant leeway in exactly how long they wait before retransmitting packets. The proof-of-concept tools Ring and Cron-OS are available to exploit this. They send a SYN packet to an open port, then ignore the SYN/ACK they receive rather than acknowledging it with an ACK (to complete the connection) or a RST (to kill it). The target host will resend the SYN/ACK several more times, and these tools track every subsecond of the wait. While some information can indeed be gleaned from this technique, there are several reasons that I haven't incorporated the patch into Nmap:

- It usually requires modifying the source host firewall rules to prevent your system from replying with a RST packet to the SYN/ACK it receives. That is hard to do in a portable way. And even if it was easy, many users don't appreciate applications mucking with their firewall rules.
- It can be very slow. The retransmissions can go on for several minutes. That is a long time to wait for a test that doesn't give all that much information in the first place.
- It can be inaccurate because packet drops and latency (which you have to expect in real-world environments) can lead to bogus results.

I have enumerated these reasons here because they also apply to some other proposed OS detection methods. I would love to add new tests, but they must be quick and require few packets. Messing with host firewall is unacceptable. I try to avoid making full TCP connections for stack fingerprinting, though that is done for OS detection as part of the version scanning system.

## IP FRAGMENTATION

IP fragmentation is a complex system and implementations are riddled with bugs and inconsistencies. Possible tests could examine how overlapping fragments are assembled or time the defragmentation time outs. These tests are avoided for Nmap because many firewalls and other inline devices defragment traffic at gateways. Thus Nmap may end up fingerprinting the firewall rather than the true destination host. In addition, fragments are difficult to send on some operating systems. Linux 2.6 kernels have a tendency to queue the fragments you are trying to send and assemble them itself before transmission.

## OPEN PORT PATTERNS

The target host OS can often be guessed simply by looking at the ports which are open. Microsoft Windows machines often have TCP ports 135 and 139 open. Windows 2000 and newer also listen on port 445. Meanwhile, a machine running services on port 22 and 631 (Internet Printing Protocol) is likely running Unix.

While this heuristic is often useful, it just isn't reliable enough for Nmap. Combinations of ports can be obscured by firewall rules, and most mainstream protocols are available on multiple platforms.

OpenSSH servers can be run on Windows, and the "Windows SMB" ports can be serviced by Samba running on a Unix machine. Port forwarding clouds the issue even further. A machine which appears to be running Microsoft IIS might be a Unix firewall simply forwarding port 80 to a Windows machine.

For these reasons, Nmap does not consider open port numbers during TCP/IP stack fingerprinting. However, Nmap can use version detection information to separately discover operating system and device type information. By keeping the OS detection results discovered by OS detection and version detection separate, Nmap can gracefully handle a Checkpoint firewall which uses TCP port forwarding to a Windows web server. The stack fingerprinting results should be"Checkpoint Firewall-1" while version detection should suggest that the OS is Windows. Keep in mind that only a IP fragmentation is a complex system and implementations are riddled with bugs and inconsistencies.

Possible tests could examine how overlapping fragments are assembled or time the defragmentation timeouts. These tests are avoided for Nmap because many firewalls and other inline devices defragment traffic at gateways. Thus Nmap may end up fingerprinting the firewall rather than the true destination host. In addition, fragments are difficult to send on some operating systems. Linux 2.6 kernels have a tendency to queue the fragments you are trying to send and assemble them itself before transmission.

## OPEN PORT PATTERNS

The target host OS can often be guessed simply by looking at the ports which are open. Microsoft Windows machines often have TCP ports 135 and 139 open. Windows 2000 and newer also listen on port 445. Meanwhile, a machine running services on port 22 (ssh) and 631 (Internet Printing Protocol) is likely running Unix.

While this heuristic is often useful, it just isn't reliable enough for Nmap. Combinations of ports can be obscured by firewall rules, and most mainstream protocols are available on multiple platforms. OpenSSH servers can be run on Windows, and the "Windows SMB" ports can be serviced by Samba running on a Unix machine. Port forwarding clouds the issue even further. A machine which appears to be running Microsoft IIS might be a Unix firewall simply forwarding port 80 to a Windows machine.

For these reasons, Nmap does not consider open port numbers during TCP/IP stack fingerprinting. However, Nmap can use version detection information to separately discover operating system and device type information. By keeping the OS detection results discovered by OS detection and version detection separate, Nmap can gracefully handle a Checkpoint firewall which uses TCP port forwarding to a Windows web server.

The stack fingerprinting results should be"Checkpoint Firewall-1" while version detection should suggest that the OS is Windows. Keep in mind that only a small fraction of version detection signatures include OS and device type information-we can only populate these fields when the application divulges the information or when it only runs on one OS or device type.

## RETIRED TESTS

There are some tests that were once performed by Nmap, but which have been retired because they were found not to help in distinguishing operating systems and only took up space in the database. Two tests in the IE line were removed: DLI checked the length of the data payload in returned packets and SI checked the ICMP sequence numbers. They were never found to vary from the values sent. In the U1line, the RUL test checked the length of the UDP packet returned. It was different from what was sent in only one case out of more than 1,700. These tests were removed in March 2009.

Other tests were removed because they were *too* discriminating; they caused false differences to be measured that harmed detection accuracy. Both of these had to do with the TOS (type of service) field in responses. TOS did this for the U1 probe and TOSI did it for IE. Although the test values did legitimately differ between operating systems, often false differences were recorded because the TOS was modified by an intermediate host. Better results were had overall when these tests were removed in October 2008.

## UNDERSTANDING AN NMAP FINGERPRINT

When Nmap stores a fingerprint in memory, Nmap uses a tree of attributes and values in data structures that users need not even be aware of. But there is also a special ASCII-encoded version which Nmap can print for users when a machine is unidentified. Thousands of these serialized fingerprints are also read back every time Nmap runs (with OS detection enabled) from the nmap-os-db database. The fingerprint format is a compromise between human comprehension and brevity. The format is so terse that it looks like line noise to many inexperienced users, but those who read this document should be able to decipher fingerprints with ease. There are actually two types of fingerprints, though they have the same general structure. The fingerprints of known operating systems that Nmap reads in are called reference fingerprints, while the fingerprint Nmap displays after scanning a system is a subject fingerprint. The reference fingerprints are a bit more complex since they can be tailored to match a whole class of operating systems by adding leeway to (or omitting) tests that aren't so reliable while allowing only a single possible value for other tests. The reference fingerprints also have OS details and classifications. Since the subject tests are simpler, we describe them first.

## DECODING THE SUBJECT FINGERPRINT FORMAT

If Nmap performs OS fingerprinting on a host and doesn't get a perfect OS matches despite promising conditions (such as finding both open and closed ports accessible on the target), Nmap prints a subject fingerprint that shows all of the test results that Nmap deems relevant, then asks the user to submit the data to Nmap.Org. Tests aren't shown when Nmap has no useful results, such as when the relevant probe responses weren't received. A special line named SCAN gives extra details about the scan (such as Nmap version number) that provide useful context for integrating fingerprint submissions into nmap-os-db. A typical subject fingerprint is shown in Example.

**Example. A typical subject fingerprint**

```
OS:SCAN(V=5.05BETA1%D=8/23%OT=2
2%CT=1%CU=42341%PV=N%DS=0%DC=L%G=Y%TM=4A91CB
OS:90%P=i686-pc-linux
gnu)SEQ(SP=C9%GCD=1%ISR=CF%TI=Z%
CI=Z%II=I%TS=A)OPS(O1
OS:=M400CST11NW5%O2=M400CST11NW5%O3=M400CN
NT11NW5%O4=M400CST11NW5%O5=M400CS
OS:T11NW5%O6=M400CST11)WIN(W1=8000%W
2=8000%W3=8000%W4=8000%W5=8000%W6=8000)
OS:ECN(R=Y%DF=Y%T=40%W=8018%O=M400CNNSNW5%C
C=N%Q=)T1(R=Y%DF=Y%T=40%S=O%
A=S+
OS:%F=AS%RD=0%Q=)T2(R=N)T3(R=Y%DF=Y%T=40%W=
8000%S=O%A=S+%F=AS%O=M400CST11NW
OS:5%RD=0%Q=)T4(R=Y%DF=Y%T=40%W=0%S=A%
A=Z%F=R%O=%RD=0%Q=)T5(R=Y%DF=Y%T=40%W
OS:=0%S=Z%A=S+%F=AR%O=%RD=0%Q=)T6(R=Y%DF=Y%T
=40%W=0%S=A%A=Z%F=R%O=%RD=0%Q=)
OS:T7(R=Y%DF=Y%T=40%W=0%S=Z%A=S+%F=AR
%O=%RD=0%Q=)U1(R=Y%DF=N%T=40%IPL=164%U
OS:N=0%RIPL=G%RID=G%RIPCK=G%RU
CK=G%RUD=G)IE(R=Y%DFI=N%T=40%CD=S)
```

Now you may look at this fingerprint and immediately understand what everything means. If so, you can simply skip this section. But I have never seen such a reaction. Many people probably think some sort of buffer overflow or unterminated string error is causing Nmap to spew garbage data at them. This section helps you decode the information so you can immediately tell that blind TCP sequence prediction attacks against this machine are moderately hard, but it may make a good idle scan (-sI) zombie. The first step in understanding this fingerprint is to fix the line wrapping. The tests are all squished together, with each line wrapped at 71 characters. Then OS: is prepended to each line, raising the length to 74 characters. This makes fingerprints easy to cut and paste into the Nmap fingerprint submission form the section called "When Nmap Fails to Find a Match and Prints a Fingerprint". Removing the prefix and fixing the word wrapping (each line should end with a right parenthesis) leads to the cleaned-up version inExample.

**Example. A cleaned-up subject fingerprint**

```
SCAN(V=5.05BETA1%D=823%OT=22%CT=1%CU=42341%
PV=N%DS=0%DC=L%G=Y%TM=4A91CB90%
P=i686-pc-linux-gnu)
SEQ(SP=C9%GCD=1%ISR=CF%TI=Z%CI=Z%II=I%TS=A)
OPS(O1=M400CST11NW5%O2=M40
0CST11N W5%O3=M400CNNT11NW5%
O4=M400CST11NW5%O5=M400CST11NW5%O6=M400CST11)
WIN(W1=8000%W2=8000%W3=8000%W4=8000%W5=8000%W6=8000)
ECN(R=Y%DF=Y%T=40%W=8018%O=M400CNNSNW5%CC=N%Q=)
T1(R=Y%DF=Y%T=40%S=O%A=S+%F=AS%RD=0%Q=)
T2(R=N)
T3(R=Y%DF=Y%T=40%W=8000%S=O%A=S+%F=AS%
O=M400CST11NW5%RD=0%Q=)
T4(R=Y%DF=Y%T=40%W=0%S=A%A=Z%F=R%O=%RD=0%Q=)
T5(R=Y%DF=Y%T=40%W=0%S=Z%A=S+%F=AR%O=%RD=0%Q=)
T6(R=Y%DF=Y%T=40%W=0%S=A%A=Z%F=R%O=%RD=0%Q=)
T7(R=Y%DF=Y%T=40%W=0%S=Z%A=S+%F=AR%O=%RD=0%Q=)
U1(R=Y%DF=N%T=40%IPL=164%UN=0%RIPL=G%RID=
G%RIPCK=G%RUCK=G%RUD=G)
IE(R=Y%DFI=N%T=40%CD=S)
```

While this still isn't the world's most intuitive format (we had to keep it short), the format is much clearer now. Every line is a category, such as SEQ for the sequence generation tests, T3 for the results from that particular TCP probe, and IE for tests related to the two ICMP echo probes.

Following each test name is a pair of parentheses which enclose results for individual tests. The tests take the format <testname>=<value>. All of the possible categories, tests, and values are described in the section called "TCP/IP Fingerprinting Methods Supported by Nmap".

Each pair of tests are separated by a percentage symbol (%). Tests values can be empty, leading to a percentage symbol or category-terminating right-parenthesis immediately following the equal sign.

The string "O=%RD=0%Q=)" in T4 of our example shows two of these empty tests. A blank test value must match another blank value, so this empty TCP quirks Q value wouldn't match a fingerprint with Q set to RU.

In some cases, a whole test is missing rather than just its value. For example, T2 of our sample fingerprint has no W (TCP window), S (sequence number), A (acknowledgment number), T (TTL), or TG (TTL guess) tests. This is because the one test and value it does include, R=N, means that no response was returned for the T2 probe.

So including a window value or sequence number would make little sense. Similarly, tests which aren't well supported on the system running Nmap are skipped. An example is the RID (IP ID field returned in ICMP packet) test, which doesn't work well on Solaris because that system tends to corrupt the ID field Nmap sends out. Tests which are inconclusive (such as failing to detect the IP ID sequence for the TI, CI, and II tests) are also omitted.

## DECODING THE SCAN LINE OF A SUBJECT FINGERPRINT

The SCAN line is a special case in a subject fingerprint. Rather than describe the target system, these tests describe various conditions of the scan. These help us integrate fingerprints submitted to Nmap.Org.

*The tests in this line are:*

- Nmap version number (V).
- Date of scan (D) in the form month/day.
- Open and closed TCP ports (on target) used for scan (OT and CT). Unlike most tests, these are printed in decimal format. If Nmap was unable to find an open or a closed port, the test is included with an empty value (even when Nmap guesses a possibly closed port and sends a probe there).
- Closed UDP port (CU). This is the same as CT, but for UDP. Since the majority of scans don't include UDP, this test's value is usually empty.
- Private IP space (PV) is Y if the target is on the 10.0.0.0/8, 172.16.0.0/12, or 192.168.0.0/16 private networks (RFC 1918). Otherwise it is N.
- Network distance (DS) is the network hop distance from the target. It is 0 if the target is localhost, 1 if directly connected on an ethernet network, or the exact distance if discovered by Nmap. If the distance is unknown, this test is omitted.
- The distance calculation method (DC) indicates how the network distance (DS) was calculated. It can take on these values: L for localhost (DS=0); D for a direct subnet connection (DS=1); I for a TTL calculation based on an ICMP response to the U1 OS detection probe; and T for a count of traceroute hops. This test exists because it is possible for the ICMP TTL calculation to be incorrect when intermediate machines change the TTL; it distinguishes between a host that is truly directly connected and what may be just a miscalculation.
- Good results (G) is Y if conditions and results seem good enough to submit this fingerprint to Nmap.Org. It is N otherwise. Unless you force them by enabling debugging (-d) or extreme verbosity (-vv), G=N fingerprints aren't printed by Nmap.
- Target MAC prefix (M) is the first six hex digits of the target MAC address, which correspond to the

vendor name. Leading zeros are not included. This field is omitted unless the target is on the same ethernet network (DS=1).

- The OS scan time (TM) is provided in Unix time_t format (in hexadecimal).
- The platform Nmap was compiled for is given in the P field.

## DECODING THE REFERENCE FINGERPRINT FORMAT

When Nmap scans a target to create a subject fingerprint, it then tries to match that data against the thousands of *reference fingerprints* in the nmap-os-db database. Reference fingerprints are initially formed from one or more subject fingerprints and thus have much in common. They do have a bit of extra information to facilitate matching and of course to describe the operating systems they represent. For example, the subject fingerprint we just looked at might form the basis for the reference fingerprint in Example.

**Example. A typical reference fingerprint**

```
Fingerprint Sony PlayStation 3 game console
Class Sony | embedded || game console
SEQ(SP=F7-101%GCD=1-6%ISR=FC-106%TI=RD%TS=21)
OPS(O1=M5B4NNSNW1NNT11%O2=M5B4NNSNW1NNT11%
O3=M5B4NW1NNT11%O4=M5B4NNSNW1NNT11%O5
=M5B4NNSNW1NNT11%O6=M5B4NNSNNT11)
WIN(W1=FFFF%W2=FFFF%W3=FFFF%W4=FFFF%W5=FFF
F%W6=FFFF)
ECN(R=Y%DF=N%T=3C-46%TG=40%W=FFFF%
O=M5B4NNSNW1%CC=N%Q=)
T1(R=Y%DF=N%T=3C-46%TG=40%S=O%A=S+%F=AS%RD=0%Q=)
T2(R=Y%DF=N%T=3C46%TG=40%W=0%S=Z%
A=O|S%F=AR%O=%RD=0%Q=)
T3(R=Y%DF=N%T=3C
46%TG=40%W=FFFF%S=O%A=S+%F=AS%O=M5B4
NNSNW1NNT11%RD=0%Q=)
T4(R=Y%DF=N%T=3C46%TG=40%W=0%S=A|O%
A=Z%F=R%O=%RD=0%Q=)
```

```
T5(R=Y%DF=N%T=3B45%TG=40%W=0%S=Z%A
=O|S+%F=AR%O=%RD=0%Q=)
T6(R=Y%DF=N%T=3B45%TG=40%W=0%S
=A|O%A=Z%F=R%O=%RD=0%Q=)
T7(R=Y%DF=N%T=3B45%TG=40%W=0%S=
Z%A=O|S%F=AR%O=%RD=0%Q=)
U1(DF=N%T=FA-
104%TG=FF%TOS=0%IPL=38%UN=0%RIPL=
G%RID=G%RIPCK=G%RUCK=G%RUL=G%RUD=G)
IE(DFI=N%T=FA-104%TG=FF%TOSI=S%CD=S%SI=S%DLI=S)
```

Some differences are immediately obvious. Line wrapping is not done because that is only important for the submission process. The SCAN line is also removed, since that information describes a specific scan instance rather than general target OS characteristics.

You probably also noticed the two new lines, Fingerprint and Class, which are new to this reference fingerprint. A more subtle change is that some of the individual test results have been removed while others have been enhanced with logical expressions.

## FREE-FORM OS DESCRIPTION (FINGERPRINT LINE)

The Fingerprint line first serves as a token so Nmap knows to start loading a new fingerprint. Each fingerprint only has one such line. Immediately after the Fingerprint token (and a space) comes a textual description of the operating system(s) represented by this fingerprint. These are in free-form English text, designed for human interpretation rather than a machine parser. Nevertheless, Nmap tries to stick with a consistent format including the vendor, product name, and then version number. Version number ranges and comma-separated alternatives discussed previously can be found in this field. Here are some examples:

```
Fingerprint HP LaserJet printer (4050, 4100, 4200,
or 8150)
Fingerprint Sun Solaris 9 or 10 (SPARC)
Fingerprint Linux 2.6.22-2.6.24
Fingerprint Microsoft Windows Server 2003 SP1
```

```
Fingerprint Microsoft Windows XP Professional SP1
Fingerprint Minolta Di550 laser printer
```

In an ideal world, every different OS would correspond to exactly one unique fingerprint. Unfortunately, OS vendors don't make life so easy for us. The same OS release may fingerprint differently based on what network drivers are in use, user-configurable options, patch levels, processor architecture, amount of RAM available, firewall settings, and more. Sometimes the fingerprints differ for no discernible reason. While the reference fingerprint format has an expression syntax for coping with slight variations, creating multiple fingerprints for the same OS is often preferable when major differences are discovered.

Just as multiple fingerprints are often needed for one OS, sometimes a single fingerprint describes several systems. If two systems give the exact same results for every single test, Nmap has little choice but to offer up both as possibilities. This commonly occurs for several reasons. One is that vendors may release a new version of their OS without any significant changes to their IP stack. Maybe they made important changes elsewhere in the system, or perhaps they did little but want to make a bunch of money selling "upgrades". In these cases, Nmap often prints a range such as Apple Mac OS X 10.4.8-10.4.11 or Sun Solaris 9 or 10.

Another cause of duplicate fingerprints is embedded devices which share a common OS. For example, a printer from one vendor and an ethernet switch from another may actually share an embedded OS from a third vendor. In many cases, subtle differences between the devices still allow them to be distinguished. But sometimes Nmap must simply list a group of possibilities such as Cisco 1200-series WAP, HP ProCurve 2650 switch, or Xerox Phaser 7400N or 8550DT printer.

There are also cases where numerous vendors private label the exact same OEM device with their own brand name and model number. Here again, Nmap must simply list the possibilities. But distinguishing these is less important because they are all fundamentally the same device.

- *Tip:* If the description printed by Nmap (which comes

from the Fingerprint line) isn't informative enough for you, more detailed information may be available in comments above the fingerprint itself in nmap-os-db. You can find it installed on your system or look up the latest version at. Search for the exact OS description that Nmap gives you. Keep in mind that there may be several Fingerprint lines with exactly the same description, so you may have to examine them all. Or use the Nmap XML output, which shows the line number of each match.

## DEVICE AND OS CLASSIFICATION (CLASS LINES)

While the Fingerprint description works great for analysts reading Nmap output directly, many people run Nmap from other scripts andapplications. Those applications might use the OS information to check for OS-specific vulnerabilities or just create a pretty graph or report.

A more structured OS classification system exists for these purposes. It is also useful when there are multiple matches. If you only get a partial fingerprint (maybe no open ports were found on the target so many tests had to be skipped), it might match dozens of different fingerprints in thenmap-os-db database. Printing the details for all of those fingerprints would be a mess. But thanks to OS classification, Nmap can find commonality. If all of the matches are classified as Linux, Nmap will simply print that the target is a Linux box.

Every fingerprint has one or more Class lines. Each contains four well-defined fields: vendor, OS family, OS generation, and device type. The fields are separated by the pipe symbol (|).

The vendor is the company which makes an OS or device. Examples are Apple, Cisco, Microsoft, and Linksys. For community projects such as OpenBSD and Linux without a controlling vendor, the OS family name is repeated for the vendor column.

OS family includes products such as Windows, Linux, IOS (for Cisco routers), Solaris, and OpenBSD. There are also hundreds of devices such as switches, broadband routers, and printers which use undisclosed operating systems. When the underlying OS isn't clear, embedded is used. OS generation is a more granular description of the OS. Generations of Linux include 2.4.X and 2.6.X, while Windows generations include 95, 98,Me, 2000, XP, and Vista. FreeBSD uses generations such as 4.X and 5.X. For obscure operating systems which we haven't subdivided into generations (or whenever the OS is listed simply as embedded), this field is left blank.

The device type is a broad classification such as router, printer, or game console and was discussed previously in this chapter. General-purpose operating systems such as Linux and Windows which can be used for just about anything are classified as general purpose.

Each field may contain just one value. When a fingerprint represents more than one possible combination of these four fields, multiple Class lines are used. Example provides some example Fingerprint lines followed by their corresponding classifications.

**Example. Some typical fingerprint descriptions and corresponding classifications**

```
Fingerprint D-Link DSL-500G ADSL router
Class D-Link | embedded || broadband router
Fingerprint Linksys WRT54GC or TRENDnet TEW-431BRP
WAP
Class Linksys | embedded || WAP
Class TRENDnet | embedded || WAP
Fingerprint Apple Mac OS X 10.3.9 (Panther)-10.4.7
(Tiger)
Class Apple | Mac OS X | 10.3.X | general purpose
Class Apple | Mac OS X | 10.4.X | general purpose
Fingerprint Sony PlayStation 3 game console
Class Sony | embedded || game console
```

If these examples aren't enough, a listing of classifications recognized by the latest version of Nmap is maintained at.

## TEST EXPRESSIONS

The test expressions don't have to change between a subject and reference fingerprint, but they almost always do. The reference fingerprint often needs to be generalized a little bit to match all instances of a particular OS, rather than just the machine you are scanning. For example, some Windows XP machines return a Window size of F424 to the T1 probe, while others return FAF0. This may be due to the particular ethernet device driver in use, or maybe how much memory is available. In any case, we would like to detect Windows XP no matter which window size is used.

One way to generalize a fingerprint is to simply remove tests that produce inconsistent results. Remove all of the window size tests from a reference fingerprint, and systems will match that print no matter what size they use. The downside is that you can lose a lot of important information this way. If the only Window sizes that a particular system ever sends are F424 and FAF0, you really only want to allow those two values, not all 65,536 possibilities.

While removing tests is overkill in some situations, it is useful in others. The R=Y test value, meaning there was a response, is usually removed from theU1 and IE tests before they are added to nmap-os-db. These probes are often blocked by a firewall, so the lack of a response should not count against the OS match.

When removing tests is undesirable, Nmap offers an expression syntax for allowing a test to match multiple values. For example, W=F424|FAF0would allow those two Windows XP window values without allowing any others. Table shows the permitted operators in test values.

**Table. Reference Fingerprint Test Expression operators**

| Op | Symbol | Example | Description |
|---|---|---|---|
| Name | | | Matches if the corresponding |
| Or | \| | O=\|ME\| MNNTNW | subject fingerprint test takes the value of any of the clauses. In this example, the initial pipe symbol means that an empty options list will match too. |
| Range | - | SP=7-A | Matches if the print's subject finger corresponding test produces a numeric value |

| | | | |
|---|---|---|---|
| | | | which falls within the range specified. |
| Greater than | > | SP=>8 | Matches if the subject fingerprint's corresponding test produces a numeric value which is greater than the one specified. |
| Less | < | GCD=<5 | Matches if the subject than fingerprint's corresponding test produces a numeric value which is less than the one specified. |

Expressions can combine operators, as in GCD=1-6|64|256|>1024, which matches if the GCD is between one and six, exactly 64, exactly 256, or greater than 1024.

## DEVICE TYPES

As stated in the section called "Device and OS classification (Class lines)", every reference fingerprint is classified with one or more device types. This list contains the device types used by Nmap and the criteria for classifying a device as each type. These same rules are used to classify the device types in version detection; see the description of the d/ /field in the section called "match Directive".

### GENERAL PURPOSE

This category contains general-purpose operating systems like Linux and Windows. In the nmap-service-probes file this class is indicated by a lack of a d//field.

### BRIDGE

A bridge combines two or more subnetworks into one. With a bridge this happens at a lower level than with a router. This category also includes things like Ethernet-to-serial bridges.

### BROADBAND ROUTER

Devices in this category connect a network to the Internet via cable, ADSL, fibre optics, etc. Some of these devices provide network address translation, a firewall, port forwarding, or other services.

### FIREWALL

A firewall controls what traffic is allowed into or out of a network. Some also have additional capabilities. This category doesn't include general-purpose operating systems that happen to come with a firewall, but it does include OS distributions purpose-built to work only as a firewall.

### GAME CONSOLE

A video game console like the Xbox or PlayStation.

### HUB

A hub joins network segments by re-broadcasting all traffic. Hubs are distinct from switches, which selectively transmit packets only to relevant destinations.

### LOAD BALANCER

A device that distributes inbound traffic to multiple devices to ease the load on those devices.

### MEDIA DEVICE

This category includes all kinds of audiovisual equipment, including portable music players, home audio systems, TVs, and projectors.

### PBX

A private branch exchange, or PBX, routes telephone calls within a private organization and connects them to the public telephone network or VoIP.

### PDA

A handheld computer. Devices that are also telephones go in the "phone" category.

### PHONE

A network-capable telephone that is not a VoIP phone. Devices in this category are typically mobile phones.

**POWER-DEVICE**

Miscellaneous power devices like uninterruptable power supplies and surge protectors.

**PRINTER**

Network-enabled printers, including printers with an embedded print server.

**PRINT SERVER**

A print server connects a printer to a network. Printers that contain their own print server go in the "printer" category instead.

**PROXY SERVER**

Any kind of proxy, including web proxies and other servers that cache data or understand high-level protocols.

**REMOTE MANAGEMENT**

Devices that allow servers or other equipment to be monitored or managed remotelv.

**ROUTER**

Routers connect multiple networks. They are distinct from hubs and switches because they route packets between different networks as opposed to extending one network.

**SECURITY-MISC**

Any security device that doesn't fall into the "firewall" category belongs in this category. This includes intrusion detection and prevention systems.

**SPECIALIZED**

The catch-all category. If a device doesn't fall into one of the other categories, it is specialized. Examples in this category are diverse and include such things as clocks, oscilloscopes, climate sensors, and more.

**STORAGE-MISC**

Data storage devices like tape decks and network-attached storage appliances.

### SWITCH

A device that extends a network by selectively re-broadcasting packets. Switches are distinct from hubs, which broadcast all packets.

### TELECOM-MISC

Devices used by telephone systems that aren't PBXs, like voice-mail and ISDN systems.

### TERMINAL

A device with a keyboard and monitor with the primary purpose of communicating directly with a terminal server or mainframe.

### TERMINAL SERVER

A device providing terminal facilities to clients over a network.

### VOIP ADAPTER

A device that converts between voice over IP (VoIP) protocols and normal telephone traffic. Also may convert different VoIP protocols.

### VOIP PHONE

A phone capable of a VoIP protocol.

### WAP

Wireless access points offer a wireless connection to a network. Most work with radio technology like 802.11b but some use infra-red or something else. Devices that could also be put in another category, like wireless broadband routers, are put in the WAP category because WAPs require special network considerations.

### WEBCAM

Any kind of camera that stores or transmits pictures or video. This includes everything from consumer webcams to security system cameras.

## OS MATCHING ALGORITHMS

Nmap's algorithm for detecting matches is relatively simple. It takes a subject fingerprint and tests it against every single reference fingerprint in nmap-os-db. When testing against a reference fingerprint, Nmap looks at each probe category line from the subject fingerprint (such as SEQ or T1) in turn. Any probe lines which do not exist in the reference fingerprint are skipped. When the reference fingerprint does have a matching line, they are compared.

For a probe line comparison, Nmap examines every individual test (R, DF, W, etc.) from the subject category line in turn. Any tests which donot exist in the reference line are skipped. Whenever a matching test is found, Nmap increments the PossiblePoints accumulator by the number of points assigned to this test. Then the test values are compared. If the reference test has an empty value, the subject test only matches if its value is empty too. If the reference test is just a plain string or number (no operators), the subject test must match it exactly.

If the reference string contains operators (|, -, >, or <), the subject must match as described in the section called "Test expressions". If a test matches, the NumMatchPoints accumulator is incremented by the test's point value. Once all of the probe lines are tested for a fingerprint, Nmap divides NumMatchPoints by PossiblePoints. The result is a confidence factor describing the probability that the subject fingerprint matches that particular reference fingerprint. It is treated as a percentage, so 1.00is a perfect match while 0.95 is very close.

Test point values are assigned by a special MatchPoints entry (which may only appear once) in nmap-os-db. This entry looks much like a normal fingerprint, but instead of providing results for each test, it provides point values (non-negative integers) for each test. Tests listed in the MatchPoints structure only apply when found in the same test they are listed in. So a value given for the W (Window size) test in T1doesn't affect the W test in T3. A test can be effectively disabled by assigning it a point value of 0. An example MatchPoints structure is given in Example.

**Example. The MatchPoints structure**

```
MatchPoints
SEQ(SP=25%GCD=75%ISR=25%TI=100%CI=50%I
I=100%SS=80%TS=100)
OPS(O1=20%O2=20%O3=20%O4=20%O5=20%O6=20)
WIN(W1=15%W2=15%W3=15%W4=15%W5=15%W6=15)
ECN(R=100%DF=20%T=15%TG=15%W=15%O=15%CC=100%Q=20)
T1(R=100%DF=20%T=15%TG=15%S=20%A=2
0%F=30%RD=20%Q=20)
T2(R=80%DF=20%T=15%TG=15%W=25%S=
20%A=20%F=30%O=10%RD=20%Q=20)
T3(R=80%DF=20%T=15%TG=15%W=25%S=20%A=20%F=30%
O=10%RD=20%Q=20)
T4(R=100%DF=20%T=15%TG=15%W=25%S=
20%A=20%F=30%O=10%RD=20%Q=20)
T5(R=100%DF=20%T=15%TG=15%W=25%S=
20%A=20%F=30%O=10%RD=20%Q=20)
T6(R=100%DF=20%T=15%TG=15%W=25%S=20%
A=20%F=30%O=10%RD=20%Q=20)
T7(R=80%DF=20%T=15%TG=15%W=25%S=2
0%A=20%F=30%O=10%RD=20%Q=20)
U1(R=50%DF=20%T=15%TG=15%TOS=0%IPL=100%UN=100%RI
PL=100%RID=100%RIPCK=100%RUCK=100%RUL=100%RUD=100)
IE(R=50%DFI=40%T=15%TG=15%TOSI=0%CD=100%SI=100%DLI=100)
```

Once all of the reference fingerprints have been evaluated, Nmap orders them and prints the perfect matches (if there aren't too many).

If there are no perfect matches, but some are very close, Nmap may print those. Guesses are more likely to be printed if the —osscan-guess option is given.

## DEALING WITH MISIDENTIFIED AND UNIDENTIFIED HOSTS

While Nmap has a huge database, it cannot detect everything. Nmap has no chance to detect most toasters, refrigerators, chairs, or automobiles because they have no IP stack. Yet I wouldn't rule any of these out, given the ever-expanding list of connected devices.

The Nmap fingerprint DB includes plenty of game consoles, phones, thermometers, cameras, interactive toys, and media players.

Having an IP address is necessary but not sufficient to guarantee a proper fingerprint. Nmap may still guess wrong or fail to produce any guess at all. Here are some suggestions for improving your results:

## UPGRADE TO THE LATEST NMAP

Many Linux distributions and other operating systems ship with ancient versions of Nmap. The Nmap OS database is improved with almost every release, so check your version number by running nmap -V and then compare that to the latest available from. Installing the newest version takes only a few minutes on most platforms.

## SCAN ALL PORTS

When Nmap detects OS detection problems against a certain host, it will issue warnings. One of the most common is: "Warning: OS detection will be MUCH less reliable because Scan all ports we did not find at least 1 open and 1 closed TCP port". It is possible that such ports really are unavailable on the machine, but retrying your scan with -p- to scan all ports may find some that are responsive for OS detection. Doing a UDP scan (-sU) too can help even more, though it will slow the scan substantially.

## TRY A MORE AGGRESSIVE GUESS

If Nmap says there are no matches close enough to print, something is probably wrong. Maybe a firewall or NAT box in the way is modifying the probe or response packets. This can cause a hybrid situation where one group of tests look like they are from one OS, while another set look completely different. Adding the —osscan-guess may give more clues as to what is running.

## SCAN FROM A DIFFERENT LOCATION

The more network hops your packet has to go through to

reach its target, the greater the chances that a network device will modify (or drop) the probe or response. NAT gateways, firewalls, and especially port forwarding can confuse OS detection. If you are scanning the IP of a load balancing device which simply redirects packets to a diverse network of servers, it isn't even clear what the"correct" OS detection result would be.

Many ISPs filter traffic to "bad" ports, and others use transparent proxies to redirect certain ports to their own servers. The port 25 or 80 you think are open on your target may actually be spoofed from your ISP to connect to ISP proxy servers.

Another behaviour which can confuse OS detection is when firewalls spoof TCP reset packets as if they are coming from the destination host. This is particularly common from port 113 (identd). Both the reset spoofing and transparent proxies can often be detected by noticing that every machine on a target network seems to exhibit the behaviour—even those which otherwise seem to be down.

If you detect any such nonsense, be sure to exclude these ports from your scan so they don't taint your results. You may also want to try from a completely different network location. The closer you are to the target, the more accurate the results will be.

In a perfect case, you would always scan the target from the same network segment it resides on.

## WHEN NMAP GUESSES WRONG

Occasionally Nmap will report an OS guess which you know is wrong. The errors are usually minor (such as reporting a machine running Linux 2.4.16 as "Linux kernel 2.4.8-2.4.15"), but there have been reports of Nmap being completely off (such as reporting your web server as an AppleWriter printer).

When you encounter such problems (minor or major), please report them so everyone can benefit.

The only reason the Nmap DB is so comprehensive is that thousands of users have spent a few minutes each to submit new information. Please follow these instructions.

## HAVE A RECENT VERSION OF NMAP

- *Run nmap*: V to determine which version of Nmap you have. You don't need to be running the absolute latest version of Nmap (though that would be ideal), but make sure your version is 4.20 or higher because we only need second generation OS fingerprints, not the old style produced by previous versions. You can determine the latest available version of Nmap by visiting. If you upgrade, you might find that the identification has already been fixed.

Be absolutely certain you know what is running Invalid "corrections" can corrupt the OS DB. If you aren't certain exactly what is running on the remote machine, please find out before submitting.

## GENERATE A FINGERPRINT

Run the command nmap -O -sSU -T4 -d <target>, where <target> is the misidentified system in question. Look at the OS detection results to ensure that the misidentification is still present. If the Nmap output for the host OS results says (JUST GUESSING), it is expected that results may be a little off. Don't submit a correction in this case. Otherwise, the map command should have produced results including the line OS fingerprint:.

Below that is the fingerprint (a series of lines which each start with OS:). Check that OS detection works against other hosts Try scanning a couple other hosts on the target network which you know have a different OS. If they aren't detected properly, maybe there is some network obstruction between the systems which is corrupting the packets. If you have gotten this far and are still able to submit, good for you! Please submit the information at.

## MODIFYING THE NMAP-OS-DB DATABASE YOURSELF

People often ask about integrating a fingerprint themselves rather than (or in addition to) submitting it to

Nmap.Org. While we don't offer detailed instructions or scripts for this, it is certainly possible after you become intimately familiar with the section called "Understanding an Nmap Fingerprint". I hope this is useful for your purposes, but there is no need to send your own reference fingerprint creations to us. We can only integrate raw subject fingerprint submissions from the web form.

# 3

# XCG Programing

## INTRODUCTION

*This chapter has the following four sections:*

- "What Is Cg?" introduces the Cg programming language.
- "Vertices, Fragments, and the Graphics Pipeline" describes the data flow of modern graphics hardware and explains how Cg fits into this data flow.
- "Cg's Historical Development" provides some background on how Cg was developed.
- "The Cg Environment" explains how applications go about using Cg programs through the Cg runtime and existing 3D application programming interfaces (APIs).

## WHAT IS CG

This book teaches you how to use a programming language called Cg. The Cg language makes it possible for you to control the shape, appearance, and motion of objects drawn using programmable graphics hardware. It marries programmatic control of these attributes with the incredible speed and capabilities of today's graphics processors. Never before have computer graphics practitioners, whether artists or programmers, had so much control over the real-time images they generate.

Cg provides developers with a complete programming platform that is easy to use and enables the fast creation of special effects and real-time cinematic-quality experiences on multiple platforms. By providing a new level of abstraction, Cg removes the need for developers to program directly to the graphics hardware assembly language, and thereby more easily target OpenGL, DirectX, Windows, Linux, Macintosh OS X, and console platforms such as the Xbox. Cg was developed in close collaboration with Microsoft Corporation and is compatible with both the OpenGL API and Microsoft's High-Level Shading Language (HLSL) for DirectX 9.0.

Cg stands for "C for graphics." The C programming language is a popular, general-purpose language invented in the 1970s. Because of its popularity and clean design, C provided the basis for several subsequent programming languages. For example, C++ and Java base their syntax and structure largely on C. The Cg language bases itself on C as well. If you are familiar with C or one of the many languages derived from C, then Cg will be easy to learn.

On the other hand, if you are not familiar with C or even programming languages in general but you enjoy computer graphics and want to learn something new, read on anyway. Cg programs tend to be short and understandable.

Much of this chapter is background that provides valuable context for understanding Cg and using it effectively. On the other hand, you may find Cg is easier to learn by doing. Feel free to skip to Chapter 2 at any time if you feel more comfortable just diving into the tutorial.

## A Language for Programming Graphics Hardware

Cg is different from C, C++, and Java because it is very specialized. No one will ever write a spreadsheet or word processor in Cg. Instead, Cg targets the ability to programmatically control the shape, appearance, and motion of objects rendered using graphics hardware. Broadly, this type of language is called a *shading language*. However, Cg can do more than just shading. For example, Cg programs can perform physical simulation, compositing, and other nonshading tasks.

Think of a Cg program as a detailed recipe for how to render an object by using programmable graphics hardware.

For example, you can write a Cg program to make a surface appear bumpy or to animate a virtual character. Later, in Section 1.3, you will learn more about the history of shading languages and where Cg fits into this history.

### Cg's Data-Flow Model

In addition to being specialized for graphics, Cg and other shading languages are different from conventional programming languages because they are based on a data-flow computational model. In such a model, computation occurs in response to data that flows through a sequence of processing steps.

Cg programs operate on vertices and fragments (think "pixels" for now if you do not know what a fragment is) that are processed when rendering an image. Think of a Cg program as a black box into which vertices or fragments flow on one side, are somehow transformed, and then flow out on the other side. However, the box is not really a black box because you get to determine, by means of the Cg programs you write, exactly what happens inside.

Every time a vertex is processed or the rasterizer generates a fragment while rendering a 3D scene, your corresponding vertex or fragment Cg program executes. Section 1.3 explains Cg's data-flow model further. Most recent personal computers—and all recent game consoles—contain a graphics processing unit (GPU) that is dedicated to graphics tasks such as transforming and rasterizing 3D models. Your Cg programs actually execute within the GPU of your computer.

### GPU Specialization and CPU Generalization

Whether or not a personal computer or game console has a GPU, there must be a CPU that runs the operating system and application programs. CPUs are, by design, general purpose. CPUs execute applications (for example, word processors and accounting packages) written in general-purpose languages, such as C++ or Java. Because of the GPU's specialized design, it is much faster at graphics tasks, such as rendering 3D scenes, than a general-purpose CPU would be.

New GPUs process tens of millions of vertices per second and rasterize hundreds of millions or even billions of fragments per second. Future GPUs will be even speedier. This is overwhelmingly faster than the rate at which a CPU could process a similar number of vertices and fragments. However, the GPU cannot execute the same arbitrary, general-purpose programs that a CPU can.

The specialized, high-performance nature of the GPU is why Cg exists. General-purpose programming languages are too open-ended for the specialized task of processing vertices and fragments. In contrast, the Cg language is fully dedicated to this task. Cg also provides an abstract execution model that matches the GPU's execution model. You will learn about the unique execution model of GPU.

## The Performance Rationale for Cg

To sustain the illusion of interactivity, a 3D application needs to maintain an animation rate of 15 or more images per second. Generally, we consider 60 or more frames per second to be "real time," the rate at which interaction with applications appears to occur instantaneously. The computer's display may have a million or more pixels that require redrawing. For 3D scenes, the GPU typically processes every pixel on the screen many times to account for how objects occlude each other, or to improve the appearance of each pixel. This means that real-time 3D applications can require hundreds of millions of pixel updates per second. Along with the required pixel processing, 3D models are composed of vertices that must be transformed properly before they are assembled into polygons, lines, and points that will be rasterized into pixels. This can require transforming tens of millions of vertices per second.

Moreover, this graphical processing happens in addition to the considerable amount of effort required of the CPU to update the animation for each new image. The reality is that we need both the CPU and the GPU's specialized graphics-oriented capabilities. Both are required to render scenes at the interactive rates and quality standards that users of 3D applications and games demand. This means a developer can write a 3D application or game in C++ and then use Cg to make the most of the GPU's additional graphics horsepower.

### Coexistence with Conventional Languages

In no way does Cg replace any existing general-purpose languages. Cg is an auxiliary language, designed specifically for GPUs. Programs written for the CPU in conventional languages such as C or C++ can use the Cg runtime (described in Section 1.4.2) to load Cg programs for GPUs to execute. The Cg runtime is a standard set of subroutines used to load, compile, manipulate, and configure Cg programs for execution by the GPU. Applications supply Cg programs to instruct GPUs on how to accomplish the programmable rendering effects that would not otherwise be possible on a CPU at the rendering rates a GPU is capable of achieving.

Cg enables a specialized style of parallel processing. While your CPU executes a conventional application, that application also orchestrates the parallel processing of vertices and fragments on the GPU, by programs written in Cg.

If a real-time shading language is such a good idea, why didn't someone invent Cg sooner? The answer has to do with the evolution of computer graphics hardware. Prior to 2001, most computer graphics hardware—certainly the kind of inexpensive graphics hardware in PCs and game consoles—was hard-wired to the specific tasks of vertex and fragment processing. By "hard-wired," we mean that the algorithms were fixed within the hardware, as opposed to being programmable in a way that is accessible to graphics applications. Even though these hard-wired graphics algorithms could be configured by graphics applications in a variety of ways, the applications could not reprogram the hardware to do tasks unanticipated by the designers of the hardware. Fortunately, this situation has changed.

Graphics hardware design has advanced, and vertex and fragment processing units in recent GPUs are truly programmable. Before the advent of programmable graphics hardware, there was no point in providing a programming language for it. Now that such hardware is available, there is a clear need to make it easier to program this hardware. Cg makes it much easier to program GPUs in the same manner that C made it much easier to program CPUs.

Before Cg existed, addressing the programmable capabilities of the GPU was possible only through low-level assembly language. The cryptic instruction syntax and manual hardware register manipulation required by assembly languages—such as DirectX 8 vertex and pixel shaders and some OpenGL extensions—made it a painful task for most developers. As GPU technology made longer and more complex assembly language programs possible, the need for a high-level language became clear. The extensive low-level programming that had been required to achieve optimal performance could now be delegated to a compiler, which optimizes the code output and handles tedious instruction scheduling. Figure is a small portion of a complex assembly language fragment program used to represent skin. Clearly, it is hard to comprehend, particularly with the specific references to hardware registers.

### *Example*

A Snippet of Assembly Language Code

```
...
DEFINE LUMINANCE = {0.299, 0.587, 0.114, 0.0};
TEX H0, f[TEX0], TEX4, 2D;
TEX H1, f[TEX2], TEX5, CUBE;
DP3X H1.xyz, H1, LUMINANCE;
MULX H0.w, H0.w, LUMINANCE.w;
MULX H1.w, H1.x, H1.x;
MOVH H2, f[TEX3].wxyz;
MULX H1.w, H1.x, H1.w;
DP3X H0.xyz, H2.xzyw, H0;
MULX H0.xyz, H0, H1.w;
TEX H1, f[TEX0], TEX1, 2D;
TEX H3, f[TEX0], TEX3, 2D;
MULX H0.xyz, H0, H3;
MADX H1.w, H1.w, 0.5, 0.5;
MULX H1.xyz, H1, {0.15, 0.15, 1.0, 0.0};
```

```
MOVX H0.w, H1.w;
TEX H1, H1, TEX7, CUBE;
TEX H3, f[TEX3], TEX2, 1D;
MULX H3.w, H0.w, H2.w;
MULX H3.xyz, H3, H3.w;
...
```

In contrast, well-commented Cg code is more portable, more legible, easier to debug, and easier to reuse. Cg gives you the advantages of a high-level language such as C while delivering the performance of low-level assembly code.

## Other Aspects of Cg

Cg is a language for programming "in the small." That makes it much simpler than a modern general-purpose language such as C++. Because Cg specializes in transforming vertices and fragments, it does not currently include many of the complex features required for massive software engineering tasks. Unlike C++ and Java, Cg does not support classes and other features used in object-oriented programming. Current Cg implementations do not provide pointers or even memory allocation (though future implementations may, and keywords are appropriately reserved). Cg has absolutely no support for file input/output operations. By and large, these restrictions are not permanent limitations in the language, but rather are indicative of the capabilities of today's highest performance GPUs. As technology advances to permit more general programmability on the GPU, you can expect Cg to grow appropriately. Because Cg is closely based on C, future updates to Cg are likely to adopt language features from C and C++.

Cg provides arrays and structures. It has all the flow-control constructs of a modern language: loops, conditionals, and function calls.

Cg natively supports vectors and matrices because these data types and related math operations are fundamental to graphics and most graphics hardware directly supports vector data types. Cg has a library of functions, called the Standard Library, that is well suited for the kind of operations required for graphics. For example, the Cg Standard Library includes a reflect function for computing reflection vectors.

Cg programs execute in relative isolation. This means that the processing of a particular vertex or fragment has no effect on other vertices or fragments processed at the same time. There are no side effects to the execution of a Cg program. This lack of interdependency among vertices and fragments makes Cg programs extremely well suited for hardware execution by highly pipelined and parallel hardware.

## The Limited Execution Environment of Cg Programs

When you write a program in a language designed for modern CPUs using a modern operating system, you expect that a more-or-less arbitrary program, as long as it is correct, will compile and execute properly. This is because CPUs, by design, execute general-purpose programs for which the overall system has more than sufficient resources.

However, GPUs are specialized rather than general-purpose, and the feature set of GPUs is still evolving. Not everything you can write in Cg can be compiled to execute on a given GPU. Cg includes the concept of hardware "profiles," one of which you specify when you compile a Cg program. Each profile corresponds to a particular combination of GPU architecture and graphics API. Your program not only must be correct, but it also must limit itself to the restrictions imposed by the particular profile used to comj ile your Cg program. For example, a given fragment profile may limit you to no more than four texture accesses per fragment.

As GPUs evolve, additional profiles will be supported by Cg that correspond to more capable GPU architectures. In the future, profiles will be less important as GPUs become more full-featured. But for now Cg programmers will need to limit programs to ensure that they can compile and execute on existing GPUs. In general, future profiles will be supersets of current profiles, so that programs written for today's profiles will compile without change using future profiles.

This situation may sound limiting, but in practice the Cg programs shown in this book work on tens of millions of GPUs and produce compelling rendering effects. Another reason for limiting program size and scope is that the smaller and more efficient your Cg programs are, the faster they will run. Real-time graphics is often about balancing increased scene complexity, animation rates, and improved shading. So it's always good to maximize rendering efficiency through judicious Cg programming.

Keep in mind that the restrictions imposed by profiles are really limitations of current GPUs, not Cg. The Cg language is powerful enough to express shading techniques that are not yet possible with all GPUs. With time, GPU functionality will evolve far enough that Cg profiles will be able to run amazingly complex Cg programs. Cg is a language for both current and future GPUs.

## VERTICES, FRAGMENTS, AND THE GRAPHICS PIPELINE

To put Cg into its proper context, you need to understand how GPUs render images. This section explains how graphics hardware is evolving and then explores the modern graphics hardware-rendering pipeline.

## THE EVOLUTION OF COMPUTER GRAPHICS HARDWARE

Computer graphics hardware is advancing at incredible rates. Three forces are driving this rapid pace of innovation, as shown in Figure. First, the semiconductor industry has committed itself to doubling the number of transistors (the basic unit of computer hardware) that fit on a microchip every 18 months. This constant redoubling of computer power, historically known as Moore's Law, means cheaper and faster computer hardware, and is the norm for our age.

The second force is the vast amount of computation required to simulate the world around us. Our eyes consume and our brains comprehend images of our 3D world at an astounding rate and with startling acuity. We are unlikely ever to reach a point where computer graphics becomes a substitute for reality. Reality is just too real. Undaunted, computer graphics practitioners continue to rise to the challenge. Fortunately, generating images is an embarrassingly parallel problem. What we mean by "embarrassingly parallel" is that graphics hardware designers can repeatedly split up the problem of creating realistic images into more chunks of work that are smaller and easier to tackle. Then hardware engineers can arrange, in parallel, the ever-greater number of transistors available to execute all these various chunks of work.

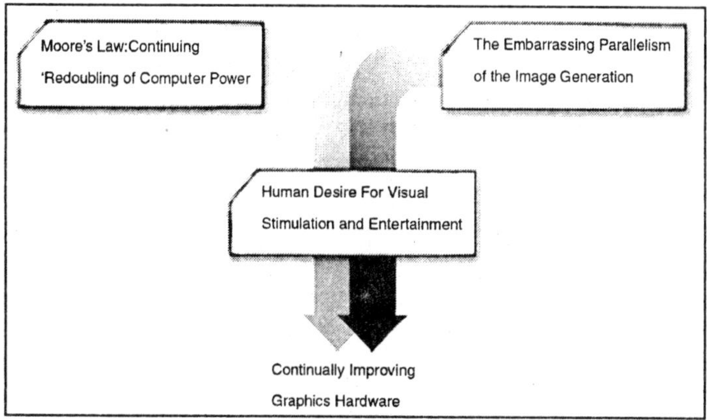


**Fig**:Forces Driving Graphics Hardware Innovation

Our third force is the sustained desire we all have to be stimulated and entertained visually. This is the force that "connects" the source of our continued redoubling of computer hardware resources to the task of approximating visual reality ever more realistically than before. As Figure illustrates, these insights let us confidently predict that computer graphics hardware is going to get much faster. These innovations whet our collective appetite for more interactive and compelling 3D experiences. Satisfying this demand is what motivated the development of the Cg language.

## FOUR GENERATIONS OF COMPUTER GRAPHICS HARDWARE

In the mid-1990s, the world's fastest graphics hardware consisted of multiple chips that worked together to render images and display them to a screen. The most complex computer graphics systems consisted of dozens of chips spread over several boards. As time progressed and semiconductor technology improved, hardware engineers incorporated the functionality of complicated multichip designs into a single graphics chip. This development resulted in tremendous economies of integration and scale.

You may be surprised to learn that the GPU now exceeds the CPU in the number of transistors present in each microchip. Transistor count is a rough measure of how much computer hardware is devoted to a microchip. For example, Intel packed its 2.4 GHz Pentium 4 with 55 million transistors; NVIDIA used over 125 million transistors in the original GeForce FX GPU. NVIDIA introduced the term "GPU" in the late 1990s when the legacy term "VGA controller" was no longer an accurate description of the graphics hardware in a PC. IBM had introduced Video Graphics Array (VGA) hardware in 1987. At that time, the VGA controller was what we now call a "dumb" frame buffer. This meant that the CPU was responsible for updating all the pixels. Today the CPU rarely manipulates pixels directly. Instead, graphics hardware designers build the "smarts" of pixel updates into the GPU.

Industry observers have identified four generations of GPU evolution so far. Each generation delivers better performance and evolving programmability of the GPU feature set. Each generation also influences and incorporates the functionality of the two major 3D programming interfaces, OpenGL and DirectX. OpenGL is an open standard for 3D programming for Windows, Linux, UNIX, and Macintosh computers. DirectX is an evolving set of Microsoft multimedia programming interfaces, including Direct3D for 3D programming.

## PRE-GPU GRAPHICS ACCELERATION

Prior to the introduction of GPUs, companies such as Silicon Graphics (SGI) and Evans and Sutherland designed specialized and expensive graphics hardware. The graphics systems developed by these companies introduced many of the concepts, such as vertex transformation and texture mapping, that we take for granted today. These systems were very important to the historical development of computer graphics, but because they were so expensive, they did not achieve the mass-market success of single-chip GPUs designed for PCs and video game consoles. Today, GPUs are far more powerful and much cheaper than any prior systems.

## FIRST-GENERATION GPUS

The first generation of GPUs (up to 1998) includes NVIDIA's TNT2, ATI's Rage, and 3dfx's Voodoo3. These GPUs are capable of rasterizing pre-transformed triangles and applying one or two textures. They also implement the DirectX 6 feature set. When running most 3D and 2D applications, these GPUs completely relieve the CPU from updating individual pixels. However, GPUs in this generation suffer from two clear limitations. First, they lack the ability to transform vertices of 3D objects; instead, vertex transformations occur in the CPU. Second, they have a quite limited set of math operations for combining textures to compute the colour of rasterized pixels.

## SECOND-GENERATION GPUS

The second generation of GPUs (1999-2000) includes NVIDIA's GeForce 256 and GeForce2, ATI's Radeon 7500, and S3's Savage3D. These GPUs offload 3D vertex transformation and lighting (T&L) from the CPU. Fast vertex transformation was one of the key capabilities that differentiated high-end workstations from PCs prior to this generation. Both OpenGL and DirectX 7 support hardware vertex transformation. Although the set of math operations for combining textures and colouring pixels expanded in this generation to include cube map textures and signed math operations, the possibilities are still limited. Put another way, this generation is more configurable, but still not truly programmable.

## THIRD-GENERATION GPUS

The third generation of GPUs (2001) includes NVIDIA's GeForce3 and GeForce4 Ti, Microsoft's Xbox, and ATI's Radeon 8500. This generation provides vertex programmability rather than merely offering more configurability. Instead of supporting the conventional transformation and lighting modes specified by OpenGL and DirectX 7, these GPUs let the application specify a sequence of instructions for processing vertices. Considerably more pixel-level configurability is available, but these modes are not powerful enough to be considered truly programmable. Because these GPUs support vertex programmability but lack true pixel programmability, this generation is transitional. DirectX 8 and the multivendor ARB_vertex_programOpenGL extension expose vertex-level programmability to applications. DirectX 8 pixel shaders and various vendor-specific OpenGL extensions expose this generation's fragment-level configurability.

## FOURTH-GENERATION GPUS

The fourth and current generation of GPUs (2002 and on) includes NVIDIA's GeForce FX family with the CineFX architecture and ATI's Radeon 9700. These GPUs provide both vertex-level and pixel-level programmability. This level of programmability opens up the possibility of offloading complex vertex transformation and pixel-shading operations from the CPU to the GPU. DirectX 9 and various OpenGL extensions expose the vertex-level and pixel-level programmability of these GPUs. This is the generation of GPUs where Cg gets really interesting. Table 1-1 lists selected NVIDIA GPUs representing these various GPU generations.

**Table. Features and Performance Evolution of Selected NVIDIA GPUs, by Generation**

| Generation | Year | Product Name | Process | Transistors | Antialiasi-ngFillRate | Polygon Rate | Note |
|---|---|---|---|---|---|---|---|
| First | Late 1998 | RIVA TNT | 0.25 m | 7 M | *50 M* | 6 M | [1] |
| First | Early 1999 | RIVA TNT2 | 0.22 m | 9 M | *75 M* | 9 M | [2] |
| Second | Late 1999 | GeForce 256 | 0.22 m | 23 M | *120 M* | 15 M | [3] |
| Second | Early 2000 | Ge Force2 | 0.18 m | 25 M | *200 M* | 25 M | [4] |

| | | | | | | | |
|---|---|---|---|---|---|---|---|
| Third | Early 2001 | GeForce3 | 0.15 m | 57 M | 800 M | 30 M | [5] |
| Third | Early 2002 | GeForce4 Ti | 0.15 m | 63 M | 1200 M | 60 M | [6] |
| Fourth | Early 2003 | GeForce FX | 0.13 m | 125 M | 2000 M | 200 M | [7] |

Notes

*The table uses the following terms:*

- *Process*: The minimum feature size in microns (m, millionths of a meter) for the semiconductor process used to fabricate each microchip
- *Transistors:* An approximate measure, in millions (M), of the chips' design and manufacturing complexity
- *Antialiasing fill rate*: A GPU's ability to fill pixels, measured in millions (M) of 32-bit RGBA pixels per second, assuming two-sample antialiasing; numbers in *italics* indicate fill rates that are de-rated because the hardware lacks true antialiased rendering
- *Polygon rate:* A GPU's ability to draw triangles, measured in millions (M) of triangles per second

The notes highlight the most significant improvements in each design. Performance rates may not be comparable with designs from other hardware vendors. Future GPUs will further generalize the programmable aspects of current GPUs, and Cg will make this additional programmability easy to use.

## THE GRAPHICS HARDWARE PIPELINE

A *pipeline* is a sequence of stages operating in parallel and in a fixed order. Each stage receives its input from the prior stage and sends its output to the subsequent stage. Like an assembly line where dozens of automobiles are manufactured at the same time, with each automobile at a different stage of the line, a conventional graphics hardware pipeline processes a multitude of vertices, geometric primitives, and fragments in a pipelined fashion.

Figure shows the graphics hardware pipeline used by today's GPUs. The 3D application sends the GPU a sequence of vertices batched into geometric primitives: typically polygons, lines, and points. As shown in Figure, there are many ways to specify geometric primitives.

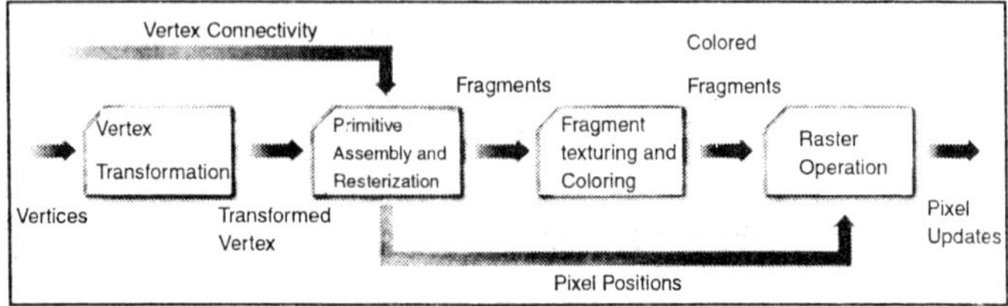


**Fig:** The Graphics Hardware Pipeline

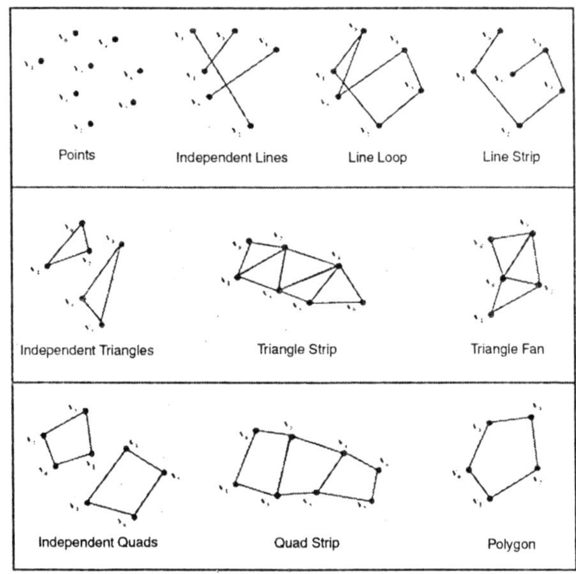


**Fig:** Types of Geometric Primitives

Every vertex has a position but also usually has several other attributes such as a colour, a secondary (or *specular*) colour, one or multiple texture coordinate sets, and a normal vector. The normal vector indicates what direction the surface faces at the vertex, and is typically used in lighting calculations.

## VERTEX TRANSFORMATION

*Vertex transformation* is the first processing stage in the graphics hardware pipeline. Vertex transformation performs a sequence of math operations on each vertex. These operations include transforming the vertex position into a screen position for use by the rasterizer, generating texture coordinates for texturing, and lighting the vertex to determine its colour. We will explain many of these tasks in subsequent chapters.

## PRIMITIVE ASSEMBLY AND RASTERIZATION

The transformed vertices flow in sequence to the next stage, called *primitive assembly and rasterization*. First, the primitive assembly step assembles vertices into geometric primitives based on the geometric primitive batching information that accompanies the sequence of vertices. This results in a sequence of triangles, lines, or points. These primitives may require clipping to the *view frustum* (the view's visible region of 3D space), as well as any enabled application-specified clip planes. The rasterizer may also discard polygons based on whether they face forward or backward. This process is known as *culling*.

Polygons that survive these clipping and culling steps must be rasterized. Rasterization is the process of determining the set of pixels covered by a geometric primitive. Polygons, lines, and points are each rasterized according to the rules specified for each type of primitive. The results of rasterization are a set of pixel locations as well as a set of fragments. There is no relationship between the number of vertices a primitive has and the number of fragments that are generated when it is rasterized. For example, a triangle made up of just three vertices could take up the entire screen, and therefore generate millions of fragments!

Earlier, we told you to think of a fragment as a pixel if you did not know precisely what a fragment was. At this point, however, the distinction between a fragment and a pixel becomes important. The term *pixel* is short for "picture element." A pixel represents the contents of the frame buffer at a specific location, such as the colour, depth, and any other values associated with that location. A *fragment* is the state required potentially to update a particular pixel.

The term "fragment" is used because rasterization breaks up each geometric primitive, such as a triangle, into pixel-sized fragments for each pixel that the primitive covers. A fragment has an associated pixel location, a depth value, and a set of interpolated parameters such as a colour, a secondary (specular) colour, and one or more texture coordinate sets. These various interpolated parameters are derived from the transformed vertices that make up the particular geometric primitive used to generate the fragments. You can think of a fragment as a "potential pixel." If a fragment passes the various rasterization tests (in the raster operations stage, which is described shortly), the fragment updates a pixel in the frame buffer.

## INTERPOLATION, TEXTURING, AND COLOURING

Once a primitive is rasterized into a collection of zero or more fragments, the*interpolation, texturing, and colouring* stage interpolates the fragment parameters as necessary, performs a sequence of texturing and math operations, and determines a final colour for each fragment. In addition to determining the fragment's final colour, this stage may also determine a new depth or may even discard the fragment to avoid updating the frame buffer's corresponding pixel. Allowing for the possibility that the stage may discard a fragment, this stage emits one or zero coloured fragments for every input fragment it receives.

## RASTER OPERATIONS

The *raster operations* stage performs a final sequence of per-fragment operations immediately before updating the frame buffer. These operations are a standard part of OpenGL and Direct3D. During this stage, hidden surfaces are eliminated through a process known as *depth testing*. Other effects, such as blending and stencil-based shadowing, also occur during this stage.

The raster operations stage checks each fragment based on a number of tests, including the scissor, alpha, stencil, and depth tests. These tests involve the fragment's final colour or depth, the pixel location, and per-pixel values such as the depth value and stencil value of the pixel. If any test fails, this stage discards the fragment without updating the pixel's colour value (though a stencil write operation may occur). Passing the depth test may replace the pixel's depth value with the fragment's depth. After the tests, a blending operation combines the final colour of the fragment with the corresponding pixel's colour value. Finally, a frame buffer write operation replaces the pixel's colour with the blended colour. Figure shows this sequence of operations.

Fragment & Associated DAta
Pixel Ownership Test
Scissor Test
Alpha Test
Depth Test
Stencil Test
Depth Buffer
Stencil Test
Depth Buffer
Blending
Dithering
Logic Op
Color Buffer

**Fig:** Standard OpenGL and Direct3D Raster Operations

Figure shows that the raster operations stage is actually itself a series of pipeline stages. In fact, all of the previously described stages can be broken down into substages as well.

## VISUALIZING THE GRAPHICS PIPELINE

Figure depicts the stages of the graphics pipeline. In the figure, two triangles are rasterized. The process starts with the transformation and colouring of vertices. Next, the primitive assembly step creates triangles from the vertices, as the dotted lines indicate. After this, the rasterizer "fills in" the triangles with fragments. Finally, the register values from the vertices are interpolated and used for texturing and colouring. Notice that many fragments are generated from just a few vertices.

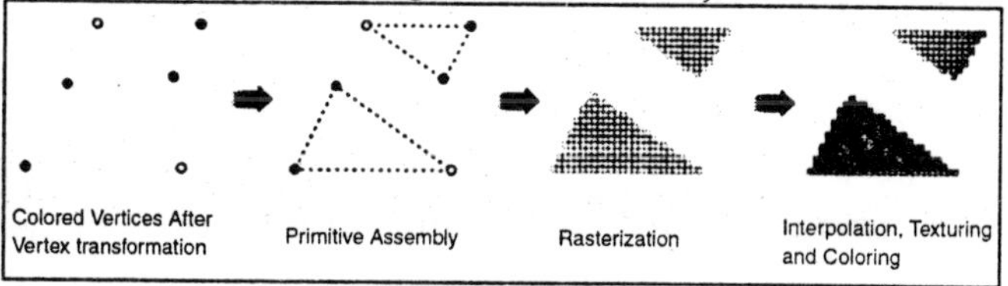


**Fig:** Visualizing the Graphics Pipeline

## The Programmable Graphics Pipeline

The dominant trend in graphics hardware design today is the effort to expose more programmability within the GPU. Figure shows the vertex processing and fragment processing stages in the pipeline of a programmable GPU.

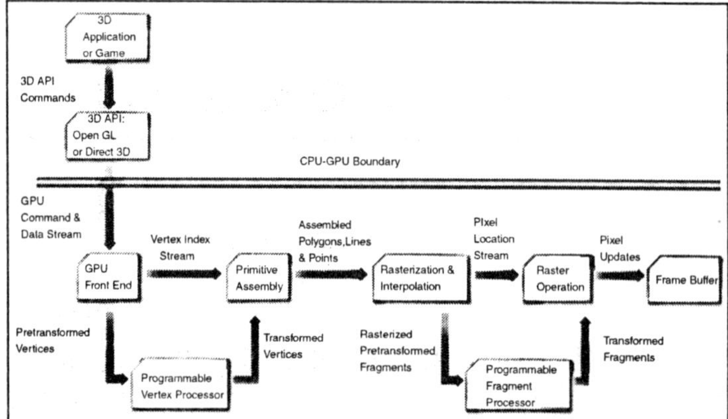


**Fig:** The Programmable Graphics Pipeline

Figure shows more detail than Figure, but more important, it shows the vertex and fragment processing broken out into programmable units. The *programmable vertex processor* is the hardware unit that runs your Cg vertex programs, whereas the *programmable fragment processor* is the unit that runs your Cg fragment programs.

As explained in GPU designs have evolved, and the vertex and fragment processors within the GPU have transitioned from being configurable to being programmable. The descriptions in the next two sections present the critical functional features of programmable vertex and fragment processors.

## THE PROGRAMMABLE VERTEX PROCESSOR

Figure shows a flow chart for a typical programmable vertex processor. The data-flow model for vertex processing begins by loading each vertex's attributes (such as position, colour, texture coordinates, and so on) into the vertex processor.

The vertex processor then repeatedly fetches the next instruction and executes it until the vertex program terminates. Instructions access several distinct sets of registers banks that contain vector values, such as position, normal, or colour. The vertex attribute registers are read-only and contain the application-specified set of attributes for the vertex. The temporary registers can be read and written and are used for computing intermediate results.

The output result registers are write-only. The program is responsible for writing its results to these registers. When the vertex program terminates, the output result registers contain the newly transformed vertex. After triangle setup and rasterization, the interpolated values for each register are passed to the fragment processor.

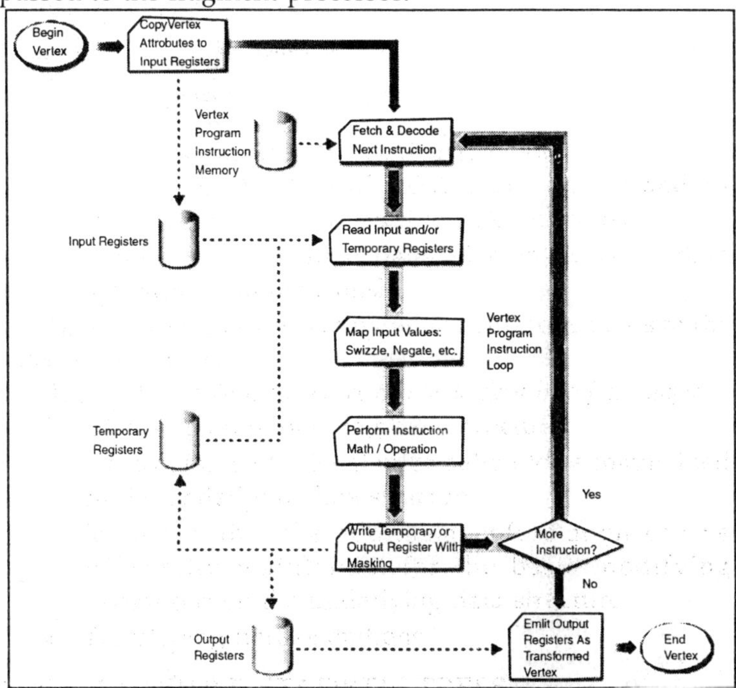


**Fig**: Programmable Vertex Processor Flow Chart

Most vertex processing uses a limited palette of operations. Vector math operations on floating-point vectors of two, three, or four components are necessary. These operations include add, multiply, multiply-add, dot product, minimum, and maximum.

Hardware support for vector negation and component-wise swizzling (the ability to reorder vector components arbitrarily) generalizes these vector math instructions to provide negation, subtraction, and cross products. Component-wise write masking controls the output of all instructions.

Combining reciprocal and reciprocal square root operations with vector multiplication and dot products, respectively, enables vector-by-scalar division and vector normalization. Exponential, logarithmic, and trigonometric approximations facilitate lighting, fog, and geometric computations. Specialized instructions can make lighting and attenuation functions easier to compute.

Further functionality, such as relative addressing of constants and flow-control support for branching and looping, is also available in more recent programmable vertex processors.

## THE PROGRAMMABLE FRAGMENT PROCESSOR

Programmable fragment processors require many of the same math operations as programmable vertex processors do, but they also support texturing operations. Texturing operations enable the processor to access a texture image using a set of texture coordinates and then to return a filtered sample of the texture image.

Newer GPUs offer full support for floating-point values; older GPUs have more limited fixed-point data types. Even when floating-point operations are available, fragment operations are often more efficient when using lower-precision data types.

GPUs must process so many fragments at once that arbitrary branching is not available in current GPU generations, but this is likely to change over time as hardware evolves. Cg still allows you to write fragment programs that branch and iterate by simulating such constructs with conditional assignment operations or loop unrolling.

Figure shows the flow chart for a current programmable fragment processor. As with a programmable vertex processor, the data flow involves executing a sequence of instructions until the program terminates. Again, there is a set of input registers.

However, rather than vertex attributes, the fragment processor's read-only input registers contain interpolated per-fragment parameters derived from the per-vertex parameters of the fragment's primitive.

Read/write temporary registers store intermediate values. Write operations to write-only output registers become the colour and optionally the new depth of the fragment. Fragment program instructions include texture fetches.

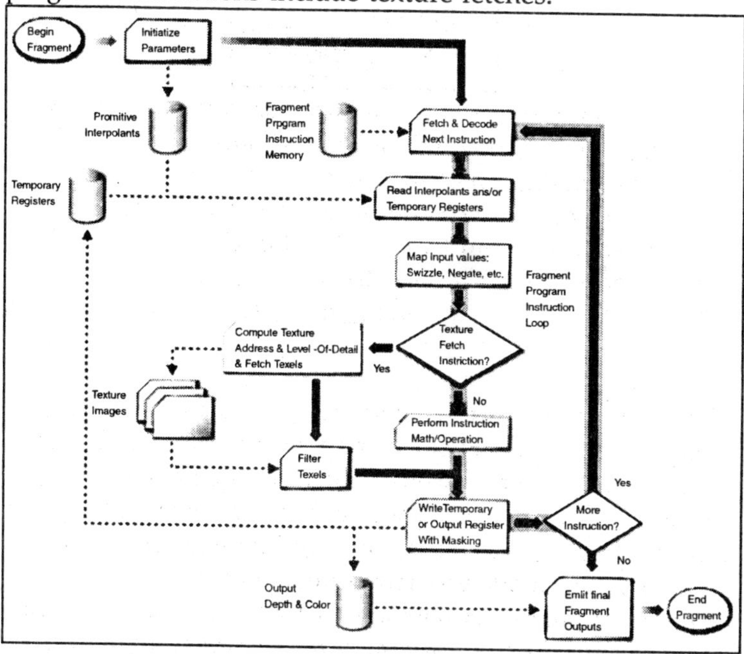


**Fig**: Programmable Fragment Processor Flow Chart

## Cg Provides Vertex and Fragment Programmability

These two programmable processors in your GPU require you, the application programmer, to supply a program for each processor to execute. What Cg provides is a language and a compiler that can translate your shading algorithm into a form that your GPU's hardware can execute. With Cg, rather than program at the level shown in Figures you can program in a high-level language very similar to C.

## CG'S HISTORICAL DEVELOPMENT

Cg's heritage comes from three sources, as shown in Figure. First, Cg bases its syntax and semantics on the general-purpose C programming language. Second, Cg incorporates many concepts from offline shading languages such as the RenderMan Shading Language, as well as prior hardware shading languages developed by academia. Third, Cg bases its graphics functionality on the OpenGL and Direct3D programming interfaces for real-time 3D.

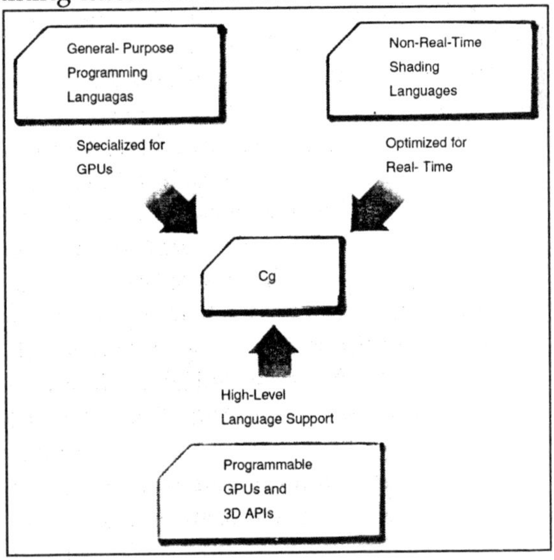

**Fig**: Sources of Cg's Technology Heritage

Figure shows the general-purpose programming languages, 3D application programming interfaces, and shading languages that inspired Cg's development. Earlier, we mentioned how Cg leverages C's syntax and semantics. Over the course of this book, you will find that Cg mostly does what C programmers expect. Cg differs from C in situations where either Cg's specialization for GPUs or performance justifies a change.

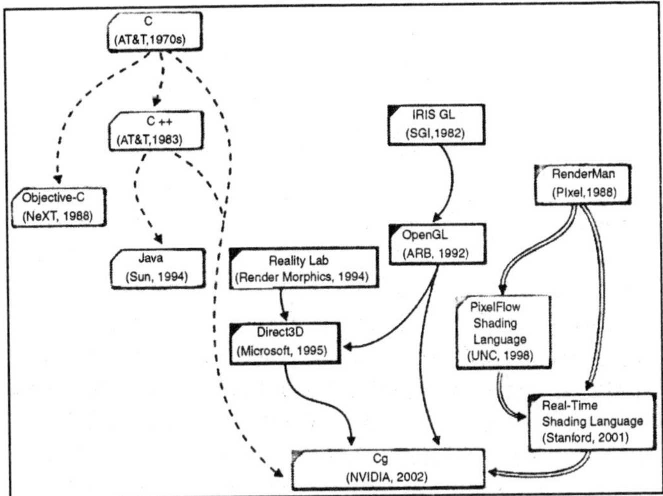


**Fig:** Inspirations for Cg's Development

## MICROSOFT AND NVIDIA'S COLLABORATION TO DEVELOP CG AND HLSL

NVIDIA and Microsoft collaborated to develop the Cg language. Microsoft calls its implementation High-Level Shading Language, or HLSL for short. HLSL and Cg are the same language but reflect the different names each company uses to identify the language and its underlying technology. HLSL is a part of Microsoft's DirectX Graphics, a component of the DirectX 9 multimedia framework. Direct3D is the 3D component of Microsoft's DirectX Graphics. Cg is indє pendent of the 3D programming interface and fully integrates with either Direct3D or OpenGL. A properly written Cg application can be written once and then work with either OpenGL or Direct3D.

This flexibility means that NVIDIA's Cg implementation provides a way to author programs that work with both dominant 3D programming interfaces and whatever operating system you choose. Cg works whether you choose Windows, Linux, Mac OS X, a game console, or embedded 3D hardware as your 3D computing platform. Cg programs work with hardware from multiple hardware vendors because Cg layers cleanly upon either Direct3D or OpenGL. Cg programs work on programmable GPUs from all the major graphics hardware vendors, such as 3Dlabs, ATI, Matrox, and NVIDIA.

The multivendor, cross-API, and multiplatform nature of the Cg language makes it the best choice when writing programs for programmable GPUs.

### Noninteractive Shading Languages

The RenderMan Interface Standard describes the best-known shading language for noninteractive shading. Pixar developed the language in the late 1980s to generate high-quality computer animation with sophisticated shading for films and commercials. Pixar has created a complete rendering system with its implementation of the RenderMan Interface Standard, the offline renderer PRMan (PhotoRealistic RenderMan). The RenderMan Shading Language is just one component of this system.

## SHADE TREES

The inspiration for the RenderMan Shading Language came from an earlier idea called*shade trees*. Rob Cook, then at Lucasfilm Ltd., which later spun off Pixar, published a SIGGRAPH paper about shade trees in 1984. A shade tree organizes various shading operations as nodes within a tree structure.

Figure shows a shade tree for rendering a copper surface. The leaf nodes are data inputs to the shade tree. The nonleaf nodes represent simple shading operations. During the process of rendering, the renderer evaluates the shade tree associated with a given surface to determine the colour of the surface in the rendered image.

To evaluate a shade tree, a renderer performs the shading operation associated with the topmost node in the shade tree. However, to evaluate a given node, the renderer must first evaluate the node's child nodes. This rule is applied recursively to evaluate the shade tree fully. The result of a shade tree evaluation at a given point on a surface is the colour of that point.

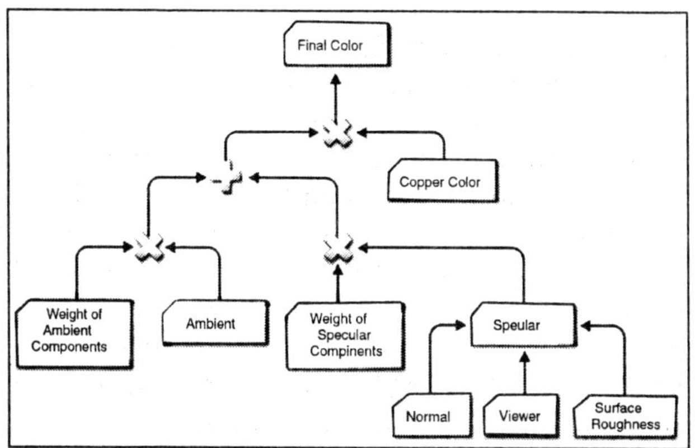


**Fig**: A Shade Tree Example, Based on Rob Cook's Original SIGGRAPH Paper

Shade trees grew out of the realization that a single predefined shading model would never be sufficient for all the objects and scenes one might want to render. Shade tree diagrams are great for visualizing a data flow of shading operations. However, if the shade trees are complex, their diagrams become unwieldy. Researchers at Pixar and elsewhere recognized that each shade tree is a limited kind of program. This realization provided the impetus for a new kind of programming language known as a shading language.

## THE RENDERMAN SHADING LANGUAGE

The RenderMan Shading Language grew out of shade trees and the realization that open-ended control of the appearance of rendered surfaces in the pursuit of photorealism requires programmability. Today most offline renderers used in actual production have some type of support for a shading language. The RenderMan Shading Language is the most established and best known for offline rendering, and it was significantly overhauled and extended in the late 1990s.

## HARDWARE-AMENABLE SHADING LANGUAGES

A hardware implementation of an algorithm is most efficient when the task decomposes into a long sequence of stages in which each stage's communication is limited to its prior stage and its subsequent stage (that is, when it can be pipelined). The vertex-based and fragment-based pipeline described in Section 1.2 is extremely amenable to hardware implementation. However, the Reyes algorithm used by PhotoRealistic RenderMan is not very suitable for efficient hardware implementation, primarily due to its higher-level geometry handling. Contemporary GPUs rely completely on a graphics pipeline based on vertices and fragments.

Researchers at the University of North Carolina (UNC) began investigating programmable graphics hardware in the mid-1990s, when UNC was developing a new programmable graphics hardware architecture called PixelFlow. This project fostered a new line of computer graphics research into hardware-amenable shading languages by Marc Olano and others at UNC. Unfortunately, PixelFlow was too expensive and failed commercially. Subsequently, researchers at Silicon Graphics worked on a system to translate shaders into multiple passes of OpenGL rendering. Although the targeted OpenGL hardware was not programmable in the way GPUs are today, the OpenGL Shader system orchestrates numerous rendering passes to achieve a shader's intended effect.

Researchers at Stanford University, including Kekoa Proudfoot, Bill Mark, Svetoslav Tzvetkov, and Pat Hanrahan, began building a shading language designed specifically for second-generation and third-generation GPUs. This language, known as the Stanford Real-Time Shading Language (RTSL), could compile shaders written in RTSL into one or more OpenGL rendering passes. The research at Stanford inspired NVIDIA's own effort to develop a commercial-quality hardware-amenable shading language. Bill Mark joined NVIDIA in 2001 to lead the effort to define and implement the shading language we now call Cg. During this time, NVIDIA collaborated with Microsoft to agree on a common language syntax and feature set.

## PROGRAMMING INTERFACES FOR 3D GRAPHICS

The third influence on Cg was the pair of standard 3D programming interfaces, OpenGL and Direct3D. The influence of these programming interfaces on Cg is ongoing, as is explained in the next section.

## THE CG ENVIRONMENT

Cg is just one component of the overall software and hardware infrastructure for rendering complex 3D scenes with programmable GPUs at real-time rates. This section explains how Cg interacts with actual 3D applications and games.

## STANDARD 3D PROGRAMMING INTERFACES: OPENGL AND DIRECT3D

In the old days of 3D graphics on a PC (before there were GPUs), the CPU handled all the vertex transformation and pixel-pushing tasks required to render a 3D scene. The graphics hardware provided only the buffer of pixels that the hardware displayed to the screen. Programmers had to implement their own 3D graphics rendering algorithms in software. In a sense, everything about vertex and fragment processing back then was completely programmable. Unfortunately, the CPU was too slow to produce compelling 3D effects. These days, 3D applications no longer implement their own 3D rendering algorithms using the CPU; rather, they rely on either OpenGL or Direct3D, the two standard 3D programming interfaces, to communicate rendering commands to the GPU.

## OPENGL

In the early 1990s, Silicon Graphics developed OpenGL in coordination with an organization called the OpenGL Architecture Review Board (ARB), which comprised all the major computer graphics system vendors. Originally, OpenGL ran only on powerful UNIX graphics workstations. Microsoft, a founding member of the ARB, then implemented OpenGL as a way to support 3D graphics for its Windows NT operating system. Microsoft later added OpenGL support to Windows 95 and all of Microsoft's desktop operating systems.

OpenGL is not limited to a single operating or windowing system. In addition to supporting UNIX workstations and

Windows PCs, OpenGL is supported by Apple for its Macintosh personal computers. Linux users can use either the Mesa open-source implementation of OpenGL or a hardware-accelerated implementation such as NVIDIA's OpenGL driver for Linux. This flexibility makes OpenGL the industry's best cross-platform programming interface for 3D graphics.

Over the last decade, OpenGL has evolved along with graphics hardware. OpenGL is extensible, meaning that OpenGL implementers can add new functionality to OpenGL in an incremental way. Today, scores of OpenGL extensions provide access to all the latest GPU features. This includes ARB-standardized extensions for vertex and fragment programmability.

As extensions are established, they are often rolled into the core OpenGL standard so that the standard as a whole advances. At the time of this writing, the current version of OpenGL is 1.4. Ongoing work to evolve OpenGL is underway in various OpenGL ARB working groups. This work includes both assembly-level and high-level programmable interfaces. Because Cg operates as a layer above such interfaces, it will continue to function with future revisions of OpenGL in a compatible manner.

## DIRECT3D

Microsoft began developing the Direct3D programming interface about 1995 as part of its DirectX multimedia initiative. Direct3D is one of the programming interfaces that make up DirectX. Microsoft introduced DirectX and Direct3D to jump-start the consumer market for 3D graphics, particularly gaming, on Windows PCs. Microsoft's Xbox game console also supports Direct3D. Direct3D is the most popular graphics API for games on Windows, due to its history of closely matching the capabilities of available graphics hardware. Every year or so, Microsoft has updated DirectX, including Direct3D, to keep up with the rapid pace of PC hardware innovation. The current version of DirectX at the time of this writing is DirectX 9, which includes HLSL, Microsoft's implementation of the same language syntax and constructs found in Cg.

## 3D PROGRAMMING INTERFACE DÉTENTE

A few years ago, OpenGL and Direct3D competed to see which programming interface would dominate, particularly in the domain of Windows PCs. The competition continues to be good for both programming interfaces, and each has improved in performance, quality, and functionality. In the area of GPU programmability that Cg addresses, both programming interfaces have comparable capabilities. This is because both OpenGL and Direct3D run on the same GPU hardware and the graphics hardware determines the available functionality and performance. OpenGL has a slight advantage in functionality because hardware vendors are better able to expose their entire feature set through OpenGL, though vendor-specific extensions do add some complexity for developers.

Most software developers now choose a 3D programming interface based on programmer preference, history, and their target market and hardware platform, rather than on technical grounds.

Cg supports either programming interface. You can write Cg programs so that they work with either the OpenGL or Direct3D programming interface. This is a huge boon for 3D content developers. They can pair their 3D content with programs written in Cg and then render the content no matter what programming interface the final application uses for 3D rendering.

## THE CG COMPILER AND RUNTIME

No GPU can execute Cg programs directly from their textual form. A process known as compilation must translate Cg programs into a form that the GPU can execute. The Cg compiler first translates your Cg program into a form accepted by the application's choice of 3D programming interface, either OpenGL or Direct3D. Then your application transfers the OpenGL or Direct3D translation of your Cg program to the GPU using the appropriate OpenGL or Direct3D commands. The OpenGL or Direct3D driver performs the final translation into the hardware-executable form your GPU requires.

The details of this translation depend on the combined capabilities of the GPU and 3D programming interface. How a Cg program compiles its intermediate OpenGL or Direct3D form depends on the type and generation of GPU in your computer.

It may be that your GPU is not capable of supporting a particular valid Cg program because of limitations of the GPU itself. For example, your Cg fragment program will not compile if your program accesses more texture units than your target GPU supports.

## SUPPORT FOR DYNAMIC COMPILATION

When you compile a program with a conventional programming language such as C or C++, compilation is an offline process. Your compiler compiles the program into an executable that runs directly on the CPU. Once compiled, your program does not need to be recompiled, unless you change the program code. We call this *static compilation.*

Cg is different because it encourages *dynamic compilation,* although static compilation is also supported. The Cg compiler is not a separate program but part of a library known as the Cg runtime. 3D applications and games using Cg programs must link with the Cg runtime. Applications using Cg then call Cg runtime routines, all prefixed with the letters cg, to compile and manipulate Cg programs. Dynamic compilation allows Cg programs to be optimized for the particular model of GPU installed in the user's machine.

## CGGL AND CGD3D, THE 3D-API-SPECIFIC CG LIBRARIES

In addition to the core Cg runtime, Cg provides two closely related libraries. If your application uses OpenGL, you will use the CgGL library to invoke the appropriate OpenGL routines to pass your translated Cg program to the OpenGL driver.

Likewise, if your application uses Direct3D, you will use the CgD3D library to invoke the appropriate Direct3D routines to pass your translated Cg program to the Direct3D driver.

Normally, you would use either the CgGL or the CgD3D library, but not both, because most applications use either OpenGL or Direct3D, not both.

Compared with the core Cg runtime library that contains the Cg compiler, the CgGL and CgD3D libraries are relatively small. Their job is to make the appropriate OpenGL or Direct3D calls for you to configure Cg programs for execution. These calls transfer a translated Cg program to the appropriate driver that will further translate the program into a form your GPU can execute.

For the most part, the CgGL and CgD3D libraries have similar routines. The routines in the CgGL library begin with cgGL; the routines in the CgD3D library begin with cgD3D.

## HOW THE CG RUNTIME FITS INTO YOUR APPLICATION

Figure shows how a typical 3D application uses the Cg libraries. If you are a programmer, you will want to learn more about the Cg runtime and the specific library for the 3D API your application uses to render 3D graphics. Most of this book focuses on the Cg language itself and on how to write Cg programs, but Appendix B has more information about the Cg runtime library.

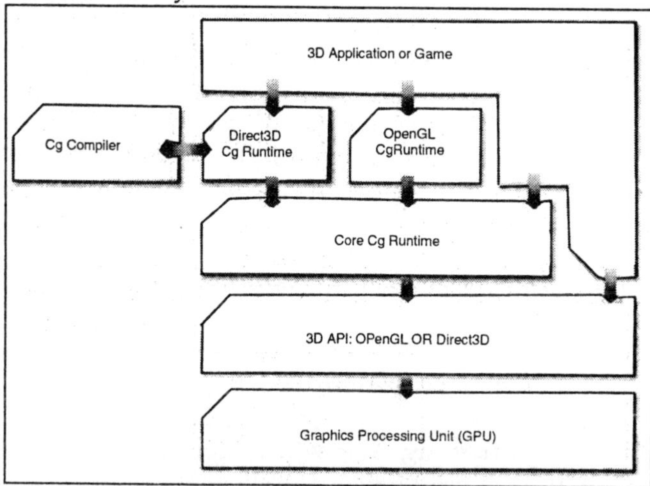


**Fig**: How Cg Fits into a Standard Cg Application

## The CgFX Toolkit and File Format

Cg programs need 3D models, textures, and other data to operate on. A Cg program without any associated data is useless. Cg programs and data also require the correct 3D programming interface configuration and state. It is often helpful to have a way to bundle all the information required to render a 3D model, including its associated Cg program.

## WHAT CGFX PROVIDES

CgFX is a standardized file format for representing complete effects and appearances. As they did with Cg, Microsoft and NVIDIA collaborated to develop the CgFX format. CgFX files are text-based, with a syntax that is a superset of Cg's, and may contain any number of Cg programs. The.fx suffix identifies CgFX files. A CgFX file describes the complete render state for a particular effect: multiple passes, texture states, and any number of individual vertex and fragment programs may be defined to create a complete appearance or effect. An accompanying development toolkit is provided for using and parsing CgFX files. The toolkit exposes user-interface hooks to host applications, so that CgFX-aware applications can automatically supply meaningful controls and semantics to users and developers alike.

Cg programs describe the vertex or fragment processing that takes place in a single rendering pass, but some complex shading algorithms require multiple rendering passes. CgFX offers a format to encode complex multipass effects, including designating which Cg program is used for each rendering pass.

*More specifically, CgFX supports three additional capabilities beyond what the core Cg language supports:*

- CgFX provides a mechanism for specifying multiple rendering passes and optional multiple implementations for a single effect.
- CgFX allows you to specify nonprogrammable rendering states, such as alpha-test modes and texture-filtering. The settings for these render states may take the form of simple expressions, which are evaluated on the CPU when the effect is initialized.

- CgFX allows annotations to be added to shaders and shader parameters. These annotations provide additional information to applications, including content creation applications. For example, an annotation can specify the allowed range of values for a shader parameter.

## MULTIPLE SHADER INSTANCING

The CgFX file format encapsulates multiple implementations of Cg programs for a given shader. This means you can have one Cg shader program written for a third-generation or fourth-generation GPU, while also including a simpler program that supports a less capable, second-generation GPU. An application loading the CgFX file can determine at runtime the most appropriate shader implementation to use based on the computer's available GPU.

Multiple instancing of Cg programs with CgFX is one way to address the functional variations in GPUs of different generations or different hardware vendors. Multiple instancing also lets you develop a Cg program specialized for a particular 3D API-for example, if OpenGL exposes extra functionality through an extension. Cg programs specialized for Direct3D, standard OpenGL, or OpenGL with extensions can all be contained in a single CgFX file.

## CGFX AND DIGITAL CONTENT CREATION

The CgFX Toolkit consists of the CgFX compiler, which supports the full CgFX syntax; the CgFX runtime API, for loading and manipulating CgFX files; and plug-in modules for major digital content creation (DCC) applications such as Alias I Wavefront's Maya and Discreet's 3ds max. Figure shows these applications making use of CgFX. Softimage I XSI 3.0 provides direct support for Cg compilation in its Render Tree.

Prior to CgFX, there was no standard way for a DCC application to export 3D content with all the associated shading knowledge necessary to render the content in real time. Now the major DCC applications use CgFX in their content creation process and support the CgFX file format.

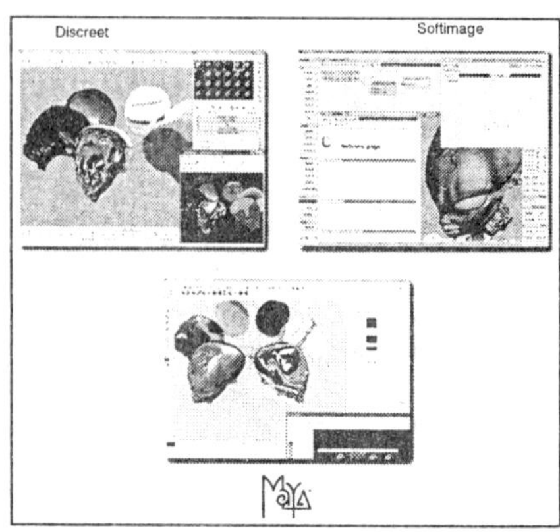


**Fig**: Digital Content Creation Applications That Use Cg and CgFX

This means that CgFX can significantly improve the artistic workflow from DCC applications to real-time games and other 3D applications. Using CgFX, artists can view and tweak Cg shaders and associated 3D content to see, from within the DCC tool of their choice, how their work will appear in a 3D game or application.

## HOW CGFX FITS INTO YOUR APPLICATION

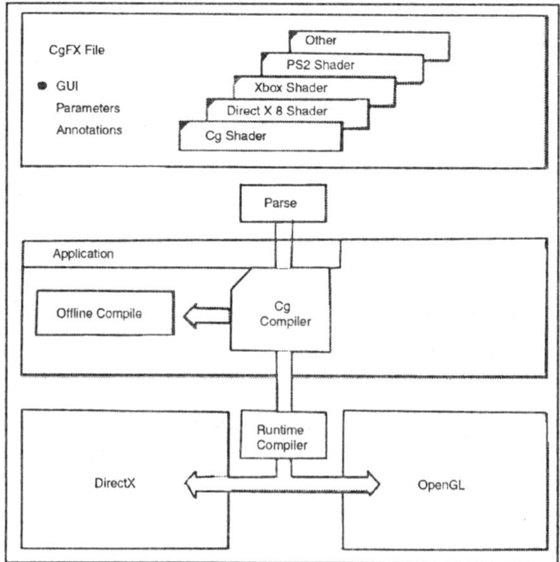


**Fig**: How CgFX Fits into a Standard Application

Figure shows how a CgFX file containing multiple instanced shaders is used by an application in conjunction with the Cg runtime and your choice of rendering API. Most of this book focuses on the Cg language itself and on how to write Cg programs, rather than CgFX, but see Appendix C for more information about the CgFX file format and its associated runtime API.

## ONWARD TO THE TUTORIAL

Having finished this introduction to the Cg programming language, you are now ready to take on the tutorial chapters, which will teach you how to write Cg programs.

## EXERCISES

*The exercises at the end of each chapter help you review your knowledge and develop practical programming skills:*

- *Answer this*: Name two standard 3D programming interfaces for which you can compile Cg programs. What operating systems does each programming interface support?
- *Answer this*: What are the major stages of the graphics pipeline? In what order are the stages arranged?
- *Answer this:* Where do vertex and fragment programs fit into the pipeline?
- *Answer this*: What is a vertex? What is a fragment? Distinguish a fragment from a pixel.
- *Try this Yourself:* We haven't begun writing Cg programs yet (we'll get there soon enough in the next chapter), so take a break and watch a good feature-length computer graphics animation such as Monsters, Inc.

## FURTHER READING

Cg builds on a host of concepts in computer language design, computer hardware design, and computer graphics. Doing justice to all these contributions in the context of this tutorial is not always practical. What we attempt in the "Further Reading" section at the end of each chapter is to offer you pointers to learn more about the contributions that underlie the topics in each chapter. There are plenty of books on C.

The C Programming Language, Third Edition (Prentice Hall, 2000), by Brian Kernighan and Dennis Ritchie, is a classic; the authors invented the C language. Cg includes concepts from both C and C++.

There now may actually be more books about C++ than about C. The classic C++ book is The C++ Programming Language, Third Edition (Addison-Wesley, 2000), by Bjarne Stroustrup, who invented the language.

To learn more about the RenderMan Shading Language, read The RenderMan Companion: A Programmer's Guide to Realistic Computer Graphics (Addison-Wesley, 1989), by Steve Upstill.

Pat Hanrahan and Jim Lawson published a SIGGRAPH paper about RenderMan called "A Language for Shading and Lighting Calculations" (ACM Press) in 1990. Robert Cook's 1984 SIGGRAPH paper titled "Shade Trees" (ACM Press) motivated the development of RenderMan.

The development of programmable graphics hardware and its associated languages has been an active and fruitful research area for almost a decade. Anselmo Lastra, Steven Molnar, Marc Olano, and Yulan Wang at UNC published an early research paper in 1995 titled "Real-Time Programmable Shading" (ACM Press).

Researchers at UNC also published several papers about their programmable PixelFlow graphics architecture. Marc Olano and Anselmo Lastra published a SIGGRAPH paper titled "A Shading Language on Graphics Hardware: The PixelFlow Shading System" (ACM Press) in 1998.

Kekoa Proudfoot, Bill Mark, Svetoslav Tzvetkov, and Pat Hanrahan published a SIGGRAPH paper in 2001 titled "A Real-Time Procedural Shading System for Programmable Graphics Hardware" (ACM Press) that describes a GPU-oriented shading language developed at Stanford. Real-Time Rendering, Second Edition (A. K. Peters, 2002), written by Eric Haines and Tomas Akenine-Möller, is an excellent resource for further information about graphics hardware and interactive techniques.

The OpenGL Graphics System: A Specification documents the OpenGL 3D programming interface. The best tutorial for learning OpenGL programming is theOpenGL Programming Guide: The Official Guide to Learning OpenGL, Third Edition(Addison-Wesley, 1999), by Mason Woo, Jackie Neider, Tom Davis, and Dave Shreiner.

# 4

# Cocoa Programming

## DESCRIPTION

This challenge is simple—type in the code provided, add the bindings in Interface Builder, and go... that is, until the "make sure to add sorting!" comment at the end.

Sorting the RaiseMan application that does not use NSArrayController requires only a careful reading of the "For the More Curious: Sorting without NSArrayController" section in Chapter.

The key sentence here, which I missed several times, is, "An optional table view dataSource method is triggered when the user clicks the header of a column with a sort descriptor:"

*There are a couple of things to notice and do:*

- *TableView*: SortDescriptorsDidChange: is a delegate method... so this means that you have to set MyDocument to be the delegate of the table view. Presumably you already did that if you set up the bindings correctly.
- You need to enter the code that appears just above the "Challenge 13 header on page 135 into MyDocument.m–this is the delegate method called when you click the column header.
- You cannot use the delegate method code as it appears in the book if you entered the code in Challenge 2, because you have a pointer to an IBOutlet object called tableView and this delegate

method waits for a call from the interface element, not from your pointer, if that makes sense. Think about it this way—the flow of information happens in two directions: that coming in from the interface to the method, and that going from the method back to the interface. You'll receive a compile warning if you call it tableView. Change it to aTableView. (You probably noticed similar changes in the code under Challenge 2.)

When referring to the incoming messages, those should be called aTableView.

When referring to outgoing messages, those should be tableView because that is what your IBOutlet pointer is called. Therefore, the final line,[tableView reloadData] needs to remain tableView and not change to aTableView because you now want to call on the IBOutlet pointer to send instructions back to the interface.

- The line [myArray sort Using Descriptors: new Descriptors]; needs to contain the name of your array... employees. It should read:[employees sort Using Descriptors: new Descriptors]; so that it sorts your array.

The final point tripped me up longer than any of the rest of it because I thought that the purpose of the exercise was to avoid using key coding. I was wrong.

The point of the exercise is to not use NSArrayController. To sort your columns, you have to have sort descriptors. Those are entered in the same spot as in the previous challenge and the chapter exercise.

In other words, when you have the name column in the table selected, the Interface Builder Table Column Attributes should look like this: The same discussion about compare: vs. localized Standard Compare: is valid here, so you can change it to the latter if you don't want Z to appear before a when you sort. .

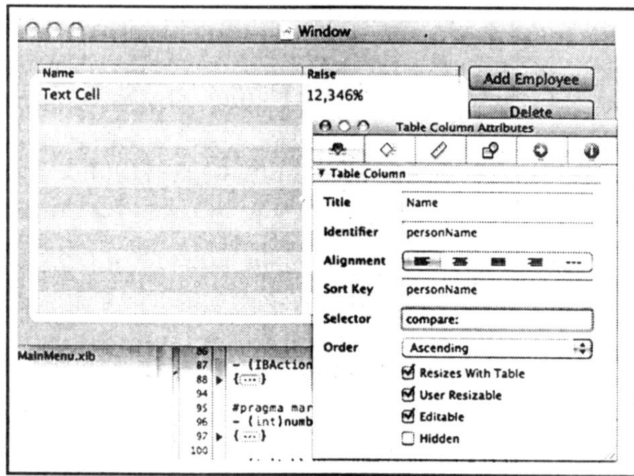


The full code follows the break:

*Here's the code:*

Person.h

```
#import <Foundation/Foundation.h>
@interface Person: NSObject {
 NSString *personName;
 float expectedRaise;
}
@property (readwrite) float expectedRaise;
@end Person.m
#import "Person.h"
@implementation Person
- (id)init
{
[super init];
 expectedRaise = 0.5;
 personName = @"New Person";
 return self;
}
```

```
- (void)dealloc
{
[personName release];
[super dealloc];
}
- (void)setNilValueForKey:(NSString *)key
{
 if ([key isEqual:@"expectedRaise"]) {
[self setExpectedRaise:0.0];
} else {
[super setNilValueForKey:key];
}
}
@synthesize personName;
@synthesize expectedRaise;
@end
```

MyDocument.h (Notice the important @class Person; line at the top… it won't compile without it.)

```
#import <Cocoa/Cocoa.h>
@class Person;
@interface MyDocument: NSDocument
{
 NSMutableArray *employees;
 IBOutlet NSTableView *tableView;
}
- (IBAction)createEmployee:(id)sender;
- (IBAction)deleteSelectedEmployees:(id)sender;
@end
```

MyDocument.m (note: some of these methods automatically appear when you create a new project that uses the Document template… I left them alone.)

view source
print?

```
#import "MyDocument.h"

@implementation MyDocument

- (id)init
{
 self =[super init];
 if (self) {
 employees =[[NSMutableArray alloc]init];
}
 return self;
}

- (void)dealloc
{
[employees release];
[super dealloc];
}

- (NSString *)windowNibName
{
 return @"MyDocument";
}

- (void)windowControllerDidLoadNib:(NSWindowController *) aController
{
[super windowControllerDidLoadNib: aController];
}

- (NSData *)dataOfType:(NSString *)typeName error:(NSError **)outError
{

```

```
if ( outError != NULL) {
*outError =[NSError error With Domain: NSOS
StatusErrorDomain code:unimpErr userInfo:NULL];
}
return nil;
}
- (BOOL)readFromData:(NSData *)data
ofType:(NSString *)typeName error:(NSError
**)outError
{
if ( outError != NULL) {
*outError =[NSError errorWithDomain: NSOS
StatusErrorDomain code:unimpErr userInfo:NULL];
}
return YES;
}
#pragma mark Action methods
- (IBAction)deleteSelectedEmployees:(id)sender
{
//Which row is selected?
NSIndexSet *rows =[tableView selected Row
Indexes];
//Is the selection empty?
if ([rows count]== 0) {
NSBeep();
return;
}
[employees removeObjectsAtIndexes:rows];
[tableView reloadData];
}
- (IBAction)createEmployee:(id)sender
{
Person *newEmployee =[[Person alloc]init];
```

```
[employees addObject:newEmployee];
[newEmployee release];
[tableView reloadData];
}
#pragma mark Table view dataSource methods
- (int)numberOfRowsInTableView:(NSTableView *)aTableView
{
 return[employees count];
}
- (id)tableView:(NSTableView *)aTableView
objectValueForTableColumn:(NSTableColumn *)aTableColumn
 row:(int)rowIndex
{
//What is the identifier for the column?
 NSString *identifier =[aTableColumn identifier];
//What person?
 Person *person =[employees objectAtIndex:rowIndex];
//What is the value of the attributenamed identifier?
 return[person valueForKey:identifier];
}
- (void)tableView:(NSTableView *)aTableView
 setObjectValue:(id)anObject
 forTableColumn:(NSTableColumn *)aTableColumn
 row:(int)rowIndex
{
 NSString *identifier =[aTableColumn identifier];
 Person *person =[employees object At Index:
```

```
rowIndex];

//Set the value for the attribute named identifier
[person setValue:anObject forKey:identifier];
}

- (void)tableView:(NSTableView *)atableView
sortDescriptorsDidChange:(NSArray *)oldDescriptors
{
 NSArray *newDescriptors =[atableView sortDescriptors];
[employees sortUsingDescriptors:newDescriptors];
[tableView reloadData];
}

@end
```

## USING MAC OS X APPLICATIONS

Mac OS X comes with many accessible applications that you can use with VoiceOver, such as Mail, iChat, and iTunes. This chapter provides information about using some of the Mac OS X applications. For information about other applications that are compatible with VoiceOver, click the following link to visit the VoiceOver Application Support webpage.

## NAVIGATING IN MAIL

The Mail window is organized like a Finder window. A table on the left contains your mailboxes.

As you move up or down the mailboxes table, the contents of each mailbox are listed in a column on the right. Below the messages list is a splitter and then a pane for previewing the selected message.

- *To navigate mailboxes and messages*:
  - When the VoiceOver cursor is on the mailboxes table, interact with the table.

- Interacting with content areas
- To move to a mailbox, press VO-arrow keys.
- To expand or collapse a mailbox to navigate to mailboxes within it, press VO-\.
- When the mailbox whose messages you want to read is in the VoiceOver cursor, jump to the messages table.
- Press VO-J. If you're using VoiceOver gestures, keep a finger on the trackpad and press the Control key. To jump back to the mailboxes table, repeat the command or the gesture.
- Move across or down each row in the table by pressing VO-arrow keys.
- To hear a description of everything in that row, press VO-R.
- When the VoiceOver cursor is on a message you want to read, jump to the message preview.

Press VO-J. If you're using VoiceOver gestures, keep a finger on the trackpad and press the Control key. To jump back to the messages table, repeat the command or the gesture.

## ADDRESSING MESSAGES IN MAIL

When you start typing e-mail addresses in a New Message window in Mail, some recipient names may appear as Smart Addresses. Smart Addresses are names and addresses that are in your address book, your Previous Recipients list, or available mail servers. Smart Addresses show the name within a blue field, which includes a pop-up menu of related commands, such as Reply to Sender or New Message.

- *To address a message:*
  - In Mail, open a New Message window.
  - The window opens with the VoiceOver cursor in the To field.
  - Start typing the recipient's e-mail address.
  - You hear the name and e-mail address of the first name that matches what you're typing. If more than one address is available for the recipient, you hear "Mail has new window" and a pop-up

menu of addresses becomes available. Use the Down Arrow or Up Arrow key to navigate the list of addresses.

- To enter the selected address in the field, press Return.
- To delete an address you just entered, press the Delete key once to highlight the address and a second time to delete it. If a recipient has a Smart Address, you hear "menu button," which refers to the pop-up menu in the Smart Address.
- To add another address, repeat steps 2 and 3.
- You can add as many addresses in the field as you want. If you enter multiple addresses that aren't Smart Addresses, separate them with a comma.
- To move to the next text field, press VO-Down Arrow.
- To open the pop-up menu in a Smart Address, press VO-Shift-M.

If it's easier to type e-mail addresses than to use Smart Addresses, turn off Smart Addresses. In Mail, choose Mail > Preferences > Viewing, and then deselect the "Use Smart Addresses" checkbox.

## READING MESSAGES IN MAIL

You can use VoiceOver commands or gestures to read messages in Mail.

- *To read a message in Mail:*
  - Move the VoiceOver cursor to the message you want to read in the messages list.
  - Jump to the message preview to start reading the message.
  - Press VO-J. If you're using VoiceOver gestures, keep a finger on the trackpad and press the Control key.
  - When you're done reading, jump back to the messages list.

Press VO-J, or keep a finger on the trackpad and press

the Control key. To quickly read through the messages list, press VO-Shift-Down Arrow to interact with it. Then press VO-Right Arrow or VO-Left Arrow until you're in the column you want to hear, such as the Subject column, and then press the Down Arrow or Up Arrow key to move up or down in that column.

## USING DATA DETECTORS IN MAIL MESSAGES

Mail can detect specific information or data in messages and makes it easier for you to use the data. For example, Mail can recognize phone numbers and add them to your address book, or recognize a date and time and create an iCal event for it.

- *To detect data*:
  - In a message you've received, move the VoiceOver cursor over a phone number, e-mail address, street address, date, or time.
  - Mail outlines the data as a field with a pop-up menu, and VoiceOver speaks "data detector present."
  - To open a shortcut menu that contains commands for using the data, press VO-Shift-M.

For example, if the data detector is an e-mail address, you can choose New Message from the shortcut menu to open a New Message window that already has the e-mail address in the To field; you don't need to retype or add the e-mail address yourself.

## ACCEPTING ICHAT INVITATIONS

If you set iChat preferences to announce when a new invitation arrives and to speak message contents automatically, you'll hear "Chat invitation from[buddy name]" when you're invited to chat, followed by the text of the new message, and finally "iChat has new window." You can ignore the message if you're busy or you can switch to iChat and accept the invitation.

- *To accept an iChat invitation:*
  - Press VO-F1 twice to open the Application Chooser menu.

- Press VO-Down Arrow until you hear iChat, and then press VO-Space bar to select the command.
- Press VO-Down Arrow until you hear "Chat with[buddy name]new" and then select the command.
- The VoiceOver cursor moves to the iChat invitation window.
- Type your response in the text field.
- If you set the initial position of the VoiceOver cursor to be the first item in a window in VoiceOver Utility, you must navigate to and select the Accept button at the bottom of the window before you can type your response.
- Press Return to send your response.

You interact with the iChat window the same way you do with other windows. All the messages in a text chat, including yours, are displayed above the text field in an HTML content area. You can interact with the area to move up and down the messages and read them.

## HEARING ICHAT INVITATIONS AND MESSAGES

You can set iChat preferences so that iChat announces when a new chat invitation arrives, and speaks the text of new chat messages. You can also set alert preferences for other events and types of chats, such as audio and video chats.

- *To set iChat to speak invitations and messages:*
  - In iChat, choose iChat > Preferences, and then click Alerts.
  - To hear incoming invitations, click the Event pop-up menu and choose Text Invitation.
  - Select the "Speak an announcement" checkbox.
  - To hear incoming messages, click the Event pop-up menu again and choose Message Received, and then repeat step 3.

Now when you receive a chat invitation, you'll hear "Chat invitation from[buddy name]," followed by the text of the new message, and finally "iChat has new window." You can choose to ignore it if you're busy or you can accept the invitation.

When cursor tracking is turned on, iChat speaks incoming messages only when you're focused on the message portion of the chat window; if you're typing a message in the text field, incoming messages are not spoken. You can turn off cursor tracking while using iChat, which enables you to move the VoiceOver cursor to the message portion to hear incoming messages, while the keyboard focus remains in the text field where you're typing. Turning off cursor tracking You can use hot spots to be alerted of incoming messages.

## NAVIGATING ICHAT MESSAGES

You can use a VoiceOver command or gesture in iChat to jump between the text field where you type your message and the table of incoming messages. This is useful if you want to review what your buddy said before you send your own message.

- *To use the jump command in iChat:*
  - When the VoiceOver cursor is in the text field, press VO-J. If you're using VoiceOver gestures, keep a finger on the trackpad and press the Control key.
  - The VoiceOver cursor jumps to the end of the last message in the HTML content area.
  - To navigate the messages, press VO-Shift-Up Arrow or VO-Shift-Down Arrow.
  - To move the VoiceOver cursor back to the text field, press VO-J. If you're using VoiceOver gestures, keep a finger on the trackpad and press the Control key.

The next time you jump during the same chat, the VoiceOver cursor will move to the last message you read. You can turn off cursor tracking while using iChat, which enables you to move the VoiceOver cursor to the message portion to hear incoming messages, while the keyboard focus remains in the text field where you're typing.

## USING ITUNES

You can use VoiceOver with iTunes 8 to navigate the iTunes

Store to buy music, movies, TV shows, and audiobooks, or download free podcasts. You can use all of the general VoiceOver commands to navigate the iTunes window. You interact with toolbars and lists just as you would in any other window.

## CHANGING TAB STOPS IN TEXTEDIT

You can click tab stop buttons located at the right end of the TextEdit toolbar to add new tab stops.

When the VoiceOver cursor is in the ruler, you can add or move tab stops. If the ruler isn't available, open TextEdit preferences and make sure the "Show ruler" checkbox is deselected.

- *To add or change a tab stop:*
  - When the VoiceOver cursor is on a tab stop button or in the ruler, press VO-Space bar.
  - In the dialog that appears, press VO-Right Arrow to navigate to the Right Tab Stop pop-up menu, and then press VO-Space bar again to open the pop-up menu.
  - Press VO-Down Arrow or VO-Up Arrow to find the type of tab stop you want to add, and then press VO-Space bar to select it.
  - Press VO-Right Arrow until you reach the edit text field for the ruler marker value
  - Type the measurement for where you want to place the tab stop. For example, 6.25 indicates six and one quarter inches on the ruler.
  - Press VO-Right Arrow until you reach the OK button and click it.
- *To drag a tab stop to another location:*
  - Navigate to the ruler and locate the marker for the tab stop you want to move.
  - Start interacting with the marker by pressing VO-Shift-Down Arrow.
  - Press VO-Left Arrow or Right Arrow until the marker is located where you want it.
  - Stop interacting with the marker by pressing VO-Shift-Up Arrow.

## USING FRONT ROW TO PLAY MEDIA

Front Row is self-speaking; you don't use VoiceOver commands to control it. Front Row uses your default VoiceOver voice to speak what's on the screen in the Front Row menu; it outputs what's on the screen to an available braille display. You navigate the Front Row menu just as you would other menus that you're familiar with.

- *Here are tips to help you use Front Row:*
  - You can use keyboard shortcuts to control Front Row.
  - To open Front Row, press Command-Escape. To exit, press Escape. To navigate in Front Row, use the arrow keys. To select an item, press Return.
  - When you change to a new screen, you hear the title of the screen and then the selected item.
  - When you change items, Front Row speaks the new item.
  - When the selection rests on an item for several seconds, Front Row speaks details about the item, if details exist.

If your Mac computer includes Apple Remote, you can use the remote to change the sound volume, navigate lists and menus, start and pause playback, and more. For more information about Front Row, open Mac Help and search for Front Row.

## AUTOMATING TASKS WITH APPLESCRIPT

Many tasks, including those using VoiceOver, can be automated by writing scripts using the AppleScript programming language included in Mac OS X. After you enable VoiceOver to work with scripts, you can use AppleScript Editor to open the VoiceOver AppleScript dictionary of terms available to use in scripts.

- *To enable using scripts:*
  - When VoiceOver is on, open VoiceOver Utility by pressing VO-F8.
  - Click General and select the "Allow VoiceOver to be controlled with AppleScript" checkbox.

- *To open the VoiceOver AppleScript dictionary:*
  - Open AppleScript Editor.
  - You can use Spotlight to search for it and then select it from the search results.
  - Choose File > Open Dictionary and then choose VoiceOver at the bottom of the alphabetical list.

You can assign AppleScript scripts to keys on the numeric keypad or keyboard, or on a braille display. If you're using a Multi-Touch trackpad, you can assign the scripts to VoiceOver gestures.

# 5

# Mac Printing

## INTRODUCTION

Apple Mac printing is a complex topic and deserves its own chapter. The developers started on PaperCut NG for the Mac in 2006.

Developing software on the Mac was an enjoyable experience and presented very few technical challenges. The challenges instead came in the area of general printer setup and idiosyncrasies with printer configuration. Mac administrators will be all too familiar with these challenges! This chapter addresses Mac printer setup (on both the client and server) and presents solutions for common setup and deployment scenarios.

*The Chapter is split into two sections:*

- *1st Section*: Organizations hosting their print queues on a Mac (*e.g.* Mac OS X Server)
- *2nd Section*: Organizations hosting their print queues on Windows Servers but supporting Mac clients

In most cases only one section will apply on your network. Jump to the relevant section as appropriate.

## MAC HOSTED PRINT QUEUES

This section discusses printer setup on systems where the print queues are hosted on a Mac system. For example, PaperCut NG is installed on a Mac system such as Mac OS X Server. See the next section if your print queues are hosted on a Windows server. This section assumes Mac OS X Server (*e.g.* Mac OS 10.6 Server), however PaperCut NG also supports running on the workstation version of Mac OS X. These notes apply in part to both operating systems. The term 'server' is used to represent the system hosting the PaperCut NG software, and not necessarily the edition of Mac OS X. Before we delve into configuring server based print queues in a Mac environment, we'll first take a few moments to discuss common terminology:

## Print Queue

*There are typically two ways of providing shared multi-system access to a printer:*

1. Configure each system to print directly to the device. The device needs to be networkable (*e.g.* have an Ethernet connection) and support multiple connections.
2. Configure a shared print queue. In this setup, only one system connects directly to the device (*e.g.* a server) and in turn the device is shared on the network via a print queue. Other systems on the network print to the shared queue rather than directly to the device.

Option 2 is regarded as a better solution on multi-user networks as it provides a higher level of scalability, allows for centralized administration, and allows administrators to move or remap devices without needing to propagate changes to workstations. PaperCut NG requires a shared print queue as it works by intercepting the jobs as they pass through the server's queue.

## CUPS

CUPS is the print queue system used by Mac. This is the same queue system used by many other UNIX based platforms including popular Linux distributions. Apple is a major supporter of CUPS.

## IP Printing

This is a generic term used to describe a number of print protocols that are used to exchange print documents between a computer, a server queue, or a physical printer. (Note: This term is also occasionally used incorrectly to describe the "JetDirect" print protocol discussed below)

### IPP

This is an acronym for Internet Printing Protocol. This is the "native" print protocol used by CUPS and hence the Mac. It's a modern protocol designed to work well on modern networks including local networks, or even over the internet or a WAN.

### LPR

LPR/LPD is the traditional UNIX based print protocol.

### JetDirect/Socket

This is a very simple print protocol used to transmit print jobs to a physical printer on a TCP network. The printer simply accepts connections on port 9100. In Windows, this print protocol is often referred to as a Standard TCP/IP Port, and in some cases generally as IP Printing. Almost all network printers support this method.

### Bonjour Printing

This is not a print protocol, but instead is a way of publishing printers on a network so workstations can locate the device/queue.

Where possible we have designed PaperCut NG to work with all print protocols, however we do recommend some over others.

He following setup procedure highlights methods that have shown to work in most environments.

*The PaperCut NG compatible setup procedure can be summarized as follows:*

- *Step 1*: Install the printers on the server using a compatible driver
- *Step 2*: Enable Printer Sharing
- *Step 3*: Set up the printers on the workstations to point to the server's shared queue

## INSTALLING THE PRINTERS ON THE SERVER

Install the printer on the system running PaperCut NG using a compatible driver. For example, a driver supplied by Apple or the manufacturer. If there is a choice of driver, opt for a Postscript or PPD based driver. Follow the manufacturer's suggested setup procedure, or Apple's recommended Queue setup procedure (Apple Print Services Administration Guide) if running on 10.5 Server.

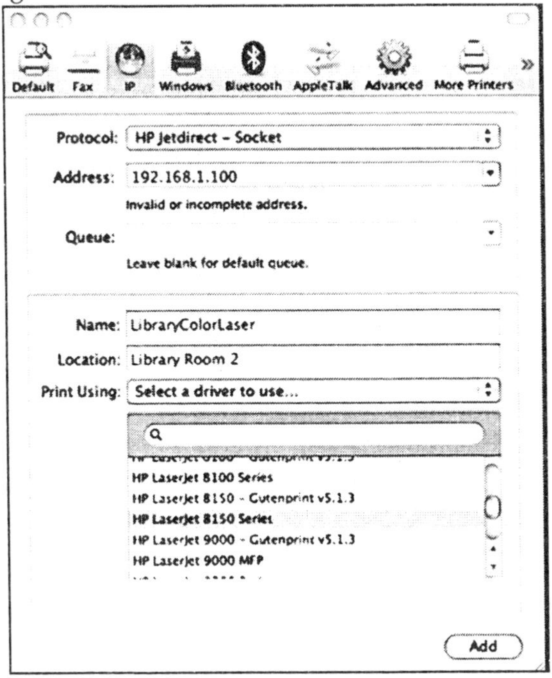

**Fig**: Setting up a Printer (direct) on Mac OS 10.5 Server using Jetdirect

If the manufacturer supports various connection methods, we recommend using JetDirect/Socket if possible. Here is an example of a procedure that will set up a standard printer using a plain JetDirect/Socket connection on all Mac versions (server/workstation 10.4/10.5):

- From the Apple Menu select System Preferences...
- Select Print and Fax
- Click on the + button to add a new printer

- Click on the IP icon on the toolbar
- Select HP Jetdirect-Socket in the Protocol list
- Enter the printer's assigned IP address
- For convenience, give the printer a simple name without spaces
- Select the driver or printer model from the list and press Add

Test printing using a local application (*e.g.* Print a web page from Safari). Confirm that printing works as expected.

## IMPORTANT

For new printers it is necessary to configure PaperCut NG to monitor the new printer. This is discussed in the section called "Adding and Removing/Deleting/Ignoring Printers". Continue to the next step only after printing from the server is working. If you have problems, see the troubleshooting section below.

## OPTIONAL HARDWARE CONFIGURATION

Some high-end printer models support other connection methods such as LPR, IPP or even direct AppleShare or Boujour printing. If the printer offers the option to disable these protocols, *e.g.* via a web based configuration page, take the time to turn these off.

This will minimize the chance of incorrect future configuration, and minimize the chance of a workstation user discovering the printer directly. Some printers also support access control via IP addresses. If available, consider setting access control so only the server IP can submit print jobs to the physical printer.

## NOTES AND TROUBLESHOOTING

- If your printer does not support JetDirect/Socket, consider using LPR as the 2nd choice.
- Some printers support proprietary connection methods (*e.g.* selected Epson printers). Always try Jetdirect/Socket first and use proprietary methods as a last resort.

- If you're not able to install or find a driver for your printer, try the Generic Postscript Driver/Printer.

## SET UP THE PRINTERS ON THE WORKSTATIONS

Once the printers are set up on the server and shared, the next step is to install the printers on the workstations. In the Windows world this is an easy process-the user just double-clicks on the print queue and the drivers are automatically deployed and configured.

The process is a little more manual on the Mac, but we'll also discuss a method of automating deployment via the Workgroup Manager. First, we'll address manual setup.

The goal is to add the printer on the workstation so it communicates with the server (its queues) rather than directly to the printer.

Protocols include, IPP, LPD, or LPD added via Bonjour. The recommended setup is to use IPP as this is the native protocol.

## RECOMMENDED MANUAL SETUP

- Log onto a workstation
- Open System Preferences Print and Fax (or the Printer Setup Utility if using Mac OS 10.4).
- Click the add new printer button (or +).
- Select IP as the type and select IPP as the Protocol.
- Enter your server name (or the server's IP Address) in the Address field.
- Enter the the printer's Queue Name prefixed with printers/in the Queue field. For example: printers/my_office_printer.*Note:* if you have selected LPR as the connection method, the printers/prefix will not be required (see the following section).

If you have problems obtaining a driver for your printer, try the Generic Postscript Driver. This option will work with most printers.

If after a test print the printer stops with a connection error, check the printer sharing permissions on the server or try the alternate method discussed below.

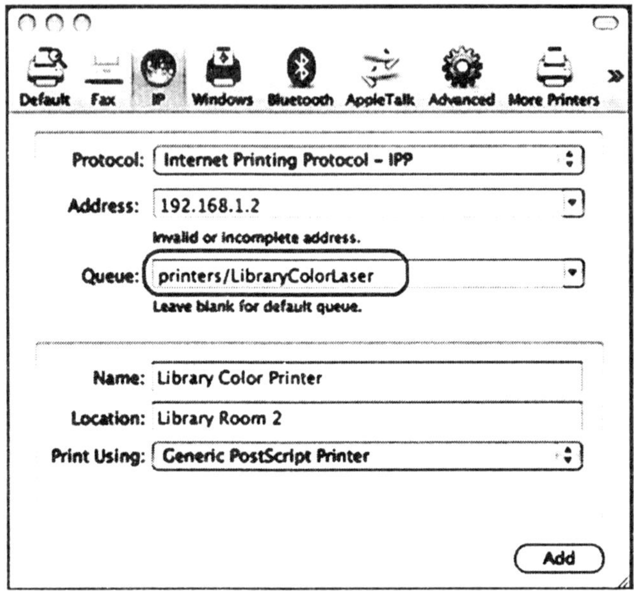


Fig: Setting up a Workstation Printer on Mac OS 10.5

## TIP

- Only publish the printer configuration after it's been tested.
- If you have problems with the manufacturer supplied driver, try the "Generic Postscript Printer"
- Always publish the printer config from a tested client workstation and never from server itself.

## UNAUTHENTICATED SYSTEMS (*e.g.* LAPTOPS)

The print queues in current Mac OS X server releases (up to and including 10.6) are unfortunately unauthenticated (editor's note: CUPS supports authentication, however Apple have decided not to expose/support this feature). Authentication in an Open Directory environment is instead performed at the time of system login. Unauthenticated systems such as laptops however fall outside this check. The introduction of unauthenticated systems on your network mandates the need for an extra layer of authentication.

*PaperCut NG offers two options:*

- Popup authentication via the client software, or
- Authentication via a release station or the web based release interface (end-user login `-> Jobs pending release`).

Network administrators must decide if the authentication policy/procedure is to be applied to all network systems, or just "untrusted" laptops.

## NETWORK-WIDE POLICY

This is the simplest solution and provides a consistent procedure/policy across all your users irrespective of their access method (workstation or their own laptop).

Select your authentication method such as popup authentication or hold/release queue and enable this option on ALL print queues. The setup procedure for both methods is summarized as follows:

### Using Popup Authentication

- Select the Unauthenticated printer option on all printers
- Ensure that all workstations have the client software installed. This includes both authenticated lab systems and laptops. The client must be running to have printer access.
- Instruct users that they will need to enter their username/password in the client when requested.

### *Using Hold/Release Queue Authentication:*

Check the Enable the hold/release queue option on all print queues.

*Jobs will not print until a user has authenticated and released the job:*

- Set up release stations, or ensure the Jobs pending release option is enabled in the end-user web interface.
- Instruct users on how to release their jobs. This procedure must be followed by all users.

## LAPTOP ONLY POLICY (ADVANCED)

One problem with the network-wide policy discussed above is that it the authentication method (*e.g.* client popup or hold/release queue) also applies to authenticated systems. In some ways this is a positive (*i.e.* provides a consistent policy), while in other ways it can be viewed as an unnecessary on trusted authenticated systems. This section discusses a solution appropriate for larger sites.

The solution is to set up two servers. One server hosts a set of queues for authenticated systems, while the other server provides queues for unauthenticated systems. Network router or firewall rules are used to ensure that only authenticated systems have access to the authenticated queues. Laptops systems must use the other queues. This is best done with partitioned IP address ranges and/or subnets. An experienced network administrator will be able to assist with restricted server access by IP address.

## FUTURE PLANS

The *Laptop Only Policy* is best described as a "hack" and is only suitable for larger sites with good network administrators. In the current release this is a supported solution. The developers do however have some ideas to streamline the setup.

*These include:*

- An ability to "endorse" the authenticated systems so the username is trusted by default. For example, a special file can be copied to these systems (readable only by the root user).
- An IP address range filter restricting systems that can use a given priter.

# MAC OS X BARE-METAL RECOVERY

## DEFINITION

While Mac OS X is similar to other flavours of Unix in many ways, the topic of backups is one where the differences stand out. Some of the available tools are the same, but familiar tools may not be the best choices. Also, as with other operating systems described in this part of the book, the methods used to record critical metadata and to boot from the recovered disk differ. Following the format of prior chapters, this chapter will show you how to make a simple and inexpensive backup of a Mac OS X system for use in bare-metal recovery.

## HOW IT WORKS

The following sections outline a procedure you can use to anticipate and conduct a full recovery of a Mac OS X system, without needing to install the OS first. The sequence is generally the same as on other platforms.

*You first prepare for the recovery*:

- Attach backup media to the system.
- Back up the important metadata.
- Back up the operating system with a native utility.

*Then, when bad things happen, you perform the recovery:*

- Boot from alternate media.
- Partition, and format the new root disk.
- Restore the operating system information.
- Set the system to boot from the new root disk.

We'll start with a general overview and then move on to a concrete example of the procedure. As with any backup method, your safety net is only as good as your last backup, so scheduling backups and testing your recovery procedures are important.

### Preparing for a Bare-Metal Recovery

This procedure can use any external hard disk drive as a backup medium. Examples include a FireWire or USB storage device of sufficient capacity to hold a full backup. Depending on your storage requirements, even an iPod makes an excellent alternative. Another option is to use a Mac laptop in FireWire Target Disk Mode, assuming it has a FireWire port. Finally, you can also use an NFS share from any Unix-type server. While the USB and FireWire drives may be excellent options for an individual user, the NFS option is usually the best for a data center. Unfortunately, an SMB share will not work, because SMB drivers aren't available from the install CD console that we will be using during the recovery, but more on that later.

To enter Target Disk Mode, click on Apple Menu →System Preferences→Startup Disk→Target Disk Mode.... Alternatively, hold down the T key while booting the Mac laptop. Hook up a FireWire cable between the laptop and the system you're backing up. The laptop then acts as an external FireWire drive. After you've attached the external backup disk, you need to collect the information necessary to format the replacement disk before you restore data to it. Save the output ofdiskutil list, pdisk device dump (on PowerPC units), and mount t hfs to files on your backup disk that you can reference during recovery.

As of the time of this writing, Apple has recently released the first Macs built around Intel x86 CPUs instead of PowerPC CPUs. If you happen to be running an Intel-based Mac, you will not be able to use pdisk, and fdisk will not supply information on the disk you're running it from, but more on that later. It's also a good idea to save Open Firmware variable settings to a file with nvram p, just in case your NVRAM gets zapped along with your root disk. And for good measure, keeping a copy of the output from System Profiler handy means you have fairly complete documentation of your system's hardware and software setup available. (Launch the System Profiler application by going to the Apple Menu and selecting About This Mac→More Info..., then use File→Save to create a profile of your configuration.)

Now it's time to back up the data you'll use to recover the operating system. There are several native backup utilities from which to choose, but for this procedure, we use one specific to Mac OS X named ditto. With Mac OS X 10.4 and later, you could conceivably choose tar instead of ditto. However, we're going to use an install disc as the boot device during recovery, and the compression tools employed by tar (gzip or compress) aren't available there, whereas ditto features have built-in PKZIP compression. In order to save space on the backup medium and for compatibility with older versions of the OS, the example procedure detailed later in this chapter uses ditto for backup and recovery. For more on backup utilities native to Mac OS X.

## PERFORMING A BARE-METAL RECOVERY

When the day comes to use your backup for a system recovery, either as practice or because something terrible has happened, your first task after replacing any failed components is to boot up the system. The easiest choice for this is to use the same optical media you would use to install a fresh copy of Mac OS X, and that's the approach we take in our example. Once the machine has booted up, it's time to partition and format the new disk using the diskutil and pdisk output you saved during backup. For this you can use the diskutil partitionDisk command. Restoring the data is pretty much the opposite of backing it up: use ditto to decompress and unpack the archive files. If you need to restore your Open Firmware setup, usenvram f filename. Finally, once all the data has been restored, use the bless command to configure the system to boot from the new disk.

### SAMPLE BARE-METAL RECOVERY

This example uses diskutil, pdisk, mount, nvram, ditto, and bless to back up and recover a complete Mac OS X system on an Apple iBook, using an iPod as the backup medium. Some alternate examples will also be provided throughout the sample procedure. All volumes are formatted as HFS+.

## RECOVER THE SYSTEM

You have a Mac OS X system with a nonfunctional root disk. If you followed the procedure covered earlier, the recovery should be straightforward. First, turn on power to the system. While the system is starting up, hold down the Option key until the machine presents a graphical list of devices from which to boot. Insert a Mac OS X installation CD or DVD (disc 1 if it's a multidisc set), and click on the reload button to make it show up in the list of boot devices. Select the installation disc, and proceed with the boot. After booting up and selecting the language to use, you reach a welcome message, and the menu bar shows up at the top of the screen. From theUtilities menu, launch Terminal to get a command line.

Now attach the backup disk. As with the backup procedure, diskarbitrationd handles the mounting. When this is done, you have the following storage devices attached: an optical drive with a Mac OS X install disc mounted on/, an external backup disk mounted on/Volumes/iPod, and a new internal hard disk with nothing mounted. (If for some reason there are partitions mounted from the internal disk, unmount them at this point with diskutil unmountDisk disk0.) An alternative to using a USB or FireWire drive, such as an iPod, is to use an NFS mount. Besides an NFS server, you will need an IP address. If you have a DHCP server available, you are given an IP address automatically. If you don't have a DHCP server, you have to manually set the IP address using the following command:

```
# ifconfig en0 ipaddress netmask netmask broadcast
broadcast-address
```

You then need to mount the NFS share. Assuming an NFS server with an IP address of 192.168.0.1, and a share called/ backups, the command to mount it is:

```
# mkdir/var/tmp/backups# mount -t nfs
192.168.0.1:/backups/var/tmp/backups
```

You then will be able to access the backups on the/backups file share. Remember to unmount the share after you've restored data from it. Refer to/Volumes/iPod/Backup/ diskutil.txt and/Volumes/iPod/Backup/pdisk.txt so that you can partition the new disk. The diskutil output provides the partition names. To determine the size of each partition, use the pdisk output to add up the partition's block size with that of the free area listed before it, then divide by two to convert 512-byte blocks to kilobytes. For example, the sizes of the first two partitions in this example are (16,515,072 + 262,144)/2 = 8,388,608, and the size of the last partition is (5,253,424 + 262,144)/2 = 2,757,784. We go through this calculation because specifying the sizes in gigabytes as shown in the diskutil output usually results in partitions sized slightly larger or smaller than you'd expect. If you're recovering an Intel Mac, though, the diskutil output may be the only information you have.

### Use Diskutil to Partition the Disk

```
# diskutil partitionDisk disk0 3 JournaledHFS+
"Mac OS X" 8388608K \
JournaledHFS+ "Mac OS X Alt" 8388608K JournaledHFS+
Local 2757784K
Started partitioning on disk disk0
Creating Partition Map 5%..
Formatting Disk 32%..
Formatting Disk 54%..
Formatting Disk 100%..
Finished partitioning on disk disk0
/dev/disk0
#: type name size identifier
0: Apple_partition_scheme *18.6 GB disk0
1: Apple_partition_map 31.5 KB disk0s1
2: Apple_HFS Mac OS X 7.9 GB disk0s3
3: Apple_HFS Mac OS X Alt 7.9 GB disk0s5
4: Apple_HFS Local 2.5 GB disk0s7
```

The diskutil manpage for more details on the command syntax and options. One thing to note is that if you'll be running Classic for Mac OS 9 support on this system, you should add the OS9Drivers parameter after the argument specifying the number of partitions. You can tell if your old disk had OS 9 drivers installed by the presence of several additional Apple_Driver partitions in diskutil.txt. After you partition the disk, the new partitions are mounted automatically. Now you're ready to restore the filesystem data. If need be, you can also reset the Open Firmware variables:

```
# ditto x k rsrc "/Volumes/iPod/Backup/Mac OS
X.zip" "/Volumes/Mac OS X"
# ditto x k rsrc "/Volumes/iPod/Backup/Mac OS X
Alt.zip" "/Volumes/Mac OS X Alt"
# ditto x k rsrc/Volumes/iPod/Backup/Local.zip/
```

```
Volumes/Local
# nvram f/Volumes/iPod/Backup/nvram.txt
```

The last step of recovery is to prepare the new disk for booting. The following bless command enters the designated folder's directory ID (an HFS+ identifier analogous to a UFS inode number) into the disk's Master Directory Block, and sets the boot-device Open Firmware variable so that the system boots from the new disk the next time it comes up:

```
# bless -folder "/Volumes/Mac OS X/System/Library/
CoreServices" -setBoot
```

Upon booting, the system will look in the blessed folder for a file of type tbxi and find BootX, which contains bootstrapping code to begin the kernel initialization process. You can use the following to see this file's type on your system if you have the Developer Tools installed:

```
%/Developer/Tools/GetFileInfo \/System/Library/
CoreServices/BootX
```

Again, if you need Mac OS 9 support on this system, you need to add something to the command line, like this:

```
# bless -folder "/Volumes/Mac OS X/System/Library/
CoreServices" -setBoot \
-folder9 "/Volumes/Mac OS 9/System Folder" \
-bootBlockFile/usr/share/misc/bootblockdata
```

Finally, reboot the system and get back to work (or play, as the case may be).

# 6

# Xnu Kernel

## INTRODUCTION

This page exists because I couuldn't find any decent, complete notes on compiling up a kernel for MacOSX and I now have people bugging me on how I did it (hi Neil!:>).

*You may wish to compile your own kernel for MacOSX because:*

- You can
- You're into self-punishment
- You want to put your own patches into the kernel to make it do things Apple's default kernel can't (*e.g.* arp-spoofing)
- You want to optimise the kernel by disabling features you don't need (not covered by this page)

*These instructions assume you have the following:*

- Some clue
- A decent package installation environment that you know how to use (*e.g.* fink or darwinports)
- An Apple Developer account_(free to sign-up)
- Xcode (1.0 comes as CD4, 1.1 came in Software Update and 1.5 you can download from ADC)
- MacOSX 10.3.5 (or something close enough)

Do not start playing with your Mac's kernel unless have some idea of what you're actually doing and you're happy taking the risks associated with it. I take absolutely no responsibility if, in following my instructions, you destory your Mac! I am, however, happy to accept comments/ corrections from people.

**Instructions**

- Make sure you've installed the Apple Development tools (XCode).
- If/usr/local/bin doesn't exist, create it:
  `mkdir/usr/local/bin`
- Make sure you have it in your path:
  `export PATH=$PATH:/usr/local/bin`
- Create a directory with nothing special in the path-name:
  `mkdir/usr/local/src·`
- Download the following packages (tar-gzips) for your version of MacOSX from the Darwin web-page (*e.g.* for 10.3.5):
  - bootstrap_cmds
  - Libstreams
  - Cctools
  - kext-tools
  - IOKitUser
  - Xnu
- Move them into your working directory,
  `/usr/local/src`
- *untar-gzip them all. Assuming you're using gnutar:*
  ```
  cd/usr/local/src; for i in *.tar do;
  tar -zxvf $i; done
  ```
- *Now do the following:*
  ```
  cd bootstrap_cmds-version/relpath.tprojmake
  sudo make install
  cd../Libstreams-version
  make
  sudo make install
  cd../ccto ols-*
  sudo cp/usr/include/sys/unistd.h
  /System/Library/Frameworks/
  Kernel.framework/Head
  ers/sys
  ```
- We now need to edit cctool's makefile to compile only what we need:
  `vi Makefile`

- Comment out the "COMMON_SUBDIRS" lines (line 28 and 29 for me) with hashes ("#"):

```
#COMMON_SUBDIRS = libstuff as gprof misc
libmacho ld dyld libdyld \
# mkshlib otool profileServer RelNotes man
cbtlibs
```

- Insert the following line just below it (line 30 for me):

  COMMON_SUBDIRS = libstuff libmacho misc·

- Write the file and exit:

```
[ESC]:wq[Enter]
```

- *Now do the the following:*

```
make RC_OS=macos
sudo cp misc/seg_hack.NEW
/usr/local/bin/seg_hack
cd ld
make RC_OS=macos kld_build
sudo cp static_kld/libkld.a/usr/local/lib
sudo ranlib/usr/local/lib/libkld.a
```

- *Time to compile up kextsymboltool:*

```
cd../.
sudo mv IOKitUser* IOKit
sudo mv IOKit/usr/include
sudo mv/usr/include/IOKit/kext.subproj
/usr/includeIOKit/kext
sudo cp -fpr cctools*/include/mach-o
/usr/include
sudo cp -fpr cctools*/include/mach/*
/usr/include/mach
cd kext_tools*
gcc kextsymboltool.c -o kextsymboltool
```

- If you get errors at the above stage, either you've made a mistake with the previous lines, I've made a mistake with the instructions or your system isn't the same as mine. Otherwise:

```
sudo cp kextsymboltool/usr/local/bin
sudo chmod 755/usr/local/bin/
kextsymboltool
```

- *Now cd into the kernel directory:*

  ```
  cd../xnu*
  ```
- *This is where you would patch the kernel source. Some patches I use include:*
  - Jeff Nathan's BIOSCHDRCMPLT patch, which allows arp-spoofing under MacOSX for apps like ettercap. Check Jeff's page for the patch that matches your kernel! The one linked above works with 10.3.5/xnu-517.7.21.
  - Peter Bartoli's FORCE_VERBOSE patch, which forces the kernel to drop the grey boot-up screen and show you verbose booting information. The above link is for 571 again. Check Peter's page for the latest patch.
- Download the patches you want and then, while still in the root of the xnu source directory, patch them with:

  ```
  patch -p0 -b —verbose —suffix=.orig </
  path/to/the/patch.patch
  ```
- Pay attention and make sure you're using the correct patch by viewing the output of the patch utility!·
- Now compile the kernel:

  ```
  make exporthdrs
  make all
  ```
- With a little luck, your kernel compiled without any errors. You will now have your freshly compiled kernel

  `at BUILD/obj/RELEASE_PPC/mach_kernel.`

  Move it into/without over-writing your defaultApple kernel:

  ```
  cp BUILD/obj/RELEASE_PPC mach_kernel/
  mach_kernel.new
  chmod 644/mach_kernel.new
  chown root.wheel/mach_kernel.new
  ```
- Credit to Jean-Pierre Mouilleseaux for the following idea: Instead of just putting it over the top of the existing kernel, you can have a second kernel and configure OpenFirmware to boot from the second

kernel, allowing you an easy way out if the new kernel is corrupt. Configure OpenFirmware to boot from the new kernel with:

```
sudo nvram boot-file='nvram boot-device |
awk -F, '{print $1}' | awk '{print
$2}' ',mach_kernel.new
```

- For those of you using a G4 iBook, it seems they always alias hd: for the boot device. However, it seems you can't use the alias when booting a custom kernel for some strange reason. The following command should fix the problem for you:

```
sudo nvram boot-file=pci2/ata-6D/
@0:3,mach_kernel.new
```

- The above command sets the OpenFirmware Variable "boot-file" to the file/kernel.new on the current boot device. If your new kernel barfs, you can back out by either:
  - During power-on, reset the entire PRAM by holding down option-apple-p-r and wait for the start-up chime to sound three times, or
  - During power-on, press option-apple-o-f to enter OpenFirmware, type "reset-all" and then "mac-boot", or
  - During power-on, reset the OpenFirmware NVRAM by holding option-apple-n-v.
- OpenFirmware defaults to booting using/ mach_kernel, which will be the default Apple kernel if you've followed the instructions above.
- So now your new kernel is installed and you can test it by restaring or simply typing "reboot" at a command line.

## MACH

XNU contains code based on Mach, the legendary architecture that originated as a research project at Carnegie Mellon University in the mid 1980s (Mach itself traces its philosophy to the Accent operating system, also developed at CMU), and has been part of many important systems. Early versions of Mach had monolithic kernels, with much of BSD's code in the kernel. Mach 3.0 was the first microkernel implementation.

XNU's Mach component is based on Mach 3.0, although it's not used as a microkernel. The BSD subsystem *is*part of the kernel and so are various other subsystems that are typically implemented as user-space servers in microkernel systems.

*XNU's Mach is responsible for various low-level aspects of the system, such as:*

- Preemptive multitasking, including kernel threads (POSIX threads on Mac OS X are implemented using kernel threads)
- Protected memory
- Virtual memory management
- Inter-process communication
- Interrupt management
- Real-time support
- Kernel debugging support (the built-in low-level kernel debugger, ddb, is part of XNU's Mach component, and so is kdp, a remote kernel debugging protocol implementation)
- Console I/O
- The sequence of events prior to the kernel is passed control is described in *Booting Mac OS X*. The secondary bootloader eventually calls the kernel's "startup" code, forwarding various boot arguments to it. This low-level code is where every processor in the system starts (from the kernel's point of view). Various important variables, like maximum virtual and physical addresses, the threshold temperature for throttling down a CPU's speed, are initialized here, BAT registers are cleared, Altivec (if present) is initialized, caches are initialized, etc. Eventually this code jumps to boot initialization code for the architecture (ppc_init() on the PowerPC). Thereafter:
- A template thread is filled in, and an initial thread

is created from this template It is set to be the "current" thread.

- Some CPU housekeeping is done.
- The "Platform Expert" is initialized (PE_init_platform()), with a flag indicating that the VM is not yet initialized. This saves the boot arguments, the device tree and display information in a state variable. Another call to PE_init_platform() is made after the VM is initialized.
- Mach VM is initialized.
- The function machine_startup() is called. It takes some actions based on the boot arguments, performs some housekeeping, starts thermal monitoring for the CPU, and calls setup_main().
- setup_main() performs a lot of work: initializing the scheduler, IPC, kernel extension loading, clock, timers, tasks, threads, etc. and finally creates a kernel thread called startup_thread that creates further kernel threads.
- Startup_thread creates a number of other threads (the idle threads, service threads for clock and device...). It also initializes the thread reaper, the stack swapin and the periodic scheduler mechanism. It is here that the BSD subsystem is initialized (via bsd_init()). startup_thread becomes the pageout daemon once it finishes its work. At this point, Mach is up and running.

In addition to BSD system calls (the syscall API, as well as the sysctl and ioctl APIs), Mach messaging and IPC can be and is used (as appropriate) to exchange. information between the user and kernel spaces.

XNU also provides various ways of memory mapping and block copying. While it may be nice (say, from an academic point of view, if nothing else) to have many APIs in a system, there is always a burden on the programmer for *choosing* wisely what API to use.

The situation is similar for user-space APIs on Mac OS X, as we shall see later.

## BSD

XNU's BSD component uses FreeBSD as the primary reference codebase (although some code might be traced to other BSDs). Darwin 7.x (Mac OS X 10.3.x) uses FreeBSD 5.x. As mentioned before, BSD runs not as an *external* (or user-level) server, but is part of the kernel itself.

*Some aspects that BSD is responsible for include:*

- Process model
- User ids, permissions, basic security policies
- POSIX API, BSD style system calls
- TCP/IP stack, BSD sockets, firewall
- VFS and filesystems for details)
- System V IPC
- Crypto framework
- Various synchronization mechanisms

Note that XNU has a unified buffer cache but it ties in to Mach's VM.

XNU uses a synchronization abstraction (built on top of Mach mutexes) called *funnels* to serialize access to the BSD portion of the kernel. The kernel variables pointing to these funnels have the _flock suffix, such askernel_flock and network_flock. When Mach initializes the BSD subsystem via a call to bsd_init(), the first operation performed is the allocation of funnels (the kernel funnel's state is set to TRUE).

*Thereafter:*

- The kernel memory allocator is initialized.
- The "Platform Expert" is called upon to see if there are any boot arguments for BSD.
- VFS buffers/hash tables are allocated and initialized.
- Process related structures are allocated/initialized. This includes the list of all processes, the list of zombie processes, hash tables for process ids and process groups.
- Process 0 is created and initialized (credentials, file descriptor table, audit information, limits, etc.). The variable kernproc points to process 0.
- The machine dependent real-time clock's time and date are initialized.

- The Unified Buffer Cache is initialized (via ubc_init(), which essentially initializes a Mach VM Zone viazinit(), which allocates a region of memory from the page-level allocator).
- Various VFS structures/mechanisms are initialized: the vnode table, the filesystem event mechanism, the vnode name cache, etc. Each present filesystem time is also initialized.
- Mbufs (memory buffers, used heavily in network memory-management) are initialized via mbinit().
- Facilities/subsystems such as syslog, audit, kqueues, aio, and System V IPC are initialized.
- The kernel's generic MIB (management information base) is initialized.
- The data link interface layer is initialized.
- Sockets and protocol families are initialized.
- XNU uses a specific type of kernel extensions, NKEs (Network Kernel Extensions), to make the 4.4BSD networking architecture fit in to Mac OS X.
- Kernel profiling is started, and BSD is "published" as a resource in the IOKit.
- Ethernet devices are initialized.
- A Mach Zone is initialized for the vnode pager.
- BSD tries to mount the root filesystem (which could be coming over the network, for example, a Mac OS X disk image (.dmg) exported over NFS).
- Devfs is mounted on/dev.
- A new process is created (cloned) from kernproc (process 0). This newly created process has pid 1, and is set to become init (actually mach_init, which starts init). mach_init is loaded and run viabsdinit_task(), which is called by the BSD asynchronous trap handler (bsd_ast()).

The rest of the user space startup is described in *Mac OS X System Startup*.I/O Kit

I/O Kit, the object-oriented device driver framework of the XNU kernel is radically different from that on traditional systems.

I/O Kit uses a restricted subset of C++ (based on Embedded C++) as its programming language. This system is implemented by the libkern library.

*Features of C++ that are not allowed in this subset include:*

- Exceptions
- Multiple inheritance
- Templates
- RTTI (run-time type information), although I/O Kit has its own run-time typing system
- The device driver model provided by the I/O Kit has several useful features (in no particular order):
- Numerous device families (ATA/ATAPI, FireWire, Graphics, HID, Network, PCI, USB, HID...)
- Object oriented abstractions of devices that can be shared
- Plug-and-play and hot-plugging
- Power management
- Preemptive multitasking, threading, symmetric multiprocessing, memory protection and data management
- Dynamic matching and loading of drivers (multiple bus types)
- A database for tracking and maintaining detailed information on instantiated objects (the I/O Registry)
- A database of all I/O Kit classes available on a system (the I/O Catalog)
- An extensive API
- Mechanisms/interfaces for applications and user-space drivers to communicate with the I/O Kit
- *Driver stacking:*
  - I/O Kit's implementation consists of three C++ libraries that are present in the kernel and available to loadable drivers: IOKit.framework, Kernel/libkern and Kernel/IOKit. The I/O Kit includes a modular, layered run-time architecture that presents an abstraction of the underlying hardware by capturing the dynamic relationships between the various hardware/software components (involved in an I/O connection).

Various tools such as ioreg, ioalloccount, ioclasscount, iostat, kextload, kextunload, kextstat,kextcache, etc. let you explore and control various aspects of I/O Kit. For example, the following command shows status of dynamically loaded kernel extensions:

```
% kextstat
Index Refs Address Size Wired Name (Version)
<Linked Against>
1 1 0x0 0x0 0x0 com.apple.kernel (7.2)
2 1 0x0 0x0 0x0 com.apple.kpi.bsd (7.2)
3 1 0x0 0x0 0x0 com.apple.kpi.iokit (7.2)
4 1 0x0 0x0 0x0 com.apple.kpi.libkern (7.2)
...
```

The following command lists the details of the I/O Kit registry in excruciating detail:

```
% ioreg -l -w 0
+-o Root <class IORegistryEntry, retain count 12>
| {
| "IOKitBuildVersion" = "IOKit Component Version
7.2:
Thu Dec 11 16:15:20 PST 2003;
root(rcbuilder):RELEASE_PPC/iokit/RELEASE
"
| "IONDRVFramebufferGeneration" = <0000000200000
002>
...
/* thousands of lines of output */
```

## PLATFORM EXPERT

The Platform Expert is an object (one can think of it as a driver) that knows the type of platform that the system is running on. I/O Kit registers a *nub* (see below) for the Platform Expert.

This nub then loads the correct platform specific driver, which further discovers the buses present on the system, registering a nub for each bus found. The I/O Kit loads a matching driver for each bus nub, which discovers the devices connected to the bus, and so on.

*Thus, the Platform Expert is responsible for actions such as:*

- Building the device tree (as described above)
- Parse certain boot arguments
- Identify the machine (including processor and bus clock speeds)
- Initialize a "user interface" to be used in case of kernel panics
- In the context of the I/O Kit, a "nub" is an object that defines an access point and communication channel for a device (a bus, a disk drive or partition, a graphics card...) or logical service (arbitration, driver matching, power management...).

## LIBKERN AND LIBSA

As described earlier, the I/O Kit uses a restricted subset of C++.

*This system, implemented by libkern, provides features such as:*

- Dynamic object allocation, construction, destruction (including data structures such as Arrays, Booleans, Dictionaries...)
- Certain atomic operations, miscellaneous functions (bcmp(), memcmp(), strlen()...)
- Provisions for tracking the number of current instances for each class
- Ways to avoid the "Fragile Base Class Problem"
- libsa provides functions for miscellaneous purposes: binary searching, symbol remangling (used for gcc 2.95 to 3.3, for example), dgraphs, catalogs, kernel extension management, sorting, patching vtables, etc.

## XNU-DEV

This project is a fork of the XNU kernel utilized by Darwin and Mac OS X whose goal is to provide additional support for hardware and functionality to users which use XNU kernel driven operating systems. Latest NewsAvailable here: Latest News We added a Wiki page for news snippets so you can keep up on the latest developments easily by subscribing to the Wiki RSS feed. User documentation. The Voodoo team has put great effort into preparing proper documentation for the end users. Please make sure to go through it as it answers several common questions.

Unfortunately currently the documentation is only available in English. We would appreciate if the community helps in translating it to other languages. We are looking for the following translations (in order of importance): Chinese, Korean, German and Russian, at the moment.

Developer documentationTwo white-papers detailing the technology that went into the kernel are being prepared and will be available soon. One of them describes the changes made in the kernel from a higher abstraction level, to enable developers to get to grips with the source tree. The second one is a highly technical paper describing the design and implementation of the vastly improved SSE3 emulator. Further documents may be available in the future.

*Bug reportsNote*: We have exceeded the attachments quota for Issues on Google Code. We're going to ask Google to extend it, and/or find alternative methods for you to get your system info or KP screenshots to us. Until then, please use SendSpace or Mediafire for the.tar.gz files, Pastie for pasting crash logs and ImageShack for putting KP screenshots.

Please go through the list of open bugs and if your problem is in the list, STAR it instead of posting a new report. Starring a bug report means voting for it and will push us to try fixing that first, and also helps avoid duplicate reports.

We are not accepting any more bug reports for sleep/ resume problems. Incomplete reports will NOT be entertained. Please be prepared to describe what steps you have taken to fix the problem yourself. Only report an issue if you believe its a bug in the kernel. We have found that almost all bug reports for the release candidate have been because of external reasons (like kexts, not updating to 10.5.5 and so on). Once ready, go to the Issues tab. Other Kernel Features (slightly outdated info)

Supports sleep/resume as well as SpeedStep on most systems (use in conjunction with the SpeedStep kext) Massively improved SSE3 Emulation layer, up to 3 times faster and fully multithread-capable (thanks Turbo) Real-time clock fix for SSE2 users (no system slowdown/stutter when SpeedStep is on, supports less than 1 GHz cpu speeds) On-the-fly cpuid opcode patching for AMD support (boot retail on AMD!) Support for 64bit on AMD Black-listing of problematic kernel extensions More secure: Execute-Disable (XD/NX) is turned on by default for supported systems HPET enabled on supported systems, cleaner boot-up code Legacy VMware support by using busratio= bootflag. Source-code is open under APSL. (Not New BSD!)

# 7

# OSX Memory

## INTRODUCTION

Memory is an important system resource that all programs use. Programs must be loaded into memory before they can run and, while running, they allocate additional memory (both explicitly and implicitly) to store and manipulate program-level data.

Making room in memory for a program's code and data requires time and resources and therefore affect the overall performance of the system. Although you cannot avoid using memory altogether, there are ways to minimize the impact your memory usage has on the rest of the system. This document provides background information about the memory systems of Mac OS X and iOS and how you use them efficiently. You can use this information to tune your program's memory usage by ensuring you are allocating the right amount of memory at the right time. This document also provides tips on how to detect memory-related performance issues in your program.

## ABOUT THE VIRTUAL MEMORY SYSTEM

Efficient memory management is an important aspect of writing high performance code in both Mac OS X and iOS. Tuning your memory usage can reduce both your application's memory footprint and the amount of CPU time it consumes. In order to properly tune your code though, you need to understand something about how the underlying system manages memory.

Both Mac OS X and iOS include a fully-integrated virtual memory system that you cannot turn off; it is always on. Both system also provide up to 4 gigabytes of addressable space per 32-bit process. In addition, Mac OS X provides approximately 18 exabytes of addressable space for 64-bit processes.

Even for computers that have 4 or more gigabytes of RAM available, the system rarely dedicates this much RAM to a single process. nTo give processes access to their entire 4 gigabyte or 18 exabyte address space, Mac OS X uses the hard disk to hold data that is not currently in use. As memory gets full, sections of memory that are not being used are written to disk to make room for data that is needed now. The portion of the disk that stores the unused data is known as the backing store because it provides the backup storage for main memory.

Although Mac OS X supports a backing store, iOS does not. In iPhone applications, read-only data that is already on the disk (such as code pages) is simply removed from memory and reloaded from disk as needed. Writable data is never removed from memory by the operating system. Instead, if the amount of free memory drops below a certain threshold, the system asks the running applications to free up memory voluntarily to make room for new data. Applications that fail to free up enough memory are terminated.

## TIPS FOR ALLOCATING MEMORY

Memory is an important resource for your application so it's important to think about how your application will use memory and what might be the most efficient allocation approaches. Most applications do not need to do anything special; they can simply allocate objects or memory blocks as needed and not see any performance degradation. For applications that use large amount of memory, however, carefully planning out your memory allocation strategy could make a big difference.

The following sections describe the basic options for allocating memory along with tips for doing so efficiently. To determine if your application has memory performance problems in the first place, you need to use the Xcode tools to look at your application's allocation patterns while it is running.

## TIPS FOR IMPROVING MEMORY-RELATED PERFORMANCE

As you design your code, you should always be aware of how you are using memory. Because memory is an important resource, you want to be sure to use it efficiently and not be wasteful. Besides allocating the right amount of memory for a given operation, the following sections describe other ways to improve the efficiency of your program's memory usage.

### Defer Your Memory Allocations

Every memory allocation has a performance cost. That cost includes the time it takes to allocate the memory in your program's logical address space and the time it takes to assign that address space to physical memory. If you do not plan to use a particular block of memory right away, deferring the allocation until the time when you actually need it is the best course of action. In particular, avoid allocating memory at launch time if you do not plan on using that memory immediately. Instead, focus your initial memory allocations on the objects needed to display your user interface and respond to input from the user.

Defer other allocations until the user issues starts interacting with your application and issuing commands. This lazy allocation of memory saves time right away and ensures that any memory that is allocated is actually used. Once place where lazy initialization can be somewhat tricky is with global variables. Because they are global to your application, you need to make sure global variables are initialized properly before they are used by the rest of your code. The basic approach often taken with global variables is to define a static variable in one of your code modules and use a public accessor function to get and set the value, as shown in Listing 1.

**Listing 1** Lazy allocation of memory through an accessor

```
MyGlobalInfo* GetGlobalBuffer()
```

```
{
static MyGlobalInfo* sGlobalBuffer = NULL;
if ( sGlobalBuffer == NULL)
{
sGlobalBuffer = malloc( sizeof( MyGlobalInfo));
}
return sGlobalBuffer;
}
```

The only time you have to be careful with code of this sort is when it might be called from multiple threads. In a multithreaded environment, you need to use locks to protect the if statement in your accessor method. The downside to that approach though is that acquiring the lock takes a nontrivial amount of time and must be done every time you access the global variable, which is a performance hit of a different kind. A simpler approach would be to initialize all global variables from your application's main thread before it spawns any additional threads.

### Initialize Memory Blocks Efficiently

Small blocks of memory, allocated using the malloc function, are not guaranteed to be initialized with zeroes. Although you could use the memset function to initialize the memory, a better choice is to use the calloc routine to allocate the memory in the first place. The calloc function reserves the required virtual address space for the memory but waits until the memory is actually used before initializing it. This approach is much more efficient than using memset, which forces the virtual memory system to map the corresponding pages into physical memory in order to zero-initialize them. Another advantage of using the calloc function is that it lets the system initialize pages as they're used, as opposed to all at once.

### Reuse Temporary Memory Buffers

If you have a highly-used function that creates a large temporary buffer for some calculations, you might want to consider reusing that buffer rather than reallocating it each time you call the function. Even if your function needs a variable buffer space, you can always grow the buffer as needed using the realloc function. For multithreaded applications, the best way to reuse buffers is to add them to your thread-local storage. Although you could store the buffer using a static variable in your function, doing so would prevent you from using that function on multiple threads at the same time. Caching buffers eliminates much of the overhead for functions that regularly allocate and free large blocks of memory. However, this technique is only appropriate for functions that are called frequently. Also, you should be careful not to cache too many large buffers. Caching buffers does add to the memory footprint of your application and should only be used if testing indicates it would yield better performance.

### Release Unused Memory

It is always important to release memory as soon as you are done using it. Forgetting to releasememory can cause memory leaks, which reduce the amount of memory available to your application and impact performance. Left unchecked, memory leaks can also put your application into a state where it cannot do anything because it cannot allocate the required memory. No matter which platform you are targeting, you should always eliminate memory leaks in your application. In iPhone applications, you should also be more diligent about releasing memory the moment it is no longer needed.

Although being lazy is fine for allocating memory, you should never be lazy about releasing memory. Use additional autorelease pools to release autoreleased objects more quickly or avoid autoreleased objects altogether and simply release the memory immediately when you are done with it. To help track down memory leaks, use the Instruments or MallocDebug applications or use the leaks command-line tool.

### Avoid Handles in Carbon

If you still have legacy code that you are moving from Mac OS 9 to Mac OS X, get rid of any code that uses handles. The benefit offered by handles in Mac OS 9 is not relevant for applications built for Mac OS X. Specifically, if you have code that calls HLock, HUnlock. HSetState, or HGetState, remove that code entirely.

## MEMORY ALLOCATION TECHNIQUES

Because memory is such a fundamental resource, Mac OS X and iOS both provide several ways to allocate it. Which allocation techniques you use will depend mostly on your needs, but in the end all memory allocations eventually use the malloc library to create the memory. Even Cocoa objects are allocated using the malloc library eventually. The use of this single library makes it possible for the performance tools to report on all of the memory allocations in your application.

If you are writing a Cocoa application, you might allocate memory only in the form of objects using the alloc method ofNSObject. Even so, there may be times when you need to go beyond the basic object-related memory blocks and use other memory allocation techniques. For example, you might allocate memory directly using malloc in order to pass it to a low-level function call. The following sections provide information about the malloc library and virtual memory system and how they perform allocations. The purpose of these sections is to help you identify the costs associated with each type of specialized allocation. You should use this information to optimize memory allocations in your code.

Note: These sections assume you are using the system supplied version of the malloc library to do your allocations. If you are using a custom malloc library, these techniques may not apply.

### Allocating Objects

For Objective-C based applications, you allocate objects using one of two techniques. You can either use the alloc class method, followed by a call to a class initialization method, or you can use the new class method to allocate the object and call its default init method in one step. Regardless of which technique you use to allocate objects, memory management for Objective-C objects is governed by the memory model you use for your application. Mac OS X applications can choose between a managed memory model or a garbage-collected memory model. (In iOS, applications can use only the managed memory model.) Which model you choose is a matter of choice but has implications on other aspects of your application's design and memory behaviour.

Applications that use the managed memory model are responsible for managing the deallocation of objects through a proper set of retain, release, and autorelease messages. For optimal performance, you should always release objects whenever possible and not autorelease them. The release method requires less overhead than the autorelease method and lets the Objective-C runtime free up objects immediately when their reference count reaches 0. If you must create large numbers of autoreleased objects, you should create more localized autorelease pools in your code so that you can release the objects they contain more frequently. In both cases, you should use the Instruments application to look for leaked objects. In Mac OS X, you can also use the leaks command-line tool to locate memory leaks.

If you are writing a Mac OS X application and choose the garbage-collected memory model, you do not have to worry about leaks but you should still be aware of other performance concerns. The garbage collector takes cues from your code when determining which objects to release and which ones to keep. You may not need to call the release method explicitly any more but you still need to set instance variables to nil when you no longer need the objects they reference. For efficiency, you should also minimize your use of finalize methods for cleaning up your objects. For more information about managing memory in Objective-C applications, see Memory Management Programming Guide. For more information on the garbage collection memory model and how to use it in Mac OS X applications.

## Allocating Small Memory Blocks

For small memory allocations, where small is anything less than a few virtual memory pages, malloc suballocates the requested amount of memory from a list (or "pool") of free blocks of increasing size. Any small blocks you deallocate using the free routine are added back to the pool and reused on a "best fit" basis. The memory pool is itself is comprised of several virtual memory pages that are allocated using the vm_allocate routine and managed for you by the system.

When allocating any small blocks of memory, remember that the granularity for blocks allocated by the malloc library is 16 bytes. Thus, the smallest block of memory you can allocate is 16 bytes and any blocks larger than that are a multiple of 16. For example, if you call malloc and ask for 4 bytes, it returns a block whose size is 16 bytes; if you request 24 bytes, it returns a block whose size is 32 bytes. Because of this granularity, you should design your data structures carefully and try to make them multiples of 16 bytes whenever possible.

Note: By their nature, allocations smaller than a single virtual memory page in size cannot be page aligned.

## Allocating Large Memory Blocks

For large memory allocations, where large is anything more than a few virtual memory pages, malloc automatically uses thevm_allocate routine to obtain the requested memory. The vm_allocate routine assigns an address range to the new block in the logical address space of the current process, but it does not assign any physical memory to those pages right away.

*Instead, the kernel does the following:*

- It maps a range of memory in the virtual address space of this process by creating a map entry; the map entry is a simple structure that defines the starting and ending addresses of the region.
- The range of memory is backed by the default pager.
- The kernel creates and initializes a VM object, associating it with the map entry.

At this point there are no pages resident in physical memory and no pages in the backing store. Everything is mapped virtually within the system. When your code accesses part of the memory block, by reading or writing to a specific address in it, a fault occurs because that address has not been mapped to physical memory. In Mac OS X, the kernel also recognizes that the VM object has no backing store for the page on which this address occurs.

*The kernel then performs the following steps for each page fault:*

- It acquires a page from the free list and fills it with zeroes.
- It inserts a reference to this page in the VM object's list of resident pages.
- It maps the virtual page to the physical page by filling in a data structure called the pmap. The pmap contains the page table used by the processor (or by a separate memory management unit) to map a given virtual address to the actual hardware address.

The granularity of large memory blocks is equal to the size of a virtual memory page, or 4096 bytes. In other words, any large memory allocations that are not a multiple of 4096 are rounded up to this multiple automatically. Thus, if you are allocating large memory buffers, you should make your buffer a multiple of this size to avoid wasting memory.

Note: Large memory allocations are guaranteed to be page-aligned. For large allocations, you may also find that it makes sense to allocate virtual memory directly using vm_allocate, rather than using malloc. The example in Listing 2 shows how to use the vm_allocate function.

Listing 2 Allocating memory with vm_allocate

```
void* AllocateVirtualMemory(size_t size)
{
char* data;
kern_return_t err;
//In debug builds, check that we have
//correct VM page alignment
check(size != 0);
check((size% 4096) == 0);
//Allocate directly from VM
err = vm_allocate( (vm_map_t) mach_task_self(),
(vm_address_t*) &data,
size,
```

```
VM_FLAGS_ANYWHERE);
//Check errors
check(err == KERN_SUCCESS);
if(err != KERN_SUCCESS)
{
data = NULL;
}
return data;
}
```

## Allocating Memory in Batches

If your code allocates multiple, identically-sized memory blocks, you can use the malloc_zone_batch_malloc function to allocate those blocks all at once. This function offers better performance than a series of calls to malloc to allocate the same memory. Performance is best when the individual block size is relatively small-less than 4K in size.

The function does its best to allocate all of the requested memory but may return less than was requested. When using this function, check the return values carefully to see how many blocks were actually allocated. Batch allocation of memory blocks is supported in Mac OS X version 10.3 and later and in iOS. For information, see the/usr/include/malloc/malloc.h header file.

## Allocating Shared Memory

Shared memory is memory that can be written to or read from by two or more processes. Shared memory can be inheritedfrom a parent process, created by a shared memory server, or explicitly created by an application for export to other applications.

*Uses for shared memory include the following:*

- Sharing large resources such as icons or sounds
- Fast communication between one or more processes

Shared memory is fragile and is generally not recommended when other, more reliable alternatives are available. If one program corrupts a section of shared memory, any programs that also use that memory share the corrupted data. The functions used to create and manage shared memory regions are in the/usr/include/sys/shm.h header file.

## Using Memory Zones

All memory blocks are allocated within a malloc zone (also referred to as a malloc heap). A zone is a variable-size range of virtual memory from which the memory system can allocate blocks. A zone has its own free list and pool of memory pages, and memory allocated within the zone remains on that set of pages. Zones are useful in situations where you need to create blocks of memory with similar access patterns or lifetimes. You can allocate many objects or blocks of memory in a zone and then destroy the zone to free them all, rather than releasing each block individually. In theory, using a zone in this way can minimize wasted space and reduce paging activity. In reality, the overhead of zones often eliminates the performance advantages associated with the zone.

Note: The term zone is synonymous with the terms heap, pool, and arena in terms of memory allocation using themalloc routines.

By default, allocations made using the malloc function occur within the default malloc zone, which is created when mallocis first called by your application. Although it is generally not recommended, you can create additional zones if measurements show there to be potential performance gains in your code. For example, if the effect of releasing a large number of temporary (and isolated) objects is slowing down your application, you could allocate them in a zone instead and simply deallocate the zone. If you are create objects (or allocate memory blocks) in a custom malloc zone, you can simply free the entire zone when you are done with it, instead of releasing the zone-allocated objects or memory blocks individually. When doing so, be sure your application data structures do not hold references to the memory in the custom zone. Attempting to access memory in a deallocated zone will cause a memory fault and crash your application.

Warning: You should never deallocate the default zone for your application.

If you are a Cocoa developer, you can use the NSCreateZone function to create a custom malloc zone and theNSDefaultMallocZone function to get the default zone for your application. To create new objects in a custom zone, use the allocWithZone: class method, which is available to all subclasses of NSObject. If your class does not descend fromNSObject, use the NSAllocateObject function to allocate the memory for your new instances. For more information, see the function descriptions in Foundation Framework Reference. At the malloc library level, support for zones is defined in/ usr/include/malloc/malloc.h. Use themalloc_create_zone function to create a custom malloc zone or the malloc_default_zone function to get the default zone for your application. To allocate memory in a particular zone, use the malloc_zone_malloc,malloc_zone_calloc, malloc_zone_valloc, or malloc_zone_realloc functions. To release the memory in a custom zone, call malloc_destroy_zone.

## COPYING MEMORY

There are two main approaches to copying memory in Mac OS X: direct and delayed. For most situations, the direct approach offers the best overall performance. However, there are times when using a delayed-copy operation has its benefits. The goal of the following sections is to introduce you to the different approaches for copying memory and the situations when you might use those approaches.

### Copying Memory Directly

The direct copying of memory involves using a routine such as memcpy or memmove to copy bytes from one block to another. Both the source and destination blocks must be resident in memory at the time of the copy.

*However, these routines are especially suited for the following situations:*

- The size of the block you want to copy is small (under 16 kilobytes).
- You intend to use either the source or destination right away.

- The source or destination block is not page aligned.
- The source and destination blocks overlap.

If you do not plan to use the source or destination data for some time, performing a direct copy can decrease performance significantly for large memory blocks. Copying the memory directly increases the size of your application's working set.

Whenever you increase your application's working set, you increase the chances of paging to disk. If you have two direct copies of a large memory block in your working set, you might end up paging them both to disk. When you later access either the source or destination, you would then need to load that data back from disk, which is much more expensive than using vm_copy to perform a delayed copy operation.

Note: If the source and destination blocks overlap, you should prefer the use of memmove over memcpy. The implementation of memmove handles overlapping blocks correctly in Mac OS X, but the implementation of memcpy is not guaranteed to do so.

## Delaying Memory Copy Operations

If you intend to copy many pages worth of memory, but don't intend to use either the source or destination pages immediately, then you may want to use the vm_copy function to do so. Unlike memmove or memcpy, vm_copy does not touch any real memory. It modifies the virtual memory map to indicate that the destination address range is a copy-on-write version of the source address range. The vm_copy routine is more efficient than memcpy in very specific situations.

Specifically, it is more efficient in cases where your code does not access either the source or destination memory for a fairly large period of time after the copy operation. The reason that vm_copy is effective for delayed usage is the way the kernel handles the copy-on-write case. In order to perform the copy operation, the kernel must remove all references to the source pages from the virtual memory system. The next time a process accesses data on that source page, a soft fault occurs, and the kernel maps the page back into the process space as a copy-on-write page. The process of handling a single soft fault is almost as expensive as copying the data directly.

### Copying Small Amounts of Data

If you need to copy a small blocks of non-overlapping data, you should prefer memcpy over any other routines. For small blocks of memory, the GCC compiler can optimize this routine by replacing it with inline instructions to copy the data by value. The compiler may not optimize out other routines such as memmove or BlockMoveData.

### Copying Data to Video RAM

When copying data into VRAM, use the BlockMoveDataUncachedfunction instead of functions such as bcopy. Thebcopy function uses cache-manipulation instructions that may cause exception errors. The kernel must fix these errors in order to continue, which slows down performance tremendously.

## RESPONDING TO LOW-MEMORY WARNINGS IN IOS

The virtual memory system in iOS does not use a backing store and instead relies on the cooperation of applications to release memory.

When the number of free pages dips below the computed threshold, the system releases unmodified pages whenever possible but may also send the currently running application a low-memory notification.

If your application receives this notification, heed the warning. Upon receiving it, your application must free up as much memory as possible by releasing objects that it does not need or clearing out memory caches that it can recreate later.

*UIKit provides several ways to receive low-memory notifications, including the following:*

- Implement the application Did Receive Memory Warning: method of your application delegate.

- Override the didReceiveMemoryWarning method in your custom UIViewController subclass.
- Register to receive the UI Application Did Receive Memory Warning Notification notification.

Upon receiving any of these notifications, your handler method should respond by immediately freeing up any unneeded memory. View controllers automatically purge any views that are currently offscreen, but you should also override thedidReceiveMemoryWarning method and use it to release objects retained by outlets or other data objects managed by your view controller.

If your custom objects have known purgeable resources, you can have those objects register for theUI Application Did Receive Memory Warning Notification notification and release their purgeable resources directly. Registering for the UIApplicationDidReceiveMemoryWarningNotification notification is appropriate if you have a few objects that manage most of your purgeable resources and it is appropriate to purge all of those resources. If you have many purgeable objects or want to coordinate the release of only a subset of those objects, however, you might want to use your application delegate to release the desired objects.

Important: Like the system applications, your applications should always handle low-memory warnings, even if they do not receive those warnings during your testing. System applications consume small amounts of memory while processing requests. When a low-memory condition is detected, the system delivers low-memory warnings to all running programs (including your application) and may terminate some background applications (if necessary) to ease memory pressure. If not enough memory is released-perhaps because your application is leaking or still consuming too much memory-the system may still terminate your application.

## TRACKING MEMORY USAGE

If you suspect your code is not using memory as efficiently as it could, the first step in determining if there is a problem is to gather some baseline data. Monitoring your code using one of the Apple-provided performance tools can give you a picture of your code's memory usage and may highlight potential problems or point to areas that need further examination. The following sections describe the tools most commonly used for memory analysis and when you might want to use them.

## TRACKING ALLOCATIONS WITH INSTRUMENTS

The Instruments application is always a good starting point for doing any sort of performance analysis. Instruments is an integrated, data-gathering environment that uses special modules (called instruments) to gather all sorts of information about a process. Instruments can operate on your application's shipping binary file-you do not need to compile special modules into your application to use it. The library of the Instruments application contains four modules that are designed specifically for gathering memory-related data.

*These modules are as follows:*

- The ObjectAlloc instrument records and displays a history of all memory allocations since the launch of your application.
- The Leaks instrument looks for allocated memory that is no longer referenced by your program's code;
- The Shared Memory instrument monitors the opening and unlinking of shared memory regions.
- The Memory Monitor instrument measures and records the system's overall memory usage.

You can add any or all of these instruments to a single trace document and gather data for each of them simultaneously. Being able to gather the data all at once lets you correlate information from one instrument with the others. For example, the Leaks instrument is often combined with the ObjectAlloc instrument so that you can both track the allocations and find out which ones were leaked. After gathering data for your application, you need to analyse it. The following sections provide tips on how to analyse data using several of the memory-related instruments. For information on how to use the Leaks instrument,

## Analysing Memory Allocations with the ObjectAlloc Instrument

The ObjectAlloc instrument to track the memory allocation activity for your application. This instrument tracks memory allocations from the time your application is launched until you stop recording data.

The instrument shows you the allocations in terms of the number of objects created and the size (or type) of the objects that were created.

In the icon viewing mode, the instrument displays a real-time histogram that lets you see changes and trends directly as they occur. It also retains a history of allocations and deallocations, giving you an opportunity to go back and see where those objects were allocated.

The information displayed by the ObjectAlloc instrument is recorded by an allocation statistics facility built into the Core Foundation framework. When this facility is active, every allocation and deallocation is recorded as it happens. For Objective-C objects, copy, retain, release, and autorelease messages are also recorded.

### Browsing Object Instances

The Detail pane of the ObjectAlloc instrument is where you go to find specific information about each memory allocation that was made.

By default, the detail pane shows the net and overall allocations for each object type. Moving the mouse over an object type in the Category column, however, reveals an arrow button that when pressed displays details about the allocated blocks of that type.

You can find out when the block was allocated along with details about the code module that allocated it. While browsing the specific block allocations, clicking the button next to the address of a given block shows you the history of the memory allocations at that address.

You can find out what type of block was allocated, when it was allocated, when it was released, who did it, and when they did it. Because allocations are tracked by address, the size and category of the block is also included. You can use this view to see all the types of data that were loaded into that particular address.

### Browsing Memory By Caller

In addition to icon mode, the ObjectAlloc instrument supports an outline mode that organizes memory allocations by type and then shows the call tree that was used to make those allocations.

Using this mode, you can look at how many blocks of a specific type were allocated within a given call tree of your application. In addition to viewing allocations for specific types of blocks, there is an entry for all allocations that mixes all of the memory allocations together into a single call tree, so you can see the total amount of memory allocated by your code at any given time.

You can use the outline mode to identify objects that were allocated by the same portion of code, whether directly by one of your routines or indirectly through a system routine. If you see some unexpected allocations in one of your application's routines, you might look to see why and adjust your own memory usage accordingly. You can also use this mode to see if a particular branch of your code is allocating more memory than you expect.

### Analysing Shared Memory Usage

For Mac OS X applications, the Shared Memory instrument tracks calls to any shm_open and shm_unlink functions, which are used for opening and closing regions of shared memory in the system. You can use this information to find out where your application is getting references to shared memory regions and to examine how often those calls are being made.

The detail pane displays the list of each function call along with information about the calling environment at the time of the call. Specifically, the pane lists the executable that initiated the call and the function parameters. Opening the Extended Detail pane shows the stack trace associated with the call.

### Analysing Data from the Memory Monitor Instrument

For Mac OS X applications, the Memory Monitor instrument displays assorted statistics about system memory usage. You can use this instrument to view the memory usage trends in your application or on the entire system. For example, you can see how much memory is currently active, inactive, wired, and free.

You can also see the amount of memory that has been paged in or out.

You might use this instrument in conjunction with other instruments to track the amount of memory your application uses with respect to specific operations.

## TRACKING ALLOCATIONS WITH MALLOCDEBUG

The MallocDebug application is an alternative to the Instruments application that you can use to inspect your program's memory allocations and look for leaks. MallocDebug shows currently allocated blocks of memory, organized by the call stack at the time of allocation.

You can use MallocDebug to determine how much memory your application allocates, where it allocates that memory, and which functions allocated large amounts of memory.

It gathers data from the Carbon Memory Manager, Core Foundation object allocations, Cocoa object allocations, and mallocallocations.

Like Instruments, MallocDebug does not require prior instrumentation of the program-that is, you don't need to link with special libraries or call special functions. Instead, MallocDebug launches your application using its own instrumented version of the malloc library calls. MallocDebug does not operate on applications running on iPhone or iPod touch devices.

Note: The custom malloc library used by MallocDebug may hold on to memory blocks longer than normal for analysis purposes. As a result, you should not try to gather metrics regarding the size of your program's memory footprint while running it under MallocDebug.

*MallocDebug includes a number of features you can use to refine your memory analysis:*

- It provides a hex-dump view for examining raw memory.
- It allows you to mark off any period of execution for analysis.
- It allows you to export performance data for detailed examination or for further analysis and refinement by command-line tools. The export feature gives you the freedom to look at or summarize the data in the form most relevant to your executable.

## Using MallocDebug

After launching MallocDebug, the main window appears. There are three basic sections in the MallocDebug window. Information about the launched program is at the top of the window. The center portion displays the call stack browser. The bottom portion displays the memory buffer browser.

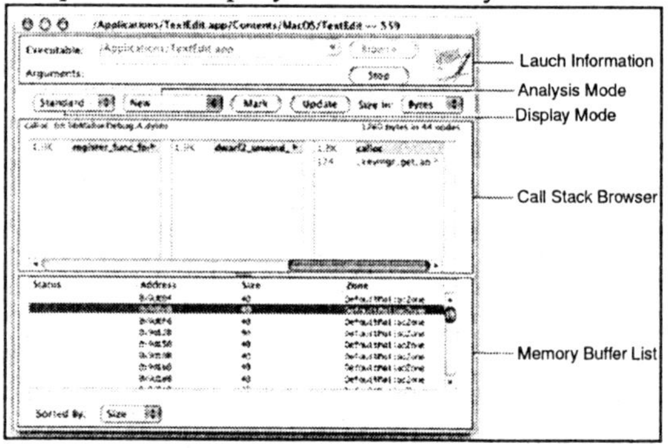


**Fig:** Malloc Debug Main Window

To start a new MallocDebug session, you must select and launch the application you want to analyse by doing the following:

- Enter the full path to the program in the Executable field, or click the Browse button and select the program using the file-system browser.
- If you want to run the executable with command-line arguments, enter them in the Arguments field.

- Click the Launch button.

MallocDebug launches the program and performs an initial query about memory usage. Further updates occur whenever you press the Update button.

## The Call Stack Browser

The main focus of memory analysis in MallocDebug is the call stack browser. This browser shows you where memory allocations occurred by gathering stack snapshots whenever one of the malloc library routines was encountered.Figure shows a sample set of data for calls to the malloc routine.

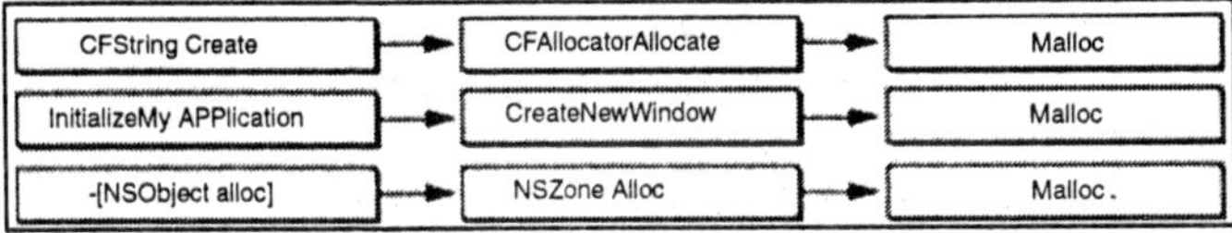


**Fig**: Function Call Stacks Gathered at Runtime

MallocDebug coalesces the call stack information it gathers into a call tree by overlapping equivalent sequences of functions. It then presents this information in the call stack browser. The call stack browser has three display modes: standard, inverted, and flat. Each display mode presents the data in a different way to help you identify trends. You can choose which mode you want from the left-most pop-up menu and toggle back and forth as needed. Standard mode presents each call stack hierarchically from the function at the top of the stack (for instance, main) to the function that performs the allocation: malloc, calloc, and so on. Each element of the browser shows the amount of memory that has been allocated in the call stack involving that method or function. Figure illustrates the structure of the call stack in standard mode.

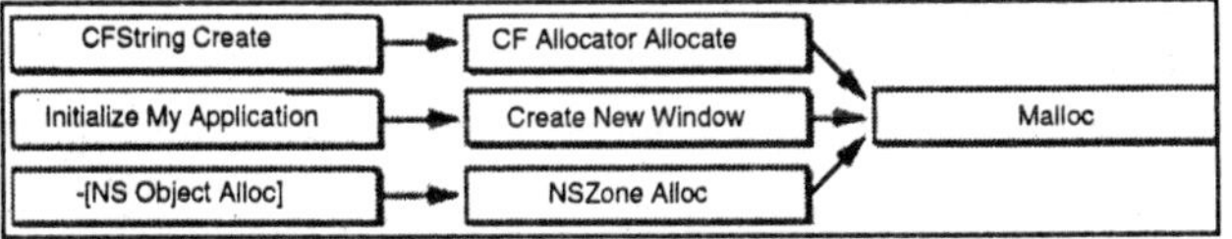


**Fig**: View of Function Call Tree in Standard Mode

Inverted mode reverses the hierarchy of standard mode and shows the call tree from the allocation functions to the bottom of each stack. This mode is useful for highlighting the ways in which specific allocation functions are called. By seeing all the calls to malloc or the Core Foundation allocators, you can more easily detect wasteful patterns in lower-level libraries. Use inverted mode if you're working on a low-level framework or if you want to focus on how you're calling malloc in your own code. Figure illustrates the structure of the call stack in inverted mode.

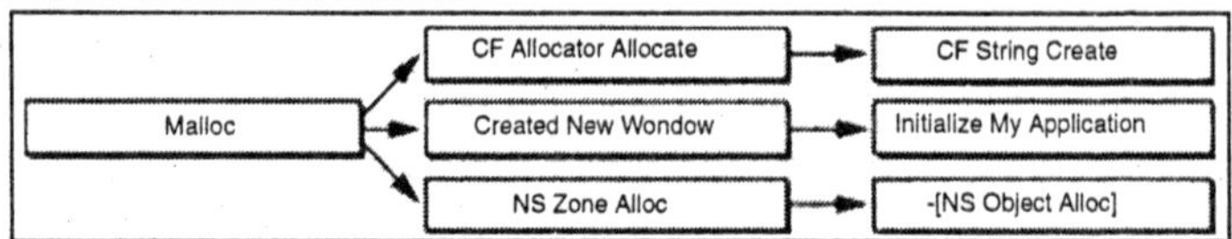


**Fig:** View of Function Call Tree in Inverted Mode

Flat mode shows memory usage for every method and function of an application in a single list, sorted by allocated amount. All of the instances of a function call are collapsed into one browser item corresponding to that function. A function's memory use includes the sum of all the allocations performed in that function and all allocations performed in functions that it calls. This allows you to see the total amount of memory allocated by a specific function and every function it called, not just those at the top or bottom of the call stack.

The analysis mode pop-up menu (located to the right of the viewing-mode pop-up menu) affects the type of allocations that are displayed in the call stack browser.

*You have several options:*

- *All Allocations*: Gives you the call trees for all currently allocated buffers in your application.
- *Allocations:* Since Mark Displays functions and methods in which an allocation has occurred since launch time or the last mark. for information on how to display allocations over a specific period of time.
- *Leaks:* This item displays a call tree showing leaked memory blocks in your program. For further discussion of this analysis mode,
- *Overruns/underruns:* Displays a call tree with a list of buffers that were written to incorrectly, caused by writing to memory before or after the buffer boundary. If the program wrote past the end of a

buffer, a right arrow (>) appears by the buffer. Similarly, if the application wrote before the start of a buffer, a left arrow (<) appears by the buffer. For more on MallocDebug's memory-detail features,

## Taking a Snapshot of Memory Usage

When you launch a program with MallocDebug, the main window displays the allocation activity that occurred during launch time. When you click the Update button, MallocDebug shows memory usage up to the current point in time.

*If you want to display allocations from a particular point in time, you can do the following:*

- Press the Mark button.
- Exercise a portion of your program.
- Select the "Allocations from mark" item from the analysis mode pop-up list.

MallocDebug shows the buffers allocated since the mark was set. Note that MallocDebug displays only the buffers that are still currently allocated, so you will see only those buffers allocated since you clicked the Mark button that have not been freed.

## Analysing Raw Memory

When you select an allocation buffer in the call stack browser, the memory buffer list might show one or more lines of data. Each line in this list represents a block of memory allocated by the currently selected function or by a function eventually called by that function. Each line contains the address of the buffer, its size (in bytes), and the zone in which it was allocated. Double-clicking one of these lines opens the Memory Viewer Panel window, which you can use to inspect the contents of memory at that location. If code attempts to write before the start or past the end of a buffer, the memory buffer list shows an appropriate indicator in the Status column. If bytes were written before the buffer, the column displays a less-than < character. If bytes were written after the buffer, the column contains a greater-than > character. Use the popup menu below the list to sort the list contents.

MallocDebug helps you catch some types of problems by writing certain hexadecimal patterns into the hex values displayed in the Memory Viewer Panel window. It overwrites freed memory with 0X55 and it guards against writing beyond a block's boundaries by putting the values 0xDEADBEEF and 0xBEEFDEAD, respectively, at the beginning and end of each allocated buffer.

The memory buffer inspector can be particularly helpful for determining why an object is leaking. For example, if a string is being leaked, the text of the string might indicate where it was created. If an event structure is leaked, you might be able to identify the type of event from the contents of memory and thus find the corresponding event-handling code responsible for the leak.

### Evaluating MallocDebug Problem Reports

Some of the reports that MallocDebug presents identify obvious problems that you should fix immediately. Some of these problems include leaks, buffer overruns, and references to freed memory.

Other problems are more subjective in nature and require you to make a determination as to whether there is a problem. To improve your program's overall allocation behaviour, use MallocDebug's detailed accounting of memory usage to explore the memory usage of your program.

This can help you identify wasted memory allocations or unexpected allocation patterns and thus optimize your program's memory usage.

*As you analyse your memory allocations, consider the following items:*

- Don't ignore small buffers. A small leaked buffer might itself contain references to larger buffers, which then also become leaks. (The leaks tool is better at reporting leaks of this nature.)
- Look at allocation patterns during specific intervals of typical program use, especially where you suspect memory usage might be a problem.
- The inverted display mode for the call stack browser

can sometimes yield results faster because it shows which routines are actually calling malloc. The normal display mode is better for seeing memory allocations in particular modules of your code.

- Keep track of important statistics, such as private memory usage and total allocated memory, so you can compare them against previous measurements.

## Limitations of MallocDebug

You can use MallocDebug to gather data for applications running in Mac OS X only. The following section describes some of the other issues you may run into when running MallocDebug.

## Allocated Memory Reporting

MallocDebug shows the current amount of allocated memory at a given point in a program's execution; it does not show thetotal amount of memory allocated by the program during its entire span of execution. Memory that has been freed is not shown. To see memory that your program has allocated and freed, use the malloc_history tool.

## Crashing Under MallocDebug

If a program crashes under MallocDebug, a diagnostic message is printed to the console that explains why the program crashed. Listing 1 gives an example of MallocDebug's crash diagnostic message. Listing 1 Diagnostic output from crashing under MallocDebug

```
MallocDebug: Target application attempted to read
address 0x55555555, which can't be read.
MallocDebug: MallocDebug trashes freed memory with
the value 0x55,
MallocDebug: strongly suggesting the application
or a library is referencing
MallocDebug: memory it already freed.
MallocDebug: MallocDebug can't do anything about
this, so the app's just going to have to be
terminated.
```

```
MallocDebug: libMallocDebug cannot help the
application recover from this error,
MallocDebug: so we'll just have to shut down the
application.
MallocDebug:*****************************************
MallocDebug: THIS IS A BUG IN THE PROGRAM BEING
RUN UNDER MALLOC DEBUG,
MallocDebug: NOT A BUG IN MALLOC DEBUG!
MallocDebug:*****************************************
```

Usually a crash results from subtle memory problems, such as referencing freed memory or dereferencing pointers found outside an allocated buffer. Check suspected buffers of memory with the memory-buffer inspector. If your program is referencing memory at 0x55555555, then it is referencing freed memory. Important: You should always investigate and fix bugs that cause your program to crash. Subtle problems may indicate a design flaw that could cost more time to fix later.

## Programs Calling Setuid or Setgid

For security reasons, the operating system does not allow programs running setuid (set the user id at execution) orsetgid (set the group id at execution) to load new libraries, such as the heap debugging library used by MallocDebug. As a result, MallocDebug cannot display information about these programs unless they are run by the target user or by a member of the target group.

*If you want to examine a setuid or setgid program with MallocDebug, you have two options:*

1. Use MallocDebug on a copy of the program without the setuid or setgid permissions set. This approach may not work if the permissions are needed to access files normally not accessible by you.
2. Run MallocDebug while logged in as the user who owns the file, or use the su tool to log in as another user. Note that you must run your program by calling the executable file directly in the latter case since the open tool runs the program as if it was launched by the user who logged in.

## Running Under libMallocDebug

If you're writing a simple program that runs from the command-line, you may need to statically link the malloc routines into your executable before MallocDebug can attach to your program.

Most programs link to the System framework, which is instrumented for use by MallocDebug. If your program does not use this framework, you can explicitly link your program with the/usr/lib/libMallocDebug.a library. (If you are running in Mac OS X 10.3.9 or later, you can also execute the command set env DYLD_INSERT_ LIBRARIES/usr/lib/ libMallocDebug.A.dylib from the debugger console to attach your program to libMallocDebug.) You should not notice any difference in your program's allocation behaviour when linking with this library.

*If you do link your application to libMallocDebug, you should be aware of the following caveats:*

- If your code runs in versions of Mac OS X prior to 10.4, you must need to set the DYLD_FORCE_FLAT_ NAMESPACE environment variable to force the linker to use the malloc routines in lib Malloc Debug. If you are running in Mac OS X v10.4 or later, you do not need to set this variable.
- When running your program in Mac OS X v10.4 or later under gdb with libMallocDebug installed, your program automatically drops into the debugger when libMallocDebug detects that memory has been corrupted by a malloc orfree call. To continue running your program, you need to jump over the affected instruction without executing it. You can do this using the jump command in GDB.
- If your program runs on a version of Mac OS X prior to version 10.3.9, you may need to execute the command " set start-with-shell 0 " in gdb to debug your program with libMallocDebug..
- In Mac OS X v10.4 and later, child processes created by a fork and exec now properly inherit theDYLD_INSERT_LIBRARIES environment variable

setting. Thus, if the parent is running under libMallocDebug, so will the child.

### Setting Environment Variables

MallocDebug does not contain any built-in mechanism for setting environment variables. You can work around this limitation by setting your environment variables from Terminal and then launching MallocDebug from there. When launched in this manner, your application inherits the Terminal environment, including any environment variables. Do not launch MallocDebug from Terminal using the open command. Instead, run the MallocDebug executable directly. The executable is located in the MallocDebug.app application bundle, usually in the MallocDebug.app/Contents/ MacOSdirectory.

## TRACKING MEMORY ALLOCATIONS WITH MALLOC_HISTORY

In Mac OS X, the malloc_history tool displays backtrace data showing exactly where your program made calls to themalloc and free functions. If you specify an address when calling malloc_history, the tool tracks memory allocations occurring at that address only. If you specify the -all_by_size or -all_by_count options, the tool displays all allocations, grouping frequent allocations together. Before using the malloc_history tool on your program, you must first enable the malloc library logging features by setting the MallocStackLogging to 1. You may also want to set the MallocStackLoggingNoCompact environment variable to retain information about freed blocks. For more information on these variables,

The malloc_history tool is best used in situations where you need to find the previous owner of a block of memory. If you determine that a particular data is somehow becoming corrupted, you can put checks into your code to print the address of the block when the corruption occurs. You can then use malloc_history to find out who owns the block and identify any stale pointers. The malloc_history tool is also suited for situations where Sampler or MallocDebug cannot be used. For example, you might use this tool from a remote computer or in situations where you want a minimal impact on the behaviour of your program. For more information on using the malloc_history tool, see malloc_history man page.

## EXAMINING MEMORY WITH THE HEAP TOOL

In Mac OS X, the heap command-line tool displays a snapshot of the memory allocated by the malloc library and located in the address space of a specified process. For Cocoa applications, this tool identifies Objective-C objects by name. For both memory blocks and objects, the tool organizes the information by heap, showing all items in the same heap together. The heap tool provides much of the same information as the ObjectAlloc instrument, but does so in a much less intrusive manner. You can use this tool from a remote session or in situations where the use of Instruments might slow the system down enough to affect the resulting output.

## FINDING MEMORY LEAKS

Memory leaks are blocks of allocated memory that the program no longer references. Memory leaks are bugs and should always be fixed. Leaks waste space by filling up pages of memory with inaccessible data and waste time due to extra paging activity. Leaked memory eventually forces the system to allocate additional virtual memory pages for the application, the allocation of which could have been avoided by reclaiming the leaked memory.

The malloc library can only reclaim the memory you tell it to reclaim. If you call malloc or any routine that allocates memory, you must balance that call with a corresponding free. A typical memory leak occurs when a developer forgets to deallocate memory for a pointer embedded in a data structure. If you allocate memory for embedded pointers in your code, make sure you release the memory for that pointer prior to deallocating the data structure itself.

Another typical memory leak example occurs when a developer allocates memory, assigns it to a pointer, and then assigns a different value to the pointer without freeing the first block of memory. In this example, overwriting the address in the pointer erases the reference to the original block of memory, making it impossible to release. Apple provides the MallocDebug application and leaks command-line tool for automatically tracking down memory leaks.

You can also track down leaks manually using other analysis tools, but that task falls under the category of finding memory problems in general and is covered in "Tracking Memory Usage." The following sections describe the MallocDebug and leakstools and show you how to use them to track down memory leaks.

## FINDING LEAKS USING INSTRUMENTS

The Instruments application can be used to find leaks in both Mac OS X and iPhone applications. To find leaks, create a new document template in the application and add the Leaks instrument to it. The Leaks instrument provides leak-detection capabilities identical to those in the leaks command-line tool. The Leaks instrument records all allocation events that occur in your application and then periodically searches the application's writable memory, registers, and stack for references to any active memory blocks. If it does not find a reference to a block in one of these places, it deems the block a "leak" and displays the relevant information in the Detail pane.

In the Detail pane, you can view leaked memory blocks using Table and Outline modes. In Table mode, Instruments displays the complete list of leaked blocks, sorted by size. Selecting an entry in the table and clicking the arrow button next to the memory address shows the allocation history for the memory block at that address.

Selecting an entry from this allocation history then shows the stack trace for that event in the Extended Detail pane of the document window. In Outline mode, the Leaks instrument displays leaks organized by call tree, which you can use to get information about the leaks in a particular branch of your code. For more information about using the Instruments application, including more information about the information displayed by the Leaks instrument.

## FINDING LEAKS WITH MALLOCDEBUG

The MallocDebug application includes a memory-leak analysis tool that you can use to identify leaks in your Mac OS X applications. The interface for MallocDebug displays potential leaks using a call-graph structure so that you can easily locate the function that generated the leak.

### Finding Leaks for Specific Features

The leak analysis tools in MallocDebug perform a global search for leaks in your program. However, there are other types of leaks that MallocDebug cannot identify. These are leaks caused by your code allocating a block and then not freeing it. You must identify these leaks yourself using the MallocDebug sampling features.

*To find these leaks, do the following:*

- In the MallocDebug window, select "Allocations from mark" from the analysis popup button.
- Click the Mark button.
- Exercise the target feature of your application.
- In MallocDebug, click the Update button to display the memory allocated since the Mark button was clicked.
- Look for any newly-allocated buffers. These may be buffers your code forgot to free after it was done with them.

## USING THE LEAKS TOOL

In Mac OS X, the leaks command-line tool searches the virtual memory space of a process for buffers that were allocated bymalloc but are no longer referenced.

*For each leaked buffer it finds, leaks displays the following information:*

- The address of the leaked memory
- The size of the leak (in bytes)
- The contents of the leaked buffer

If leaks can determine that the object is an instance of an Objective-C or Core Foundation object, it also displays the name of the object. If you do not want to view the contents of each leaked buffer, you can specify the -nocontext option when calling leaks. If the MallocStackLogging environment variable is set and you are running your application in gdb, leaksdisplays a stack trace describing where the buffer was allocated. For more information on malloc debugging options, The leaks tool has some advantages over MallocDebug when it comes to detecting leaks in complex data structures. For example, the leaks tool correctly handles leaks in circularly linked structures. It can also identify leaks in groups of connected nodes. MallocDebug may not correctly identify leaks in these types of structures.

Note: The leaks command-line tool is located in/usr/bin.

## FINDING LEAKED AUTORELEASED OBJECTS

If a Cocoa object is autoreleased without an autorelease pool in place, Xcode sends an a message to the console warning you that the object is just leaking. Even if you are not writing a Cocoa application, it is possible to see this same type of console warning. The implementation of many Cocoa classes is based on Core Foundation types. If your application uses Core Foundation, it is possible that the leaks are occurring as a result of calls to that framework. To find memory leaks of this type, use the debugger to put a breakpoint on the _NSAutoreleaseNoPool function. This function is declared in NSDebug.h in the Foundation framework. When the debugger reaches that function, you should be able to look at the stack crawl and see what piece of code caused the leak.

## TIPS FOR IMPROVING LEAK DETECTION

The following guidelines can help you find memory leaks quickly in your program. Most of these guidelines are intended to be used with the leaks tool but some are also applicable for use with MallocDebug and general use.

- Run leaks during unit testing. Because unit testing exercises all code paths in a repeatable manner, you are more likely to find leaks than you would be if you were testing your code in a production environment.

- Enable the MallocScribble and MallocPreScribble environment variables before running your leak tests. For more information,
- Use the -exclude option of leaks to filter out leaks in functions with known memory leaks. This option helps reduce the amount of extraneous information reported by leaks.
- If leaks reports a leak intermittently, set up a loop around the target code path and run the code hundreds or thousands of times. This increases the likelihood of the leak reappearing more regularly.
- Run your program against libgmalloc.dylib in gdb. This library is an aggressive debugging malloc library that can help track down insidious bugs in your code. For more information, see the libgmalloc man page.
- For Cocoa and iPhone applications, if you fix a leak and your program starts crashing, your code is probably trying to use an already-freed object or memory buffer. Set the NSZombieEnabled environment variable to YES to find messages to already freed objects.

Most unit testing code executes the desired code paths and exits. Although this is perfectly normal for unit testing, it creates a problem for the leaks tool, which needs time to analyse the process memory space. To fix this problem, you should make sure your unit-testing code does not exit immediately upon completing its tests. You can do this by putting the process to sleep indefinitely instead of exiting normally.

## ENABLING THE MALLOC DEBUGGING FEATURES

Debugging memory-related bugs can be time consuming if you do not know where to start looking. This is usually compounded by the problem that many memory bugs occur well after the memory in question was manipulated by the code. Fortunately, Mac OS X includes options for identifying memory problems closer to when those problems actually happen.

## ENABLING GUARD MALLOC

Guard Malloc is a special version of the malloc library that replaces the standard library during debugging. Guard Malloc uses several techniques to try and crash your application at the specific point where a memory error occurs. For example, it places separate memory allocations on different virtual memory pages and then deletes the entire page when the memory is freed.

Subsequent attempts to access the deallocated memory cause an immediate memory exception rather than a blind access into memory that might now hold other data. When the crash occurs, you can then go and inspect the point of failure in the debugger to identify the problem.

To enable debugging using Guard Malloc, choose the Run > Enable Guard Malloc option in Xcode before running your project. Building and running your application with this option enabled runs your application using the Guard Malloc library automatically. You can use this option both Mac OS X applications and also for iPhone applications running in the simulator.

For more information about the types of memory problems that Guard Malloc can help you track down, see the libgmallocman page in Mac OS X Man Pages.

## CONFIGURING THE MALLOC ENVIRONMENT VARIABLES

The malloc library provides debugging features to help you track down memory smashing bugs, heap corruption, references to freed memory, and buffer overruns. You enable these debugging options through a set of environment variables. With the exception of MallocCheckHeapStart and MallocCheckHeapEach, the value for most of these environment variables is ignored. To disable a variable from Terminal, use the unset command. Table 1 lists some of the key environment variables and describes their basic function. For a complete list of variables, see the malloc man page.

**Table: Malloc Environment Variables**

| Variable | Description |
|---|---|
| MallocStackLogging | If set, malloc remembers the function call stack at the time of each allocation. |
| MallocStackLogging NoCompact | This option is similar to Malloc Stack Logging but makes sure that all allo cations are logged, no matter how small or how short lived the buffer may be. |
| MallocScribble | If set, free sets each byte of every released block to the value 0x55. |
| MallocPreScribble | If set, malloc sets each byte of a newly allocated block to the value 0xAA. This increases the likelihood that a program making assumptions about freshly allocated memory fails. |
| MallocGuardEdges | If set, malloc adds guard pages before and after large allocations. |
| MallocDoNotProtect Prelude | Fine-grain control over thebehaviour of MallocGuardEdges: If set, malloc does not place a guard page at the head of each large block allocation. |
| MallocDoNotProtect Postlude | Fine-grain control over the behaviour of MallocGuardEdges: If set, malloc does not place a guard page at the tail of each large block allocation. |
| MallocCheckHeapStart | Set this variable to the number of allocations before malloc will begin validating the heap. If not set, malloc does not validate the heap. |
| MallocCheckHeapEach | Set this variable to the number of allocations before malloc should validate the heap. If not set, malloc does not validate the heap. |

The following example enables stack logging and heap checking in the current shell before running an application.

The value for MallocCheckHeapStart is set to 1 but is irrelevant and can be set to any value you want. You could also set these variables from your shell's startup file, although if you do be sure to export each variable.

```
% MallocStackLogging=1
% MallocCheckHeapStart=1000
% MallocCheckHeapEach=100
%./my_tool
```

If you want to run your program in gdb, you can set environment variables from the Xcode debugging console using the command set env, as shown in the following example:

```
% gdb
(gdb) set env MallocStackLogging 1
(gdb) run
```

Some of the performance tools require these options to be set in order to gather their data. For example, themalloc_history tool can identify the allocation site of specific blocks if the MallocStackLogging flag is set. This tool can also describe the blocks previously allocated at an address if the MallocStackLoggingNoCompact environment variable is set. The leaks command line tool will name the allocation site of a leaked buffer if MallocStackLogging is set. See the man pages for leaks and malloc_history for more details.

## Detecting Double Freed Memory

The malloc library reports attempts to call free on a buffer that has already been freed. If you have enabled theMallocStackLoggingNoCompact option, you can use the logged stack information to find out where in your code the second free call was made. You can then use this information to set up an appropriate breakpoint in the debugger and track down the problem. The malloc library reports information to stderr.

## Detecting Heap Corruption

To enable heap checking, assign values to the MallocCheckHeapStart and MallocCheckHeapEach environment variables. You must set both of these variables to enable heap checking. The MallocCheckHeapStart variable tells the malloc library how many malloc calls to process before initiating the first heap check. Set the second to the number ofmalloc calls to process between heap checks. The MallocCheckHeapStart variable is useful when the heap corruption occurs at a predictable time. Once it hits the appropriate start point, the malloc library starts logging allocation messages to the Terminal window. You can watch the number of allocations and use that information to determine approximately where the heap is being corrupted. Adjust the values for MallocCheckHeapStart and MallocCheckHeapEach as necessary to narrow down the actual point of corruption.

### Detecting Memory Smashing Bugs

To find memory smashing bugs, enable the MallocScribble variable. This variable writes invalid data to freed memory blocks, the execution of which causes an exception to occur. When using this variable, you should also set theMallocStackLogging and MallocStackLoggingNoCompact variables to log the location of the exception. When the exception occurs, you can then use the malloc_history command to track down the code that allocated the memory block. You can then use this information to track through your code and look for any lingering pointers to this block.

## VIEWING VIRTUAL MEMORY USAGE

In addition to the Instruments application, Mac OS X provides the top, vm_stat, pagestuff, and vmmap command-line tools for viewing statistics about virtual memory usage. The Memory Monitor instrument in the Instruments application lets you view all sorts of information about virtual memory usage in your application. This information displayed by this instrument is analogous to what you would see running the top command-line tool.

If you need more detailed information about virtual memory usage, you can use the vm_stat, pagestuff, and vmmapcommand-line tools for analysing your Mac OS X applications.

The information returned by these tools ranges from summary information about all the system processes to detailed information about a specific process. The following sections provide information on using the vm_stat, pagestuff, and vmmap tools to gather detailed memory information. For more information on using Instruments to analyse memory, and the other articles in this document. For information on how to use the top tool.

## VIEWING VIRTUAL MEMORY STATISTICS

The vm_stat tool displays high-level statistics about the current virtual memory usage of the system. By default, vm_statdisplays these statistics once, but you can specify an interval value (in seconds) to update these statistics continuously.

For information on the usage of this tool, see the vm_stat man page. Listing 1 shows an example of the output from vm_stat.

**Table: Listing 1 Output of Vm_Stat tool**

| Mach Virtual Memory: Statistics | (page size of 4096 bytes) |
|---|---|
| Pages free: | 3194. |
| Pages active: | 34594. |
| Pages inactive: | 17870. |
| Pages wired down: | 9878. |
| "Translation faults": | 6333197. |
| Pages copy-on-write: | 81385. |
| Pages zero filled: | 3180051. |
| Pages reactivated: | 343961. |
| Pageins: | 33043. |
| Pageouts: | 78496. |
| Object cache: | 66227 hits of 96952 lookups (68% hit rate) |

## VIEWING MACH-O CODE PAGES

The pagestufftool displays information about the specified

logical pages of a file conforming to the Mach-O executable format. For each specified page of code, symbols (function and static data structure names) are displayed. All pages in the__TEXT, __text section are displayed if no page numbers are given.

Listing 2 shows part of the output from pagestuff for the TextEdit application. This output is the result of running the tool with the -a option, which prints information about al! of the executable's code pages. It includes the virtual address locations of each page and the type of information on that page.

Listing 2 Partial output of pagestuff tool

```
File Page 0 contains Mach-O headers
File Page 1 contains Mach-O headers
File Page 2 contains contents of section
(__TEXT,__text)
Symbols on file page 2 virtual address 0x3a08 to
0x4000
File Page 3 contains contents of section
(__TEXT,__text)
Symbols on file page 3 virtual address 0x4000 to
0x5000
File Page 4 contains contents of section
(__TEXT,__text)
Symbols on file page 4 virtual address 0x5000 to
0x6000
...
File Page 22 contains contents of section
(__TEXT,__cstring)
File Page 22 contains contents of section
(__TEXT,__literal4)
File Page 22 contains contents of section
(__TEXT,__literal8)
File Page 22 contains contents of section
(__TEXT,__const)
Symbols on file page 22 virtual address 0x17000
to 0x17ffc
File Page 23 contains contents of section
(__DATA,__data)
```

```
File Page 23 contains contents of section
(__DATA,__la_symbol_ptr)
File Page 23 contains contents of section
(__DATA,__nl_symbol_ptr)
File Page 23 contains contents of section
(__DATA,__dyld)
File Page 23 contains contents of section
(__DATA,__cfstring)
File Page 23 contains contents of section
(__DATA,__bss)
File Page 23 contains contents of section
(__DATA,__common)
Symbols on file page 23 virtual address 0x18000
to 0x18d48
0x00018000 _NXArgc
0x00018004 _NXArgv
0x00018008 _environ
0x0001800c ___progname
...
```

In the preceding listing, if a page exports any symbols, those symbols are also displayed by the -a option. If you want to view the symbols for a single page, pass in the desired page number instead of the -a option. For more information about thepagestuff tool and its supported options.

## VIEWING VIRTUAL MEMORY REGIONS

The vmmap and vmmap64 tools display the virtual memory regions allocated for a specified process. These tools provide access to the virtual memory of 32-bit and 64-bit applications, respectively. You can use them to understand the purpose of memory at a given address and how that memory is being used. For each virtual-memory region, these tools display the type of page, the starting address, region size (in kilobytes), read/write permissions, sharing mode, and the purpose of the pages in that region. The following sections show you how to interpret the output from the vmmap tool. For more information about the vmmap andvmmap64 tools, see the vmmap or vmmap64 man pages.

## Sample Output From vmmap

Listing 3 shows some sample output from the vmmap tool. This example is not a full listing of the tool's output but is an abbreviated version showing the primary sections.

Listing 3 Typical output of vmmap

```
==== Non-writable regions for process 313
__PAGEZERO 0[ 4K]---/--- SM=NUL...ts/MacOS/Clock
__TEXT 1000[ 40K]r-x/rwx SM=COW...ts/MacOS/Clock
__LINKEDIT e000[ 4K]r--/rwx SM=COW...ts/w/Clock
90000[ 4K]r--/r-- SM=SHM
340000[3228K]r--/rwx SM=COW 00000100 00320...
789000[3228K]r--/rwx SM=COW 00000100 00320...
Submap 90000000-9fffffff r--/r-- machine-wide
submap
__TEXT 90000000[ 932K]r-x/r-x SM=COW/usr/lib/
libSystem.B.dylib
__LINKEDIT 900e9000[ 260K]r--/r-- SM=COW/usr/lib/
libSystem.B.dylib
__TEXT 90130000[ 740K]r-x/r-x SM=COW.../Versions/
A/CoreFoundation
__LINKEDIT 901e9000[ 188K]r--/r-- SM=COW.../
Versions/A/CoreFoundation
__TEXT 90220000[2144K]r-x/r-x SM=COW.../Versions/
A/CarbonCore
__LINKEDIT 90438000[ 296K]r--/r-- SM=COW.../
Versions/A/CarbonCore
[...data omitted...]
==== Writable regions for process 606
__DATA 18000[ 4K]rw-/rwx SM=PRV/Contents/MacOS/
TextEdit
__OBJC 19000[ 8K]rw-/rwx SM=COW/Contents/MacOS/
TextEdit
MALLOC_OTHER 1d000[ 256K]rw-/rwx SM=PRV
MALLOC_USED(DefaultMallocZone_0x5d2c0) 5d000[
256K]rw-/rwx SM=PRV
9d000[ 372K]rw-/rwx SM=COW 33320000 00000020
00000000 00001b84...
VALLOC_USED(DefaultMallocZone_0x5d2c0) ff000[
```

```
36K]rw-/rwx SM=PRV
MALLOC_USED(CoreGraphicsDefaultZone_0x10 108000[
256K]rw-/rwx SM=PRV
MALLOC_USED(CoreGraphicsRegionZone_0x148 148000[
256K]rw-/rwx SM=PRV
[...data omitted...]
Submap a000b000-a012ffff r--/r-- process-only
submap
__DATA a0130000[ 28K]rw-/rw- SM=COW.../Versions/
A/CoreFoundation
Submap a0137000-a021ffff r--/r-- process-only
submap
__DATA a0220000[ 20K]rw-/rw- SM=COW.../Versions/
A/CarbonCore
Submap a0225000-a048ffff r--/r-- process-only
submap
__DATA a0490000[ 12K]rw-/rw- SM=COW.../
IOKit.framework/Versions/A/IOKit
Submap a0493000-a050ffff r--/r-- process-only
submap
__DATA a0510000[ 36K]rw-/rw- SM=COW.../Versions/
A/OSServices
b959e000[ 4K]rw-/rw- SM=SHM
b95a0000[ 4K]rw-/rw- SM=SHM
b9630000[ 164K]rw-/rw- SM=SHM
b965a000[ 896K]rw-/rw- SM=SHM
bff80000[ 504K]rw-/rwx SM=ZER
STACK[0]bfffe000[ 4K]rw-/rwx SM=PRV
bffff000[ 4K]rw-/rwx SM=PRV
__DATA c000c000[ 4K]rw-/rwx SM=PRV.../Versions/
A/ApplicationEnhancer
STACK[1]f0001000[ 512K]rw-/rwx SM=PRV
ff002000[12272K]rw-/rw- SM=SHM
==== Legend
SM=sharing mode:
COW=copy_on_write PRV=private NUL=empty
ALI=aliased
SHM=shared ZER=zero_filled S/A=shared_alias
```

```
==== Summary for process 313
Read Only portion of Libraries: Total = 27420
KBresident=12416KB(45%) swapped_out_or_unallocated
= 15004 K B(55%)
Writable regions: Total = 21632K B written = 536K
B (2%) resident = 1916 K B (9%) swapped_out = 0
K B (0%) unallocated = 19716 K B (91%)
```

If you specify the -d parameter (plus an interval in seconds), vmmap takes two snapshots of virtual-memory usage-one at the beginning of a specified interval and the other at the end-and displays the differences.

*It shows three sets of differences:*

- Individual differences
- Regions in the first snapshot that are not in the second
- Regions in the second snapshot that are not in the first

# 8

# Interprocess Communication

## INTRODUCTION

Communication between tasks is an important element of the Mach philosophy. Mach supports a client/server system structure in which tasks (clients) access services by making requests of other tasks (servers) via messages sent over a communication channel.

The endpoints of these communication channels in Mach are called ports, while port rights denote permission to use the channel.

*The forms of IPC provided by Mach include:*

- Message queues
- Semaphores
- Notifications
- Lock sets
- Remote procedure calls (RPCs)

The type of IPC object denoted by the port determines the operations permissible on that port, and how (and whether) data transfer occurs.

- *Important:* The IPC facilities in Mac OS X are in a state of transition. In early versions of the system, not all of these IPC types may be implemented.

There are two fundamentally different Mach APIs for raw manipulation of ports-the mach_ipc family and the mach_msg family. Within reason, both families may be used with any IPC object; however, the mach_ipc calls are preferred in new code. The mach_ipc calls maintain state information where appropriate in order to support the notion of a transaction.

The mach_msg calls are supported for legacy code but deprecated; they are stateless.

## IPC TRANSACTIONS AND EVENT DISPATCHING

When a thread calls mach_ipc_dispatch, it repeatedly processes events coming in on the registered port set. These events could be an argument block from anRPC object (as the results of a client's call), a lock object being taken (as a result of some other thread's releasing the lock), a notification or semaphore being posted, or a message coming in from a traditional message queue.

These events are handled via callouts from mach_msg_dispatch. Some events imply a transaction during the lifetime of the callout. In the case of a lock, the state is the ownership of the lock. When the callout returns, the lock is released. In the case of remote procedure calls, the state is the client's identity, the argument block, and the reply port. When the callout returns, the reply is sent. When the callout returns, the transaction (if any) is completed, and the thread waits for the next event. The mach_ipc_dispatch facility is intended to support work loops.

## MESSAGE QUEUES

Originally, the sole style of interprocess communication in Mach was the message queue. Only one task can hold the receive right for a port denoting a message queue. This one task is allowed to receive (read) messages from the port queue. Multiple tasks can hold rights to the port that allow them to send (write) messages into the queue. A task communicates with another task by building a data structure that contains a set of data elements and then performing a message-send operation on a port for which it holds send rights. At some later time, the task with receive rights to that port will perform a message-receive operation.

*A message may consist of some or all of the following:*

- Pure data
- Copies of memory ranges
- Port rights

- Kernel implicit attributes, such as the sender's security token

The message transfer is an asynchronous operation. The message is logically copied into the receiving task, possibly with copy-on-write optimizations. Multiple threads within the receiving task can be attempting to receive messages from a given port, but only one thread can receive any given message.

## SEMAPHORES

Semaphore IPC objects support wait, post, and post all operations. These are counting semaphores, in that posts are saved (counted) if there are no threads currently waiting in that semaphore's wait queue. A post all operation wakes up all currently waiting threads.

## NOTIFICATIONS

Like semaphores, notification objects also support post and wait operations, but with the addition of a state field. The state is a fixed-size, fixed-format field that is defined when the notification object is created. Each post updates the state field; there is a single state that is overwritten by each post.

## LOCKS

A lock is an object that provides mutually exclusive access to a critical section. The primary interfaces to locks are transaction oriented. During the transaction, the thread holds the lock. When it returns from the transaction, the lock is released.

## REMOTE PROCEDURE CALL (RPC) OBJECTS

As the name implies, an RPC object is designed to facilitate and optimize remote procedure calls. The primary interfaces to RPC objects are transaction oriented. When an RPC object is created, a set of argument block formats is defined. When an RPC (a send on the object) is made by a client, it causes a message in one of the predefined formats to be created and queued on the object, then eventually passed to the server (the receiver). When the server returns from the transaction, the reply is returned to the sender. Mach tries to optimize the transaction by executing the server using the client's resources; this is called thread migration.

## TIME MANAGEMENT

The traditional abstraction of time in Mach is the clock, which provides a set of asynchronous alarm services based on mach_timespec_t. There are one or more clock objects, each defining a monotonically increasing time value expressed in nanoseconds. The real-time clock is built in, and is the most important, but there may be other clocks for other notions of time in the system. Clocks support operations to get the current time, sleep for a given period, set an alarm (a notification that is sent at a given time), and so forth.

The mach_timespec_t API is deprecated in Mac OS X. The newer and preferred API is based on timer objects that in turn use AbsoluteTime as the basic data type. AbsoluteTime is a machine-dependent type, typically based on the platform-native time base. Routines are provided to convert AbsoluteTime values to and from other data types, such as nanoseconds. Timer objects support asynchronous, drift-free notification, cancellation, and premature alarms. They are more efficient and permit higher resolution than clocks.

## MAC OS X VM

The VM system used in Mac OS X is a descendent of Mach VM, which was created at Carnegie Mellon University in the 1980s. To a large extent, the fundamental design is the same, although some of the details are different, particularly when enhancing the VM system.

It does, however, support the ability to request certain paging behaviour through the use of universal page lists (UPLs). for more information. The design of Mach VM centers around the concept of physical memory being a cache for virtual memory. At its highest level, Mach VM consists of address spaces and ways to manipulate the contents of those address spaces from outside the space. These address spaces are sparse and have a notion of protections to limit what tasks can access their contents. At a lower level, the object level, virtual memory is seen as a collection of VM objects and memory objects, each with a particular owner and protections. These objects can be modified with object calls that are available both to the task and (via the back end of the VM) to the pagers.

Note: While memory objects and VM objects are closely related, the terms are not equivalent and should not be confused..A VM object can be backed by one or more memory objects, which are, in turn, managed by a pager. A VM object may also be partially backed by other VM objects, as occurs in the case of shadow chains (described later in this section). The VM object is internal to the virtual memory system, and includes basic information about accessing the memory. The memory object, by contrast, is provided by the pager. The contents of the memory associated with that memory object can be retrieved from disk or some other backing store by exchanging messages with the memory object. Implicitly, each VM object is associated with a given pager through its memory object. VM objects are cached with system pages (RAM), which can be any power of two multiple of the hardware page size. In the Mac OS X kernel, system pages are the same size as hardware pages. Each system page is represented in a given address space by a map entry. Each map entry has its own protection and inheritance. A given map entry can have an inheritance of shared, copy, or none. If a page is marked shared in a given map, child tasks share this page for reading and writing. If a page is marked copy, child tasks get a copy of this page (using copy-on-write). If a page is marked none, the child's page is left unallocated.

VM objects are managed by the machine-independent VM system, with the underlying virtual to physical mappings handled by the machine-dependent pmap system. The pmap system actually handles page tables, translation lookaside buffers, segments, and so on, depending on the design of the underlying hardware.

When a VM object is duplicated (for example, the data pages from a process that has just called fork), a shadow object is created. A shadow object is initially empty, and contains a reference to another object. When the contents of a page are modified, the page is copied from the parent object into the shadow object and then modified. When reading data from a page, if that page exists in the shadow object, the page listed in the shadow object is used. If the shadow object has no copy of that page, the original object is consulted. A series of shadow objects pointing to shadow objects or original objects is known as a shadow chain.

Shadow chains can become arbitrarily long if an object is heavily reused in a copy-on-write fashion. However, since fork is frequently followed by exec, which replaces all of the material being shadowed, long chains are rare. Further, Mach automatically garbage collects shadow objccts, removing any intermediate shadow objects whose pages are no longer referenced by any (nondefunct) shadow object. It is even possible for the original object to be released if it no longer contains pages that are relevant to the chain.

The VM calls available to an application include vm_map and vm_allocate, which can be used to map file data or anonymous memory into the address space. This is possible only because the address space is initially sparse. In general, an application can either map a file into its address space (through file mapping primitives, abstracted by BSD) or it can map an object (after being passed a handle to that object). In addition, a task can change the protections of the objects in its address space and can share those objects with other tasks. In addition to the mapping and allocation aspects of virtual memory, the VM system contains a number of other subsystems. These include the back end (pagers) and the shared memory subsystem. There are also other subsystems closely tied to VM, including the VM shared memory server. These are described in "Other VM and VM-Related Subsystems".

## MEMORY MAPS EXPLAINED

Each Mach task has its own memory map. In Mach, this memory map takes the form of an ordered doubly linked list.

As described in "Mac OS X VM Overview", each of these objects contains a list of pages and shadow references to other objects.

In general, you should never need to access a memory map directly unless you are modifying something deep within the VM system. The vm_map_entry structure contains task-specific information about an individual mapping along with a reference to the backing object. In essence, it is the glue between an VM object and a VM map. While the details of this data structure are beyond the scope of this document, a few fields are of particular importance.

The field is_submap is a Boolean value that tells whether this map entry is a normal VM object or a submap. A submap is a collection of mappings that is part of a larger map. Submaps are often used to group mappings together for the purpose of sharing them among multiple Mach tasks, but they may be used for many purposes. What makes a submap particularly powerful is that when several tasks have mapped a submap into their address space, they can see each other's changes, not only to the contents of the objects in the map, but to the objects themselves. This means that as additional objects are added to or deleted from the submap, they appear in or disappear from the address spaces of all tasks that share that submap.

The field behaviour controls the paging reference behaviour of a specified range in a given map. This value changes ho pageins are clustered. Possible values are **VM_BEHAVIOUR_DEFAULT,VM_BEHAVIOUR_RANDOM, VM_BEHAVIOUR_SEQUENTIAL, and VM_BEHAVIOUR_RSEQNTL,** for default, random, sequential, or reverse-sequential pagein ordering.

The protection and max_protection fields control the permissions on the object. The protection field indicates what rights the task currently has for the object, while the max_protection field contains the maximum access that the current task can obtain for the object. You might use the protection field when debugging shared memory. By setting the protection to be read-only, any inadvertent writes to the shared memory would cause an exception. However, when the task actually needs to write to that shared region, it could increase its permissions in the protection field to allow writes. It would be a security hole if a task could increase its own permissions on a memory object arbitrarily, however. In order to preserve a reasonable security model, the task that owns a memory object must be able to limit the rights granted to a subordinate task. For this reason, a task is not allowed to increase its protection beyond the permissions granted in max_protection.

Possible values for protection and max_protection are described in detail in xnu/osfmk/mach/vm_prot.h. Finally, the use_pmap field indicates whether a submap's low-level mappings should be shared among all tasks into which the submap is mapped. If the mappings are not shared, then the structure of the map is shared among all tasks, but the actual contents of the pages are not. For example, shared libraries are handled with two submaps. The read-only shared code section has use_pmap set to true. The read-write (nonshared) section hasuse_pmap set to false, forcing a clean copy of the library's DATA segment to be mapped in from disk for each new task.

## NAMED ENTRIES

The Mac OS X VM system provides an abstraction known as a named entry. A named entry is nothing more than a handle to a shared object or a submap. Shared memory support in Mac OS X is achieved by sharing objects between the memory maps of various tasks. Shared memory objects must be created from existing VM objects by calling vm_allocate to allocate memory in your address space and then calling mach_make_memory_entry_64 to get a handle to the underlying VM object.

The handle returned by mach make_memory_entry_64 can be passed to vm_map to map that object into a given task's address space. The handle can also be passed via IPC or other means to other tasks so that they can map it into their address spaces. This provides the ability to share objects with tasks that are not in your direct lineage, and also allows you to share additional memory with tasks in your direct lineage after those tasks are created.

The other form of named entry, the submap, is used to group a set of mappings. The most common use of a submap is to share mappings among multiple Mach tasks. A submap can be created with vm_region_object_create. What makes a submap particularly powerful is that when several tasks have mapped a submap into their address space, they can see each other's changes to both the data and the structure of the map. This means that one task can map or unmap a VM object in another task's address space simply by mapping or unmapping that object in the submap.

## UNIVERSAL PAGE LISTS (UPLS)

A universal page list, or UPL, is a data structure used when communicating with the virtual memory system. UPLs can be used to change the behaviour of pages with respect to caching, permissions, mapping, and so on. UPLs can also be used to push data into and pull data from VM objects. The term is also often used to refer to the family of routines that operate on UPLs. The flags used when dealing with UPLs are described in osfmk/mach/memory_object_types.h.

*The life cycle of a UPL looks like this:*

- A UPL is created based on the contents of a VM object. This UPL includes information about the pages within that object.
- That UPL is modified in some way.
- The changes to the UPL are either committed (pushed back to the VM system) or aborted, with ubc_upl_commit or ubc_upl_abort, respectively.

If you have a control handle for a given VM object (which generally means that you are inside a pager), you can use vm_object_upl_request to get a UPL for that object. Otherwise, you must use the vm_map_get_upl call. In either case, you are left with a handle to the UPL. When a pagein is requested, the pager receives a list of pages that are locked against the object, with certain pages set to not valid. The pager must either write data into those pages or must abort the transaction to prevent invalid data in the kernel. Similarly in pageout, the kernel must write the data to a backing store or abort the transaction to prevent data loss. The pager may also elect to bring additional pages into memory or throw additional pages out of memory at its discretion.

Because pagers can be used both for virtual memory and for memory mapping of file data, when a pageout is requested, the data may need to be freed from memory, or it may be desirable to keep it there and simply flush the changes to disk. For this reason, the flag UPL_CLEAN_IN_PLACE exists to allow a page to be flushed to disk but not removed from memory. When a pager decides to page in or out additional pages, it must determine which pages to move. A pager can request all of the dirty pages by setting theRETURN_ONLY_DIRTY flag. It can also request all pages that are not in memory using the RETURN_ONLY_ABSENT flag.

There is a slight problem, however. If a given page is marked as BUSY in the UPL, a request for information on that page would normally block. If the pager is doing prefetching or preflushing, this is not desirable, since it might be blocking on itself or on some other pager that is blocked waiting for the current transaction to complete. Avoid such deadlock, the UPL mechanism provides the UPL_NOBLOCK flag. This is frequently used in the anonymous pager for requesting free memory.

The flag QUERY_OBJECT_TYPE can be used to determine if an object is physically contiguous and to get other properties of the underlying object.

The flag UPL_PRECIOUS means that there should be only one copy of the data. This prevents having a copy both in memory and in the backing store. However, this breaks the adjacency of adjacent pages in the backing store, and is thus generally not used to avoid a performance hit. The flag SET_INTERNAL is used by the BSD subsystem to cause all information about a UPL to be contained in a single memory object so that it can be passed around more easily. It can only be used if your code is running in the kernel's address space.

Since this handle can be used for multiple small transactions (for example, when mapping a file into memory block-by-block), the UPL API includes functions for committing and aborting changes to only a portion of the UPL. These functions are upl_commit_range and upl_abort_range, respectively. To aid in the use of UPLs for handling multi-part transactions, the upl_commit_range and upl_abort_range calls have a flag that causes the UPL to be freed when there are no unmodified pages in the UPL. If you use this flag, you must be very careful not to use the UPL after all ranges have been committed or aborted.

Finally, the function vm_map_get_upl is frequently used in file systems. It gets the underlying VM object associated with a given range within an address space. Since this returns only the first object in that range, it is your responsibility to determine whether the entire range is covered by the resulting UPL and, if not, to make additional calls to get UPLs for other objects. Note that while the vm_map_get_upl call is against an address space range, most UPL calls are against avm_object.

## USING MACH MEMORY MAPS

Warning: This section describes the low-level API for dealing with Mach VM maps. These maps cannot be modified in this way from a kernel extension. These functions are not available for use in a KEXT. They are presented strictly for use within the VM system and other parts of Mach. If you are not doing in-kernel development, you should be using the methods described in the chapter "Boundary Crossings".

From the context of the kernel (not from a KEXT), there are two maps that you will probably need to deal with. The first is the kernel map. Since your code is executing in the kernel's address space, no additional effort is needed to use memory referenced in the kernel map. However, you may need to add additional mappings into the kernel map and remove them when they are no longer needed. The second map of interest is the memory map for a given task. This is of most interest for code that accepts input from user programs, for example a sysctl or a Mach RPC handler. In nearly all cases, convenient wrappers provide the needed functionality, however. The low-level VM map API includes the following functions:

```
kern_return_t vm_map_copyin(vm_map_t src_map,
          vm_offset_t src_addr,
          vm_size_t len, boolean_t src_destroy,
          vm_map_copy_t *copy_result);
kern_return_t vm_map_copyout(vm_map_t map,
          vm_offset_t *addr,/* Out */
          Register vm_map_copy_t copy);
kern_return_t vm_map_copy_overwrite(vm_map_t
dst_map,
          vm_offset_t dst_address,vm_map_copy_t
          copy,
          boolean_t interruptible, pmap_t pmap);
void vm_map_copy_discard(vm_map_copy_t copy);
void vm_map_wire(vm_map_t map, vm_offset_t start,
          vm_offset_t end,
vm_prot_t access_type, boolean_t user_wire);
void vm_map_unwire(vm_map_t map, vm_offset_t
start,           vm_offset_t end,
          boolean_t user_wire);
```

The function vm_map_copyin copies data from an arbitrary (potentially non-kernel) memory map into a copy list and returns the copy list pointer in copy_result. If something goes wrong and you need to throw away this intermediate object, it should be freed with vm_map_copy_discard. In order to actually get the data from the copy list, you need to overwrite a memory object in the kernel's address space with vm_map_copy_overwrite. This overwrites an object with the contents of a copy list. For most purposes, the value passed for interruptible should be FALSE, and pmap should be NULL.

Copying data from the kernel to user space is exactly the same as copying data from user space, except that you pass kernel_map to vm_map_copyin and pass the user map to vm_map_copy_overwrite. In general, however, you should avoid doing this, since you could end up with a task's memory being fragmented into lots of tiny objects, which is undesirable.

Do not use vm_map_copyout when copying data into an existing user task's address map. The function vm_map_copyout is used for filling an unused region in an address map. If the region is allocated, then vm_map_copyout does nothing. Because it requires knowledge of the current state of the map, it is primarily used when creating a new address map (for example, if you are manually creating a new process). For most purposes, you do not need to use vm_map_copyout.

The functions vm_map_wire and vm_map_unwire can be used to wire and unwire portions of an address map. If you set the argument user_wire to TRUE, then the page can be unwired from user space. This should be set to FALSE if you are about to use the memory for I/O or for some other operation that cannot tolerate paging. In vm_map_wire, the argument access_type indicates the types of accesses that should not be allowed to generate a page fault. In general, however, you should be using vm_wire to wire memory. As mentioned earlier, this information is presented strictly for use in the heart of the kernel. You should not use anything in this section from a kernel extension.

## VM AND VM-RELATED SUBSYSTEMS

There are two additional VM subsystems: pagers and the working set detection subsystem. In addition, the VM shared memory server subsystem is closely tied to (but is not part of) the VM subsystem. This section describes these three VM and VM-related subsystems.

### PAGERS

Mac OS X has three basic pagers: the vnode pager, the default pager (or anonymous pager), and the device pager. These are used by the VM system to actually get data into the VM objects that underlie named entries. Pagers are linked into the VM system through a combination of a subset of the old Mach pager interface and UPLs. The default pager is what most people think of when they think of a VM system. It is responsible for moving normal data into and out of the backing store. In addition, there is a facility known as the dynamic pager that sits on top of the default pager and handles the creation and deletion of backing store files. These pager files are filled with data in clusters (groups of pages). When the total fullness of the paging file pool reaches a high-water mark, the default pager asks the dynamic pager to allocate a new store file. When the pool drops below its low water mark, the VM system selects a pager file, moves its contents into other pager files, and deletes it from disk.

The vnode pager has a 1:1 (onto) mapping between objects in VM space and open files (vnodes). It is used for memory mapped file I/O. The vnode pager is generally hidden behind calls to BSD file APIs. The device pager allows you to map non-general-purpose memory with the cache characteristics required for that memory (WIMG). Non-general-purpose memory includes physical addresses that are mapped onto hardware other than main memory-for example, PCI memory, frame buffer memory, and so on. The device pager is generally hidden behind calls to various I/O Kit functions.

## WORKING SET DETECTION SUBSYSTEM

To improve performance, Mac OS X has a subsystem known as the working set detection subsystem. This subsystem is called on a VM fault; it keeps a profile of the fault behaviour of each task from the time of its inception. In addition, just before a page request, the fault code asks this subsystem which adjacent pages should be brought in, and then makes a single large request to the pager. Since files on disk tend to have fairly good locality, and since address space locality is largely preserved in the backing store, this provides a substantial performance boost. Also, since it is based upon the application's previous behaviour, it tends to pull in pages that would probably have otherwise been needed later. This occurs for all pagers.

The working set code works well once it is established. However, without help, its performance would be the baseline performance until a profile for a given application has been developed. To overcome this, the first time that an application is launched in a given user context, the initial working set required to start the application is captured and stored in a file. From then on, when the application is started, that file is used to seed the working set. These working set files are established on a per-user basis. They are stored in/var/vm/app_profile and are only accessible by the super-user (and the kernel).

## VM SHARED MEMORY SERVER SUBSYSTEM

The VM shared memory server subsystem is a BSD service that is closely tied to VM, but is not part of VM. This server provides two submaps that are used for shared library support in Mac OS X. Because shared libraries contain both read-only portions (text segment) and read-write portions (data segment), the two portions are treated separately to maximize efficiency. The read-only portions are completely shared between tasks, including the underlying pmap entries. The read-write portions share a common submap, but have different underlying data objects (achieved through copy-on-write).

The three functions exported by the VM shared memory server subsystem should only be called by dyld. Do not use them in your programs. The function load_shared_file is used to load a new shared library into the system. Once such a file is loaded, other tasks can then depend on it, so a shared library cannot be unshared. However, a new set of shared regions can be created with new_system_shared_regions so that no new tasks will use old libraries. The function reset_shared_file can be used to reset any changes that your task may have made to its private copy of the data section for a file.

Finally, the function new_system_shared_regions can be used to create a new set of shared regions for future tasks. New regions can be used when updating prebinding with new shared libraries to cause new tasks to see the latest libraries at their new locations in memory. (Users of old shared libraries will still work, but they will fall off the pre-bound path and will perform less efficiently.) It can also be used when dealing with private libraries that you want to share only with your task's descendents.

## ADDRESS SPACES

This section explains issues that some developers may see when using their drivers in Panther or later. These changes were necessitated by a combination of hardware and underlying OS changes; however, you may see problems resulting from the changes even on existing hardware.

*There are three basic areas of change in Mac OS X 10.3. These are:*

1. IOMemoryDescriptor changes
2. VM system (pmap) changes
3. Kernel dependency changes

These are described in detail in the sections that follow.

## BACKGROUND INFO ON PCI ADDRESS TRANSLATION

To allow existing device drivers to work with upcoming 64-bit system architectures, a number of changes were required. To explain these, a brief introduction to PCI bus bridges is needed. When a PCI device needs to perform a data transaction to or from main memory, the device driver calls a series of functions intended to prepare this memory for I/O. In an architecture where both the device drivers and the memory subsystem use 32-bit addressing, everything just works, so long as the memory doesn't get paged out during the I/O operation. As kernel memory is generally not pageable, the preparation is largely superfluous.

On a system whose memory subsystem uses 64-bit addressing, however, this becomes a bit of a problem. Because the hardware devices on the PCI bus can only handle 32-bit addresses, the device can only "see" a 4 gigabyte aperture into the (potentially much larger) main memory at any given time. There are two possible solutions for this problem. The easy (but slow) solution would be to use "bounce buffers". In such a design, device drivers would copy data into memory specifically allocated within the bottom 4 gigs of memory. However, this incurs a performance penalty and also puts additional constraints on the lower 4 gigs of memory, causing numerous problems for the VM system.

The other solution, the one chosen in Apple's 64-bit implementation, is to use address translation to "map" blocks of memory into the 32-bit address space of the PCI devices. While the PCI device can still only see a 4 gig aperture, that aperture can then be non-contiguous, and thus bounce buffers and other restrictions are unnecessary. This address translation is done using a part of the memory controller known as DART, which stands for Device Address Resolution Table.

This introduces a number of potential problems, however. First, physical addresses as seen by the processor no longer map 1:1 onto the addresses as seen by PCI devices. Thus, a new term, I/O addresses, is introduced to describe this new view.

Because I/O addresses and physical addresses are no longer the same, the DART must keep a table of translations to use when mapping between them. Fortunately, if your driver is written according to Apple guidelines (using only documented APIs), this process is handled transparently.

*Note*: This additional addressing mode has an impact when debugging I/O Kit device drivers. For more information,

## IOMEMORYDESCRIPTOR CHANGES

When your driver calls IOMemoryDescriptor::prepare, a mapping is automatically injected into the DART. When it calls IOMemoryDescriptor::release, the mapping is removed. If you fail to do this, your driver could experience random data corruption or panics.

Because the DART requires different caching for reads and writes, the DMA direction is important on hardware that includes a DART. While you may receive random failures if the direction is wrong in general (on any system), if you attempt to call WriteBytes on a memory region whose DMA direction is set up for reading, you will cause a kernel panic on 64-bit hardware.

If you attempt to perform a DMA transaction to unwired (user) memory, on previous systems, you would only get random crashes, panics, and data corruption. On machines with a DART, you will likely get no data whatsoever. As a side-effect of changes in the memory subsystem, Mac OS X is much more likely to return physically contiguous page ranges in memory regions. Historically, Mac OS X returned multi-page memory regions in reverse order, starting with the last page and moving towards the first page. The result of this was that multi-page memory regions essentially never had a contiguous range of physical pages.

Because of the increased probability of seeing physically contiguous blocks of memory in a memory region, this change may expose latent bugs in some drivers that only show up when handling contiguous ranges of physical pages, which could result in incorrect behaviour or panics. Note that the problems mentioned above are caused by bugs in the drivers, and could result in problems on older hardware prior to Panther. These issues are more likely to occur in Panther and later versions of Mac OS X, however, because of the new hardware designs and the OS changes that were made to support those designs.

## VM SYSTEM AND PMAP CHANGES

In Panther, as a result of the changes described in detail in the section on PCI address translation, physical addresses obtained directly from the pmap layer have no useful purpose outside the VM system itself. To prevent their inadvertent use in device drivers, the pmap calls are no longer available from kernel extensions. A few drivers written prior to the addition of the IOMemoryDescriptor class still use pmap calls to get the physical pages associated with a virtual address. Also, a few developers have looked at the IOMemoryDescriptor implementation and chosen to obtain addresses directly from the pmap layer to remove what was perceived as an unnecessary abstraction layer.

Even without removing access to the pmap calls, these drivers would not function on systems with a DART (see the PCI section above for info on DARTs). To better emphasize this upcoming failure, Panther will cause these drivers to fail to load with an undefined symbol error (generally for pmap_extract) even on systems without a DART.

## KERNEL DEPENDENCY CHANGES

Beginning in Panther, device drivers that declare a dependency on version 7 (the Panther version) of the I/O Kit will no longer automatically get symbols from Mach and BSD. This change was made to discourage I/O Kit developers from relying on symbols that are not explicitly approved for use in the I/O Kit. Existing drivers are unaffected by this change. This change only affects you if you explicitly modify your device driver to declare a dependency on version 7 of the I/O Kit to take advantage of new I/O Kit features.

## SUMMARY

As described above, some device drivers may require minor modifications to support Panther and higher. Apple has made every effort to ensure compatibility with existing device drivers to the greatest extent possible, but a few drivers may break. If your driver breaks, you should first check to see if your driver includes any of the bugs described in the previous sections. If it does not, contact Apple Developer Technical Support for additional debugging suggestions.

# ALLOCATING MEMORY IN THE KERNEL

As with most things in the Mac OS X kernel, there are a number of ways to allocate memory. The choice of routines depends both on the location of the calling routine and on the reason for allocating memory. In general, you should use Mach routines for allocating memory unless you are writing code for use in the I/O Kit, in which case you should use I/O Kit routines.

## ALLOCATING MEMORY USING MACH ROUTINES

Mach routines provide a relatively straightforward interface for allocating and releasing memory. They are the preferred mechanism for allocating memory outside of the I/O Kit. BSD also offers _MALLOC and _FREE, which may be used in BSD parts of the kernel. They do not provide for forced mapping of a given physical address to a virtual address. However, if you need such a mapping, you are probably writing a device driver, in which case you should be using I/O Kit routines instead of Mach routines. These are some of the commonly used Mach routines for allocating memory:

```
kern_return_t kmem_alloc(vm_map_t map, vm_offset_t
        *addrp, vm_size_t size);
void kmem_free(vm_map_t map, vm_offset_t addr,
        vm_size_t size);
kern_return_t mem_alloc_aligned(vm_map_t map,
        vm_offset_t *addrp,
        vm_size_t size);
kern_return_t kmem_alloc_wired(vm_map_t map,
        vm_offset_t *addrp,
        vm_size_t size);
kern_return_t kmem_alloc_pageable(vm_map_t map,
        vm_offset_t *addrp,
        vm_size_t size);
kern_return_t kmem_alloc_contig(vm_map_t map,
        vm_offset_t *addrp,
        vm_size_t size, vm_offset_t mask, int
        flags);
```

These functions all take a map as the first argument. Unless you need to allocate memory in a different map, you should pass kernel_map for this argument.

All of the kmem_alloc functions except kmem_alloc_pageable allocate wired memory. The function kmem_alloc_pageable creates the appropriate VM structures but does not back the region with physical memory. This function could be combined with vm_map_copyout when creating a new address map, for example. In practice, it is rarely used. The function kmem_alloc_aligned allocates memory aligned according to the value of the size argument, which must be a power of 2.

The function kmem_alloc_wired is synonymous with kmem_alloc and is appropriate for data structures that cannot be paged out. It is not strictly necessary; however, if you explicitly need certain pieces of data to be wired, using kmem_alloc_wired makes it easier to find those portions of your code. The function kmem_alloc_contig attempts to allocate a block of physically contiguous memory. This is not always possible, and requires a full sort of the system free list even for short allocations. After startup, this sort can cause long delays, particularly on systems with lots of RAM. You should generally not use this function. The function kmem_free is used to free an object allocated with one of the kmem_alloc functions. Unlike the standard C free function, kmem_free requires the length of the object. If you are not allocating fixed-size objects (for example, sizeof struct foo), you may have to do some additional bookkeeping, since you must free an entire object, not just a portion of one.

## ALLOCATING MEMORY FROM THE I/O KIT

Although the I/O Kit is generally beyond the scope of this document, the I/O Kit memory management routines are presented here for completeness. In general, I/O Kit routines should not be used outside the I/O Kit. Similarly, Mach allocation routines should not be directly used from the I/O Kit because the I/O Kit has abstractions for those routines that fit the I/O Kit development model more closely. The I/O Kit includes the following routines for kernel memory allocation:

```
void *IOMalloc(vm_size_t size);
void *IOMallocAligned(vm_size_t size, vm_size_t
        alignment);
void *IOMallocContiguous(vm_size_t size, vm_size_t
        alignment,
        IOPhysicalAddress *physicalAddress);
void *IOMallocPageable(vm_size_t size, vm_size_t
        alignment);
void IOFree(void *address, vm_size_t size);
void IOFreeAligned(void *address, vm_size_t size);
void IOFreeContiguous(void *address, vm_size_t
        `size);
void IOFreePageable(void *address, vm_size_t
size);
```

Most of these routines are relatively transparent wrappers around the Mach allocation functions. There are two major differences, however. First, the caller does not need to know which memory map is being modified. Second, they have a separate free call for each allocation call for internal bookkeeping reasons. The functions IOMallocContiguous and IOMallocAligned differ somewhat from their Mach underpinnings. IOMallocAligned uses calls directly to Mach VM to add support for arbitrary (power of 2) data alignment, rather than aligning based on the size of the object. IOMallocContiguous adds an additional parameter, PhysicalAddress. If this pointer is not NULL, the physical address is returned through this pointer. Using Mach functions, obtaining the physical address requires a separate function call.

Important: If your KEXT allocates memory that will be shared, you should create a buffer of type IOMemory Descriptor or IOBufferMemoryDescriptor and specify that the buffer should be sharable. If you are allocating memory in a user application that will be shared with the kernel, you should use valloc orvm_allocate instead of malloc and then call mach_make_memory_entry_64.

# 9

# Building and Debugging Kernels

## DESCRIPTION

There are a number of good KEXT tutorials on Apple's developer documentation site. This chapter is about adding new in-kernel modules (optional parts of the kernel), building kernels, and debugging kernel and kernel extension builds. The discussion is divided into three sections. The first, "Adding New Files or Modules", describes how to add new functionality into the kernel itself. You should only add files into the kernel when the use of a KEXT is not possible (for example, when adding certain low-level motherboard hardware support).

The second section, "Building Your First Kernel", describes how to build a kernel, including how to build a kernel with debugger support, how to add new options, and how to obtain sources that are of similar vintage to those in a particular version of Mac OS X or Darwin.

The third section, "When Things Go Wrong: Debugging the Kernel", tells how to debug a kernel or kernel module using ddb and gdb. This is a must-read for anyone doing kernel development.

## ADDING NEW FILES OR MODULES

In this context, the term module is used loosely to refer to a collection of related files in the kernel that are controlled by a single config option at compile time. It does not refer to loadable modules (KEXTs). This section describes how to add additional files that will be compiled into the kernel, including how to add a newconfig option for an additional module.

## MODIFYING THE CONFIGURATION FILES

The details of adding a new file or module into the kernel differ according to what portion of the kernel contains the file. If you are adding a new file or module into the Mach portion of the kernel, you need to list it in various files in xnu/osfmk/conf. For the BSD portion of the kernel, you should list it in various files inxnu/bsd/conf. In either case, the procedure is basically the same, just in a different directory. This section is divided into two subsections. The first describes adding the module itself and the second describes enabling the module.

## ADDING THE FILES OR MODULES

In the appropriate conf directory, you need to add your files or modules into various files. The files MASTER, MASTER.ppc, and MASTER.i386 contain the list of configuration options that should be built into the kernel for all architectures, PowerPC, and i386, respectively. These are supplemented by files, files.ppc, and files.i386, which contain associations between compile options and the files that are related to them for their respective architectures.

The format for these two files is relatively straightforward. If you are adding a new module, you should first choose a name for that module. For example, if your module is called mach_foo, you should then add a new option line near the top of files that is whitespace (space or tab) delimited and looks like this:

```
OPTIONS/mach_foo optional mach_foo
```

The first part defines the name of the module as it will be used in #if statements in the code. for more information.) The second part is always the word optional. The third part tells the name of the option as used to turn it on or off in a MASTER file. Any line with mach_foo in the last field will be enabled only if there is an appropriate line in a MASTER file.

*Then, later in the file, you add:*

```
osfmk/foo/foo_main.c            optional mach_foo
osfmk/foo/foo_bar.c             optional mach_foo
```

and so on, for each new file associated with that module. This also applies if you are adding a file to an existing module. If you are adding a file that is not associated with any module at all, you add a line that looks like the following to specify that this file should always be included:

```
osfmk/crud/mandatory_file.c standard
```

If you are not adding any modules, then you're done. Otherwise, you also need to enable your option in one of the MASTER files.

### Enabling Module Options

To enable a module option (as described in the files files), you must add an entry for that option into one of the MASTER files. If your code is not a BSD pseudo-device, you should add something like the following:

```
options MACH_FOO
```

Otherwise, you should add something like this:

```
pseudo-device mach_foo
```

In the case of a pseudo-device (for example,/dev/random), you can also add a number. When your code checks to see if it should be included, it can also check that number and allocate resources for more than one pseudo-device. The meaning of multiple pseudo-devices is device-dependent. An example of this is ppp, which allocates resources for two simultaneous PPP connections. Thus, in the MASTER.ppc file, it has the line:

```
pseudo-device ppp 2
```

## MODIFYING THE SOURCE CODE FILES

In the Mac OS X kernel, all source code files are automatically compiled. It is the responsibility of the C file itself to determine whether its contents need to be included in the build or not. In the example above, you created a module called mach_foo. Assume that you want this file to compile only on PowerPC-based computers. In that case, you should have included the option only in MASTER.ppc and not in MASTER.i386. However, by default, merely specifying the file foo_main.c in files causes it to be compiled, regardless of compile options specified. To make the code compile only when the option mach_foo is included in the configuration, you should begin each C source file with the lines,

```
#include <mach_foo.h>
#if (MACH_FOO > 0)
```

and end it with

```
#endif/* MACH_FOO */
```

If mach_foo is a pseudo-device and you need to check the number of mach_foo pseudo-devices included, you can do further tests of the value of MACH_FOO.

Note that the file <mach_foo.h> is not something you create. It is created by the makefiles themselves. You must run make exporthdrs before make all to generate these files.

## MACH SCHEDULING AND THREAD INTERFACES

Mac OS X is based on Mach and BSD. Like Mach and most BSD UNIX systems, it contains an advanced scheduler based on the CMU Mach 3 scheduler. This chapter describes the scheduler from the perspective of both a kernel programmer and an application developer attempting to set scheduling parameters. This chapter begins with the "Overview of Scheduling", which describes the basic concepts behind Mach scheduling at a high level, including real-time priority support. The second section, "Using Mach Scheduling From User Applications", describes how to access certain key Mach scheduler routines from user applications and from other parts of the kernel outside the scheduler. The third section, "Kernel Thread APIs", explains scheduler-related topics including how to create and terminate kernel threads and describes the BSD spl macros and their limited usefulness in Mac OS X.

## OVERVIEW OF SCHEDULING

The Mac OS X scheduler is derived from the scheduler used in OSFMK 7.3. In general, much documentation about prior implementations applies to the scheduler in Mac OS X, although you will find numerous differences. The details of those differences are beyond the scope of this overview.

Mach scheduling is based on a system of run queues at various priorities that are handled in different ways. The priority levels are divided into four bands according to their characteristics, as described in Table.

**Table. Thread Priority Bands**

| Priority Band | Characteristics |
|---|---|
| Normal | Normal application thread priorities |
| System high priority | Threads whose priority has been raised above normal threads |
| Kernel mode only | Reserved for threads created inside the kernel that need to run at a higher priority than all user space threads (I/O Kit workloops, for example) |
| Real-time threads | Threads whose priority is based on getting a well-defined fraction of total clock cycles, regardless of other activity (in an audio player application, for example). |

Threads can migrate between priority levels for a number of reasons, largely as an artifact of the time sharing algorithm used. However, this migration is within a given band. Threads marked as being real-time priority are also special in the eyes of the scheduler. A real-time thread tells the scheduler that it needs to run for A cycles out of the next B cycles. For example, it might need to run for 3000 out of the next 7000 clock cycles in order to keep up. It also tells the scheduler whether those cycles must be contiguous. Using long contiguous quanta is generally frowned upon but is occasionally necessary for specialized real-time applications.

The kernel will make every effort to honour the request, but since this is soft real-time, it cannot be guaranteed. In particular, if the real-time thread requests something relatively reasonable, its priority will remain in the real-time band, but if it lies blatantly about its requirements and behaves in a compute-bound fashion, it may be demoted to the priority of a normal thread. Changing a thread's priority to turn it into a real-time priority thread using Mach calls is described in more detail in "Using Mach Scheduling From User Applications". In addition to the raw Mach RPC interfaces, some aspects of a thread's priority can be controlled from user space using the POSIX thread priority API. The POSIX thread API is able to set thread priority only within the lowest priority band (0-63). For more information on the POSIX thread priority API.

## USING MACH SCHEDULING FROM USER APPLICATIONS

There are three basic ways to change how a user thread is scheduled. You can use the BSD pthreads API to change basic policy and importance. You can also use Mach RPC calls to change a task's importance. Finally, you can use RPC calls to change the scheduling policy to move a thread into a different scheduling band.

This is commonly used when interacting with CoreAudio. The pthreads API is a user space API, and has limited relevance for kernel programmers. The Mach thread and task APIs are more general and can be used from anywhere in the kernel. The Mach thread and task calls can also be called from user applications.

## USING THE PTHREADS API TO INFLUENCE SCHEDULING

Mac OS X supports a number of policies at the POSIX threads API level. If you need real-time behaviour, you must use the Mach thread_policy_set call. This is described in "Using the Mach Thread API to Influence Scheduling". The pthreads API adjusts the priority of threads within a given task. It does not necessarily impact performance relative to threads in other tasks. To increase the priority of a task, you can use nice(1) or renice(8) from the command line or call getpriority and setpriority from your application. The API provides two functions: pthread_getschedparam and pthread_ setschedparam. Their prototypes look like this:

```
pthread_setschedparam(pthread_t thread, int
      policy, struct sched_param *param);
pthread_getschedparam(pthread_t thread, int
      *policy,struct sched_param *param)
```

The arguments for pthread_getschedparam are straightforward. The first argument is a thread ID, and the others are pointers to memory where the results will be stored. The arguments to pthread_setschedparam are not as obvious, however. As with pthread_getschedparam, the first argument is a thread ID.

The second argument to pthread_setschedparam is the desired policy, which can currently be one of SCHED_FIFO (first in, first out), SCHED_RR (round-robin), orSCHED_OTHER. The SCHED_OTHER policy is generally used for extra policies that are specific to a given operating system, and should thus be avoided when writing portable code. The third argument is a structure that contains various scheduling parameters. Here is a basic example of using pthreads functions to set a thread's scheduling policy and priority.

```
int set_my_thread_priority(int priority) {
      struct sched_param sp;
      memset(&sp, 0, sizeof(struct sched_param));
      sp.sched_priority=priority;
      if (pthread_setschedparam(pthread_self(),
      SCHED_RR, &sp) == -1) {
      printf("Failed to change priority.\n");
      return -1;
      }
      return 0;
      }
```

This code snippet sets the scheduling policy for the current thread to round-robin scheduling, and sets the thread's relative importance within the task to the value passed in through the priority argument. For more information, see the manual page for pthread(3).

## USING THE MACH THREAD API TO INFLUENCE SCHEDULING

This API is frequently used in multimedia applications to obtain real-time priority. It is also useful in other situations when the pthread scheduling API cannot be used or does not provide the needed functionality.

The API consists of two functions, thread_policy_set and thread_policy_get.

```
kern_return_t thread_policy_set(
     thread_act_t thread,
     thread_policy_flavour_t flavour,
     thread_policy_t policy_info,
```

```
    mach_msg_type_number_t count);
kern_return_t thread_policy_get(
    thread_act_t thread,
    thread_policy_flavour_t flavour,
    thread_policy_t policy_info,
    mach_msg_type_number_t *count,
    boolean_t *get_default);
```

The parameters of these functions are roughly the same, except that the thread_policy_get function takes pointers for the count and the get_defaultarguments. The count is an inout parameter, meaning that it is interpreted as the maximum amount of storage (in units of int32_t) that the calling task has allocated for the return, but it is also overwritten by the scheduler to indicate the amount of data that was actually returned.

These functions get and set several parameters, according to the thread policy chosen. The possible thread policies are listed in Table.

**Table: Thread Policies**

| Policy | Meaning |
|---|---|
| THREAD_STANDARD_POLICY | Default value |
| THREAD_TIME_CONSTRAINT _POLICY | Used to specify real-time behaviour. |
| THREAD_PRECEDENCE_POLICY | Used to indicate the importance of computation relative to other threads in a given task. |

The following code snippet shows how to set the priority of a task to teil the scheduler that it needs real-time performance. The example values provided in comments are based on the estimated needs of esd (the Esound daemon).

```
#include <mach/mach_init.h>
#include <mach/thread_policy.h>
#include <mach/sched.h>
int set_realtime(int period, int computation, int
        constraint) {
```

```
        struct thread_time_constraint_policy
        ttcpolicy;
        int ret;
        ttcpolicy.period=period;//HZ/160
        ttcpolicy.computation=computation;//HZ/
        3300;
        ttcpolicy.constraint=constraint;//HZ/
        2200;
        ttcpolicy.preemptible=1;
    if ((ret=thread_policy_set(mach_thread_self(),
        THREAD_TIME_CONSTRAINT_POLICY,
        (thread_policy_t)&ttcpolicy,
        THREAD_TIME_CONSTRAINT_POLICY_COUNT)) !=
        KERN_SUCCESS)fprintf(stderr,
        "set_realtime() failed.\n"); return 0;
    }
    return 1;
    }
```

The time values are in terms of Mach absolute time units. Since these values differ according to the bus speed of your computer, you should generally use numbers relative to HZ (a global variable containing the current number of ticks per second). You can either handle this conversion yourself by dividing this value by an appropriate quantity or use the conversion routines described in "Using Kernel Time Abstractions". Say your computer reports 133 million for the value of HZ. If you pass the example values given as arguments to this function, your thread tells the scheduler that it needs approximately 40,000 (HZ/3300) out of the next 833,333 (HZ/160) bus cycles. The preemptible value (1) indicates that those 40,000 bus cycles need not be contiguous. However, the constraint value (HZ/2200) tells the scheduler that there can be no more than 60,000 bus cycles between the start of computation and the end of computation.

*Note*: Because the constraint sets a maximum bound for computation, it must be larger than the value for computation. A straightforward example using this API is code that displays video directly to the framebuffer hardware. It needs to run for a certain number of cycles every frame to get the new data into the frame buffer. It can be interrupted without worry, but if it is interrupted for too long, the video hardware starts displaying an outdated frame before the software writes the updated data, resulting in a nasty glitch. Audio has similar behaviour, but since it is usually buffered along the way (in hardware and in software), there is greater tolerance for variations in timing, to a point.

Another policy call is THREAD_PRECEDENCE_POLICY. This is used for setting the relative importance of non-real-time threads. Its calling convention is similar, except that its structure is thread_precedence_policy, and contains only one field, an integer_t called importance. While this is a signed 32-bit value, the minimum legal value is zero (IDLE_PRI). threads set to IDLE_PRI will only execute when no other thread is scheduled to execute.

In general, larger values indicate higher priority. The maximum limit is subject to change, as are the priority bands, some of which have special purposes (such as real-time threads). Thus, in general, you should use pthreads APIs to achieve this functionality rather than using this policy directly unless you are setting up an idle thread.

## USING THE MACH TASK API TO INFLUENCE SCHEDULING

This relatively simple API is not particularly useful for most developers. However, it may be beneficial if you are developing a graphical user interface for Darwin. It also provides some insight into the prioritization of tasks in Mac OS X. It is presented here for completeness.

The API consists of two functions, `task_policy_set` and `task_policy_get`.

```
kern_return_t task_policy_set(
     task_t task,
     task_policy_flavour_t flavour,
     task_policy_t policy_info,
     mach_msg_type_number_t count);
kern_return_t task_policy_get(
```

```
task_t task,
task_policy_flavour_t flavour,
task_policy_t policy_info,
mach_msg_type_number_t *count,
boolean_t *get_default);
```

As with thread_policy_set and thread_policy_get, the parameters are similar, except that the task_policy_get function takes pointers for the count and the get_default arguments. The count argument is an inout parameter. It is interpreted as the maximum amount of storage that the calling task has allocated for the return, but it is also overwritten by the scheduler to indicate the amount of data that was actually returned. These functions get and set a single parameter, that of the role of a given task, which changes the way the task's priority gets altered over time. The possible roles of a task are listed in Table.

**Table: Task Roles**

| Role | Meaning |
|---|---|
| TASK_UNSPECIFIED | Default value |
| TASK_RENICED<br>process is executed with | This is set when a nice or is modified by renice. |
| TASK_FOREGROUND_APPLICATION | GUI application in the foreground. There can be more than one foreground application. |
| TASK_BACKGROUND_APPLICATION | GUI application in the background. |
| TASK_CONTROL_APPLICATION | Reserved for the dock or equivalent (assigned FCFS). |
| TASK_GRAPHICS_SERVER | Reserved for Window Server or equivalent (assigned FCFS). |

The following code snippet shows how to set the priority of a task to tell the scheduler that it is a foreground application (regardless of whether it really is).

```
#include <mach/mach_init.h>
#include <mach/task_policy.h>
#include <mach/sched.h>
int set_my_task_policy(void) {
    int ret;
    struct task_category_policy tcatpolicy;
    tcatpolicy.role = TASK_FOREGROUND_APPLICATION;
    if ((ret=task_policy_set(mach_task_self(),
        TASK_CATEGORY_POLICY,(thread_policy_t)
        &tcatpolicy,
        TASK_CATEGORY_POLICY_COUNT))!=
        KERN_SUCCESS)    {
        fprintf(stderr, "set_my_task_policy()
        failed.\n");
        return 0;
}
return 1;
}
```

## KERNEL THREAD APIS

The Mac OS X scheduler provides a number of public APIs. While many of these APIs should not be used, the APIs to create, destroy, and alter kernel threads are of particular importance. While not technically part of the scheduler itself, they are inextricably tied to it. The scheduler directly provides certain services that are commonly associated with the use of kernel threads, without which kernel threads would be of limited utility. For example, the scheduler provides support for wait queues, which are used in various synchronization primitives such as mutex locks and

## CREATING AND DESTROYING KERNEL THREADS

The recommended interface for creating threads within the kernel is through the I/O Kit. It provides IOCreateThread, IOThreadSelf, and IOExitThread functions that make it relatively painless to create threads in the kernel. The basic functions for creating and terminating kernel threads are:

```
IOThread IOCreateThread(IOThreadFunc function,
```

```
        void *argument);
IOThread IOThreadSelf(void);
void IOExitThread(void);
```

With the exception of IOCreateThread (which is a bit more complex), the I/O Kit functions are fairly thin wrappers around Mach thread functions. The types involved are also very thin abstractions.

IOThread is really the same as thread_t. The IOCreate Thread function creates a new thread that immediately begins executing the function that you specify. It passes a single argument to that function. If you need to pass more than one argument, you should dynamically allocate a data structure and pass a pointer to that structure. For example, the following code creates a kernel thread and executes the function myfunc in that thread:

```
#include <IOKit/IOLib.h>
#include <libkern/libkern.h>
#include <sys/malloc.h>
struct mydata {
     int three;
     char *string;
     };
static void myfunc(void *myarg) {
     struct mydata *md = (struct mydata *)myarg;
     IOLog("Passed%d =%s\n", md->three, md-
     >string);
     IOExitThread();
     }
void start_threads() {
     IOThread mythread;
     struct mydata *md = (struct mydata
     *)malloc(sizeof(*md));
     md->three = 3; md->string = (char *)malloc(2
     * sizeof(char));
     md->string[0]= '3'; md->string[1]= '\0';
//Start a thread using IOCreateThread
mythread = IOCreateThread(&myfunc, (void *)md);
     }
```

One other useful function is thread_terminate. This can be used to destroy an arbitrary thread (except, of course, the currently running thread). This can beextremely dangerous if not done correctly. Before tearing down a thread with thread_terminate, you should lock the thread and disable any outstanding timers against it. If you fail to deactivate a timer, a kernel panic will occur when the timer expires. With that in mind, you may be able to terminate a thread as follows:

```
thread_terminate(getact_thread(thread));
```

'There thread is of type thread_t. In general, you can only be assured that you can kill yourself, not other threads in the system. The function thread_terminatetakes a single parameter of type thread_act_t (a thread activation). The function getact_thread takes a thread shuttle (thread_shuttle_t) or thread_t and returns the thread activation associated with it.

## SPL AND FRIENDS

BSD-based and Mach-based operating systems contain legacy functions designed for basic single-processor synchronization. These include functions such assplhigh, splbio, splx, and other similar functions. Since these functions are not particularly useful for synchronization in an SMP situation, they are not particularly useful as synchronization tools in Mac OS X.

If you are porting legacy code from earlier Mach-based or BSD-based operating systems, you must find an alternate means of providing synchronization. In many cases, this is as simple as taking the kernel or network funnel. In parts of the kernel, the use of spl functions does nothing, but causes no harm if you are holding a funnel (and results in a panic if you are not).

In other parts of the kernel, spl macros are actually used. Because spl cannot necessarily be used for its intended purpose, it should not be used in general unless you are writing code it a part of the kernel that already uses it. You should instead use alternate synchronization primitives such as those described in "Synchronization Primitives".

## WAIT QUEUES AND WAIT PRIMITIVES

The wait queue API is used extensively by the scheduler and is closely tied to the scheduler in its implementation. It is also used extensively in locks, semaphores, and other synchronization primitives.

The wait queue API is both powerful and flexible, and as a result is somewhat large.

Not all of the API is exported outside the scheduler, and parts are not useful outside the context of the wait queue functions themselves. This section documents only the public API.

The wait queue API includes the following functions:

```
void wait_queue_init(wait_queue_t wq, int policy);
Externwait_queue_twai t_queue_
     twait_queue_alloc(int policy);
void wait_queue_free(wait_queue_t wq);
void wait_queue_lock(wait_queue_t wq);
void wait_queue_lock_try(wait_queue_t wq);
void wait_queue_unlock(wait_queue_t wq);
boolean_t wait_queue_member(wait_queue_t wq,
      wait_queue_sub_t wq_sub);
boolean_t wait_queue_member_locked(wait_queue_t
      wq, wait_queue_sub_t wq_sub);
kern_return_t wait_queue_link(wait_queue_t wq,
      wait_queue_sub_t wq_sub);
kern_return_t wait_queue_unlink(wait_queue_t wq,
      wait_queue_sub_t wq_sub);
kern_return_t wait_queue_unlink_one(wait_queue_t
      wq,
      wait_queue_sub_t *wq_subp);
void wait_queue_assert_wait(wait_queue_t wq,
      event_t event,
      int interruptible);
```

```
void wait_queue_assert_wait_locked(wait_queue_t
      wq, event_t event,
      int interruptible, boolean_t unlocked);
kern_return_t wait_queue_wakeup_all(wait_queue_t
      wq, event_t event,
      int result);
kern_return_t wait_queue_peek_locked(wait_queue_t
      wq, event_t event,
      thread_t *tp, wait_queue_t *wqp);
void wait_queue_pull_thread_locked(wait_queue_t
      wq, thread_t thread,
      boolean_t unlock);
thread_twait_queue_wakeup_identity_
      locked(wait_queue_t wq, event_t event,
      int result, boolean_t unlock);
kern_return_t wait_queue_wakeup_one(wait_queue_t
      wq, event_t event,
      int result);
kern_return_twait_queue_wakeup_one_
      locked(wait_queue_t wq, event_t event,
      int result, boolean_t unlock);
kern_return_twait_queue_wakeup_thread(wait_queue_t
       wq, event_t event,thread_t thread, int
       result);
kern_return_t wait_queue_wakeup_thread_
       locked(wait_queue_twq, event_t event,
       thread_t thread, int result, boolean_t
       unlock);
kern_return_t wait_queue_remove(thread_t thread);
```

Most of the functions and their arguments are straightforward and are not presented in detail. However, a few require special attention.

Most of the functions take an event_t as an argument. These can be arbitrary 32-bit values, which leads to the potential for conflicting events on certain wait queues. The traditional way to avoid this problem is to use the address of a data object that is somehow related to the code in question as that 32-bit integer value.

For example, if you are waiting for an event that indicates that a new block of data has been added to a ring buffer, and if that ring buffer's head pointer was calledrb_head, you might pass the value &rb_head as the event ID. Because wait queue usage does not generally cross address space boundaries, this is generally sufficient to avoid any event ID conflicts.

Notice the functions ending in _locked. These functions require that your thread be holding a lock on the wait queue before they are called.

Functions ending in_locked are equivalent to their nonlocked counterparts (where applicable) except that they do not lock the queue on entry and may not unlock the queue on exit (depending on the value of unlock). The remainder of this section does not differentiate between locked and unlocked functions.

*The wait_queue_alloc and wait_queue_init functions take a policy parameter, which can be one of the following:*

- SYNC_POLICY_FIFO-first-in, first-out
- SYNC_POLICY_FIXED_PRIORITY-policy based on thread priority
- SYNC_POLICY_PREPOST-keep track of number of wakeups where no thread was waiting and allow threads to immediately continue executing without waiting until that count reaches zero. This is frequently used when implementing semaphores.

You should not use the wait_queue_init function outside the scheduler. Because a wait queue is an opaque object outside that context, you cannot determine the appropriate size for allocation. Thus, because the size could change in the future, you should always use wait_queue_alloc and wait_queue_free unless you are writing code within the scheduler itself. Similarly, the functions wait_queue_member, wait_ queue_member_locked, wait_queue_link, wait_queue_ unlink, and wait_queue_unlink_one are operations on subordinate queues, which are not exported outside the scheduler. The function wait_queue_member determines whether a subordinate queue is a member of a queue.

The functions wait_queue_link and wait_queue_unlink link and unlink a given subordinate queue from its parent queue, respectively. The function wait_queue_unlink_one unlinks the first subordinate queue in a given parent and returns it.

The function wait_queue_assert_wait causes the calling thread to wait on the wait queue until it is either interrupted (by a thread timer, for example) or explicitly awakened by another thread. The interruptible flag indicates whether this function should allow an asynchronous event to interrupt waiting.

The function wait_queue_wakeup_all wakes up all threads waiting on a given queue for a particular event. The function wait_queue_peek_locked returns the first thread from a given wait queue that is waiting on a given event. It does not remove the thread from the queue, nor does it wake the thread.

It also returns the wait queue where the thread was found. If the thread is found in a subordinate queue, other subordinate queues are unlocked, as is the parent queue. Only the queue where the thread was found remains locked. The function wait_queue_pull_thread_locked pulls a thread from the wait queue and optionally unlocks the queue. This is generally used with the result of a previous call to wait_queue_peek_locked.

The function wait_queue_wakeup_identity_locked wakes up the first thread that is waiting for a given event on a given wait queue and starts it running but leaves the thread locked. It then returns a pointer to the thread.

This can be used to wake the first thread in a queue and then modify unrelated structures based on which thread was actually awakened before allowing the thread to execute. The function wait_queue_wakeup_one wakes up the first thread that is waiting for a given event on a given wait queue. The function wait_queue_wakeup_thread wakes up a given thread if and only if it is waiting on the specified event and wait queue (or one of its subordinates). The function wait_queue_remove wakes a given thread without regard to the wait queue or event on which it is waiting.

# 10

# Performance

## INTRODUICTION

Performance is a key aspect of any software system. Nowhere is this more true than in the kernel, where small performance problems tend to be magnified by repeated execution.

For this reason, it is extremely important that your code be as efficient as possible. This chapter discusses the importance of low interrupt latency and fine-grained locking and tells you how to determine what portions of your code would benefit most from more efficient design.

## INTERRUPT LATENCY

In Mac OS X, you will probably never need to write code that runs in an interrupt context. In general, only motherboard hardware requires this.

However, in the unlikely event that you do need to write code in an interrupt context, interrupt latency should be a primary concern. Interrupt latency refers to the delay between an interrupt being generated and an interrupt handler actually beginning to service that interrupt. In practice, the worst case interrupt latency is closely tied to the amount of time spent in supervisor mode (also called kernel mode) with interrupts off while handling some other interrupt.

Low interrupt latency is necessary for reasonable overall performance, particularly when working with audio and video. In order to have reasonable soft real-time performance (for example, performance of multimedia applications), the interrupt latency caused by every device driver must be both small and bounded.

Mac OS X takes great care to bound and minimize interrupt latency for built-in drivers. It does this primarily through the use of interrupt service threads (also known as I/O service threads).

When Mac OS X takes an interrupt, the low-level trap handlers call up to a generic interrupt handling routine that clears the pending interrupt bit in the interrupt controller and calls a device-specific interrupt handler. That device-specific handler, in turn, sends a message to an interrupt service thread to notify it that an interrupt has occurred, and then the handler returns.

When no further interrupts are pending, control returns to the currently executing thread. The next time the interrupt service thread is scheduled, it checks to see if an interrupt has occurred, then services the interrupt. As the name suggests, this actually is happening in a thread context, not an interrupt context.

*This design causes two major differences from traditional operating system design:*

- Interrupt latency is near zero, since the code executing in an interrupt context is very small.
- It is possible for an interrupt to occur while a device driver is executing. This means that traditional (threaded) device drivers can be preempted and must use locking or other similar methods to protect any shared data (although they need to do so anyway to work on computers with multiple processors).

This model is crucial to the performance of Mac OS X. You should not attempt to circumvent this design by doing large amounts of work in an interrupt context. Doing so will be detrimental to the overall performance of the system.

## LOCKING BOTTLENECKS

It is difficult to communicate data between multiple threads or between thread and interrupt contexts without using locking or other synchronization.

This locking protects your data from getting clobbered by another thread. However, it also has the unfortunate side effect of being a potential bottleneck.

In some types of communication (particularly n-way), locking can dramatically hinder performance by allowing only one thing to happen at a time. Read-write locks, discussed in "Synchronization Primitives", can help alleviate this problem in the most common situation where multiple clients need to be able to read information but only rarely need to modify that data.

However, there are many cases where read-write locks are not helpful. This section discusses some possible problems and ways of improving performance within those constraints.

## WORKING WITH HIGHLY CONTENDED LOCKS

When many threads need to obtain a lock (or a small number of threads need to obtain a lock frequently), this lock is considered highly contended. Highly contended locks frequently represent faulty code design, but they are sometimes unavoidable.

In those cases, the lock tends to become a major performance bottleneck. Take, for example, the issue of many-to-many communication that must be synchronized through a common buffer. While some improvement can be gained by using read-write locks instead of an ordinary mutex, the issue of multiple writers means that read-write locks still perform badly.

One possible solution for this many-to-many communication problem is to break the lock up into multiple locks. Instead of sharing a single buffer for the communication itself, make a shared buffer that contains accounting information for the communication (for example, a list of buffers available for reading).

Then assign each individual buffer its own lock. The readers might then need to check several locations to find the right data, but this still frequently yields better performance, since writers must only contend for a write lock while modifying the accounting information.

Another solution for many-to-many communications is to eliminate the buffer entirely and communicate using message passing, sockets, IPC, RPC, or other methods. Yet another solution is to restructure your code in a way that the locking is unnecessary.

This is often much more difficult. One method that is often helpful is to take advantage of flags and atomic increments, as outlined in the next paragraph. For simplicity, a single-writer, single-reader example is presented, but it is possible to extend this idea to more complicated designs.

Take a buffer with some number of slots. Keep a read index and a write index into that buffer. When the write index and read index are the same, there is no data in the buffer. When writing, clear the next location. Then do an atomic increment on the pointer. Write the data. End by setting a flag at that new location that says that the data is valid.

Note that this solution becomes much more difficult when dealing with multiple readers and multiple writers, and as such, is beyond the scope of this section.

## REDUCING CONTENTION BY DECREASING GRANULARITY

One of the fundamental properties of locks is granularity. The granularity of a lock refers to the amount of code or data that it protects.

A lock that protects a large block of code or a large amount of data is referred to as a coarse-grained lock, while a lock that protects only a small amount of code or data is referred to as a fine-grained lock.

A coarse-grained lock is much more likely to be contended (needed by one thread while being held by another) than a more finely grained lock.

There are two basic ways of decreasing granularity. The first is to minimize the amount of code executed while a lock is held.

For example, if you have code that calculates a value and stores it into a table, don't take the lock before calling the function and release it after the function returns. Instead, take the lock in that piece of code right before you write the data, and release it as soon as you no longer need it. Of course, reducing the amount of protected code is not always possible or practical if the code needs to guarantee consistency where the value it is writing depends on other values in the table, since those values could change before you obtain the lock, requiring you to go back and redo the work.

It is also possible to reduce granularity by locking the data in smaller units. In the above example, you could have a lock on each cell of the table. When updating cells in the table, you would start by determining the cells on which the destination cell depends, then lock those cells and the destination cell in some fixed order. (To avoid deadlock, you must always either lock cells in the same order or use an appropriate try function and release all locks on failure.)

Once you have locked all the cells involved, you can then perform your calculation and release the locks, confident that no other thread has corrupted your calculations. However, by locking on a smaller unit of data, you have also reduced the likelihood of two threads needing to access the same cell.

A slightly more radical version of this is to use read-write locks on a per-cell basis and always upgrade in a particular order. This is, however, rather extreme, and difficult to do correctly.

## CODE PROFILING

Code profiling means determining how often certain pieces of code are executed. By knowing how frequently a piece of code is used, you can more accurately gauge the importance of optimizing that piece of code.

There are a number of good tools for profiling user space applications. However, code profiling in the kernel is a very different beast, since it isn't reasonable to attach to it like you would a running process. (It is possible by using a second computer, but even then, it is not a trivial task.).

This section describes two useful ways of profiling your kernel code: counters and lock profiling. Any changes you make to allow code profiling should be done only during development. These are not the sort of changes that you want to release to end users.

## USING COUNTERS FOR CODE PROFILING

The first method of code profiling is with counters. To profile a section of code with a counter, you must first create a global variable whose name describes that piece of code and initialize it to zero.

You then add something like,

```
#ifdef PROFILING
foo_counter++; #endif
```

in the appropriate piece of code. If you then define PROFILING, that counter is created and initialized to zero, then incremented each time the code in question is executed. One small snag with this sort of profiling is the problem of obtaining the data.

This can be done in several ways. The simplest is probably to install a sysctl, using the address of foo_counter as an argument.

Then, you could simply issue the sysctl command from the command line and read or clear the variable. Adding asysctl is described in more detail in "BSD sysctl API".

In addition to using sysctl, you could also obtain the data by printing its value when unloading the module (in the case of a KEXT) or by using a remote debugger to attach to the kernel and directly inspecting the variable. However, a sysctl provides the most flexibility.

With a sysctl, you can sample the value at any time, not just when the module is unloaded.

The ability to arbitrarily sample the value makes it easier to determine the importance of a piece of code to one particular action. If you are developing code for use in the I/O Kit, you should probably use your driver's setProperties call instead of a sysctl.

## LOCK PROFILING

Lock profiling is another useful way to find the cause of code inefficiency.

*Lock profiling can give you the following information:*

- How many times a lock was taken
- How long the lock was held on average
- How often the lock was unavailable

Put another way, this allows you to determine the contention of a lock, and in so doing, can help you to minimize contention by code restructuring. There are many different ways to do lock profiling.

The most common way is to create your own lock calls that increment a counter and then call the real locking functions.

When you move from debugging into a testing cycle before release, you can then replace the functions with defines to cause the actual functions to be called directly. For example, you might write something like this:

```
extern struct timeval time;
boolean_t mymutex_try(mymutex_t *lock) {
      int ret;
      ret=mutex_try(lock->mutex);
      if (ret) {
      lock->tryfailcount++;
      }
      return ret;
      }
void mymutex_lock(mymutex_t *lock) {
      if (!(mymutex_try(lock))) {
      mutex_lock(lock->mutex);}
      lock->starttime = time.tv_sec;
}
void mymutex_unlock(mymutex_t *lock) {
      lock->lockheldtime += (time.tv_sec-lock-
      >starttime);
      lock->heldcount++;
      mutex_unlock(lock->mutex);
}
```

This routine has accuracy only to the nearest second, which is not particularly accurate. Ideally, you want to keep track of both time.tv_sec and time.tv_usecand roll the microseconds into seconds as the number gets large. From this information, you can obtain the average time the lock was held by dividing the total time held by the number of times it was held.

It also tells you the number of times a lock was taken immediately instead of waiting, which is a valuable piece of data when analysing contention.

As with counter-based profiling, after you have written code to record lock use and contention, you must find a way to obtain that information. A sysctl is a good way of doing this, since it is relatively easy to implement and can provide a "snapshot" view of the data structure at any point in time. For more information on adding a sysctl. Another way to do lock profiling is to use the built-in ETAP (Event Trace Analysis Package).

This package consists of additional code designed for lock profiling. However, since this requires a kernel recompile, it is generally not recommended.

## KERNEL PROGRAMMING STYLE

As described in "Keep Out", programming in the kernel is fraught with hazards that can cause instability, crashes, or security holes. In addition to these issues, programming in the kernel has the potential for compatibility problems. If you program only to the interfaces discussed in this document or other Apple documents, you will avoid the majority of these. However, even limiting yourself to documented interfaces does not protect you from a handful of pitfalls. The biggest potential problem that you face is namespacecollision, which occurs when your function, variable, or class name is the same as someone else's.

Since this makes one kernel extension or the other fail to load correctly (in a non-deterministic fashion), Apple has established function naming conventions for C and C++ code within the kernel. These are described in"Standard C Naming

Conventions" and "C++ Naming Conventions", respectively.\
In addition to compatibility problems, kernel extensions that misbehave can also dramatically decrease the system's overall performance or cause crashes.

Some of these issues are described in "Performance and Stability Tips". For more thorough coverage of performance and stability, you should also read the chapters "Security Considerations" and "Performance Considerations".

## C++ NAMING CONVENTIONS

Basic I/O Kit C++ naming conventions are defined in the document I/O Kit Device Driver Design Guidelines. This section refines those conventions in ways that should make them more useful to you as a programmer.

### Basic Conventions

*The primary conventions are as follows:*

- Use the Java-style reverse DNS naming convention, substituting underscores for periods. For example, com_apple_foo.
- Avoid the following reserved prefixes:
- OS
- Os
- IO
- Io
- Apple
- Apple
- AAPL
- Aapl

This ensures that you will not collide with classes created by other companies or with future classes added to the operating system by Apple. It does not protect you from other projects created within your company, however, and for this reason, some additional guidelines are suggested.

### Additional Guidelines

These additional guidelines are intended to minimize the

chance of accidentally breaking your own software and to improve readability of code by developers.

*This is particularly of importance for open source projects.*

- Begin each function name within a class with the name of the class. For example, if the class is com_apple_iokit_pickle, and the function would be eat, you should name the function pickle_eat. This makes it easier to see class associations, particularly when called from other files.
- Name classes based on project names. For example, if you are working on project Schlassen, and one of its classes was pickle, you would name the classcom_apple_driver_schlassen_pickle.
- Name families based on project names. For example, if you are working on project Schlassen, and one of its classes was pickle, you would name the classcom_apple_iokit_schlassen_pickle.
- Name classes hierarchically if your organization is large. For example, if Apple's marketing department were working on the Schlassen project, then they might name the class com_apple _driver_marketing_ schlassen_pickle. If they had another project that was in the BSD layer that interfaced with this one, then that BSD extension's class could be com_apple _bsd_marketing_schlassen_pickle.
- If you anticipate that the last part of the class name may be the same as the last part of another class name, consider beginning each function name with a larger portion of the class name. For example, you might have bsd_pickle_eat and driver_pickle_eat.

These are only suggested guidelines. Your company or organization should adopt its own set of guidelines within the constraints of the basic conventions described in the previous section. These guidelines should provide a good starting point.

## STANDARD C NAMING CONVENTIONS

The naming conventions for C++ have been defined for some time in the document I/O Kit Device Driver Design

Guidelines. However, no conventions have been given for standard C code. Because standard C has an even greater chance of namespace collision than C++, it is essential that you follow these guidelines when writing C code for use in the kernel.

Because C does not have the benefit of classes, it is much easier to run into a naming conflict between two functions.

*For this reason, the following conventions are suggested:*

- Declare all functions and (global) variables static where possible to prevent them from being seen in the global namespace. If you need to share these across files within your KEXT, you can achieve a similar effect by declaring them __private_extern__. Declare all functions and (global) variables static Each function name should use Java-style reverse DNS naming. For example, if your company is apple.com, you should begin each function withcom_apple_. Declare all functions and (global) variables static Follow the reverse DNS name with the name of your project. For example, if you work at Apple and were working on project Schlassen, you would start each function name (in drivers) with com_apple_driver_schlassen_.
  Note: The term driver is reserved for actual device drivers. For families, you should instead use iokit. For example, if project Schlassen is an I/O Kit family, function names should all begin with com_apple_iokit_schlassen_.
- Use hierarchical names if you anticipate multiple projects with similar names coming from different parts of your company or organization.
- Use macro expansion to save typing, for example PROJECT_eat could expandto `com_apple_driver_schlassen_pickle_eat.`
- If you anticipate that the last part of a function name may be the same as the last part of another function name(for example, `PROJECT1_eatandPROJECT2_eat),`

you should change the names to avoid confusion (for example, `PROJECT1_eatpickle` and `PROJECT2_eatburger`).

- *Avoid the following reserved prefixes:*
  - OS
  - Os
  - IO
  - Io
  - Apple
  - Apple
  - AAPL
  - Aapl
- Avoid conflicting with any names already in the kernel, and do not use prefixes similar to those of existing kernel functions that you may be working with.
- Never begin a function name with an underscore (_).
- Under no circumstances should you use common names for your functions without prefixing them with the name of your project in some form. These are some examples of unacceptable names:
  - Getuseridentity
  - Get_user_info
  - Print
  - Find
  - Search
  - Sort
  - Quicksort
  - Merge
  - Console_log

In short, picking any name that you would normally pick for a function is generally a bad idea, because every other developer writing code is likely to pick the same name for his or her function.

Occasional conflicts are a fact of life. However, by following these few simple rules, you should be able to avoid the majority of common namespace pitfalls.

## COMMONLY USED FUNCTIONS

One of the most common problems faced when programming in the kernel is use of "standard" functions-things like printf or bcopy. Many commonly used standard C library functions are implemented in the kernel. In order to use them, however, you need to include the appropriate prototypes, which may be different from the user space prototypes for those functions, and which generally have different names when included from kernel code.

In general, any non-I/O Kit header that you can safely include in the kernel is located in xnu/bsd/sys or xnu/osfmk/ mach, although there are a few specialized headers in other places like libkern and libsa. Normal headers (those in/usr/ include) cannot be used in the kernel. Important: If you are writing an I/O Kit KEXT, most of these functions are not what you are looking for. The I/O Kit provides its own APIs for these features, including IOLog, IOMemoryDescriptor, and IOLock. While using the lower-level functionality is not expressly forbidden, it is generally discouraged (thoughprintf is always fine). For more information about APIs available to I/O Kit KEXTs, see Kernel Framework Reference.

Table lists some commonly used C functions, variables, and types, and gives the location of their prototypes.

**Table: Commonly Used C Functions**

| Function name | Header path |
|---|---|
| Printf | <sys/systm.h> |
| Buffer cache functions (bread, bwrite, and brelse) | <sys/buf.h> <sys/systm.h> |
| Directory entries | <sys/dirent.h> |
| Error numbers | <sys/errno.h> |
| Kernel special variables | <sys/kernel.h> |
| Spinlocks | <sys/lock.h> |
| malloc | <sys/malloc.h> |
| Queues | <sys/queue.h> |
| Random number generator | <sys/rand.h> |

| | |
|---|---|
| bzero, bcopy, copyin, and copyout | <sys/systm.h> |
| timeout and untimeout | <sys/system.h> |
| Various time functions | <sys/time.h> |
| Standard type declarations | <sys/types.h> <mach/mach_types.h> |
| User credentials | <sys/ucred.h> |
| OS and system information | <sys/utsname.h> |

If the standard C function you are trying to use is not in one of these files, chances are the function is not supported for use within the kernel, and you need to implement your code in another way.

The symbols in these header files are divided among multiple symbol sets, depending on the technology area where they were designed to be used.

*To use these, you may have to declare dependencies on any of the following:*

- Com.apple.kernel-You should generally avoid this.
- Com.apple.kernel.bsd-BSD portions of the kernel.
- Com.apple.kernel.iokit-The I/O Kit.
- Com.apple.kernel.libkern-General-purpose functions.
- Com.apple.kernel.mach-Mach-specific APIs.
- Com.apple.kpi.bsd-BSD portions of the kernel (v10.4 and later).
- Com.apple.kernel.iokit-The I/O Kit (v10.4 and later).
- Com.apple.kernel.libkern-General-purpose functions (v10.4 and later).
- Com.apple.kernel.mach-Mach-specific APIs (v10.4 and later).
- Com.apple.kpi.unsupported-Unsupported legacy functionality (v10.4 and later).

Where possible, you should specify a dependency on the KPI version of these symbols. However, these symbols are only available in v10.4 and later. For the I/O Kit and libkern, this should make little difference. For other areas, such as network kernel extensions or file system KEXTs, you must use the KPI versions if you want your extension to load in Mac OS X v10.4 and later.

For a complete list of symbols in any of these dependencies, run nm(1) on the binaries in/System/Library/Extensions/System.kext/PlugIns.

## PERFORMANCE AND STABILITY TIPS

This section includes some basic tips on performance and stability. You should read the sections on security and performance for additional information.

These tips cover only style issues, not general performance or stability issues.

### Performance and Stability Tips

Programming in the kernel is subject to a number of restrictions that do not exist in application programming. The first and most important is the stack size. The kernel has a limited amount of space allocated for thread stacks, which can cause problems if you aren't aware of the limitation.

*This means the following:*

- Recursion must be bounded (to no more than a few levels).
- Recursion should be rewritten as iterative routines where possible.
- Large stack variables (function local) are dangerous. Do not use them. This also applies to large local arrays.
- Dynamically allocated variables are preferred (using malloc or equivalent) over local variables for objects more than a few bytes in size.
- Functions should have as few arguments as possible.
  - Pass pointers to structures, not the broken out elements.
  - Don't use arguments to avoid using global or class variables.
  - Do name global variables in a way that protects you from collision.
- C++ functions should be declared static.

- Functions not obeying these rules can cause a kernel panic, or in extreme cases, do not even compile.

In addition to issues of stack size, you should also avoid doing anything that would generate unnecessary load such as polling a device or address. A good example is the use of mutexes rather than spinlocks. You should also structure your locks in such a way to minimize contention and to minimize hold times on the most highly contended locks. Also, since unused memory (and particularly wired memory) can cause performance degradation, you should be careful to deallocate memory when it is no longer in use, and you should never allocate large regions of wired memory. This may be unavoidable in some applications, but should be avoided whenever possible and disposed of at the earliest possible opportunity. Allocating large contiguous blocks of memory at boot time is almost never acceptable, because it cannot be released.

There are a number of issues that you should consider when deciding whether to use floating point math or AltiVec vector math in the kernel. First, the kernel takes a speed penalty whenever floating-point math or AltiVec instructions are used in a system call context (or other similar mechanisms where a user thread executes in a kernel context), as floating-point and AltiVec registers are only maintained when they are in use.

Note: In cases where altivec or floating point has already been used in user space in the calling thread, there is no additional penalty for using them in the kernel. Thus, for things like audio drivers, the above does not apply. In general, you should avoid doing using floating-point math or AltiVec instructions in the kernel unless doing so will result in a significant speedup. It is not forbidden, but is strongly discouraged.

Second, AltiVec was not supported in the kernel prior to Mac OS X 10.3. It was not possible to detect this support from within the kernel until a later 10.3 software update. If you must deploy your KEXT on earlier versions of Mac OS X, you must either provide a non-AltiVec version of your code or perform the AltiVec instructions in user space. Finally, AltiVec data stream instructions (dst, dstt, dstst, dss, and dssall) are not supported in the kernel, even for processors that support them in user space.

Do not attempt to use them. If you decide to use AltiVec in the kernel, your code can determine whether the CPU supports AltiVec using the sysctlbyname call to get thehw.optional.altivec property. For more information, "The sysctlbyname System Call".

## Stability Tips

- Don't sleep while holding resources (locks, for example). While this is not forbidden, it is strongly discouraged to avoid deadlock.
- Be careful to allocate and free memory with matching calls. For example, do not use allocation routines from the I/O Kit and deallocation routines from BSD. Likewise, do not use IOMallocContiguous with IOFreePageable.
- Use reference counts to avoid freeing memory that is still in use elsewhere. Be sure to deallocate memory when its reference count reaches zero, but not before.
- Lock objects before operating on them, even to change reference counts.
- Never dereference pointers without verifying that they are not NULL. In particular, never do this:

```
int foo = *argptr;
```

- unless you have already verified that argptr cannot possibly be NULL.
- Test code in sections and try to think up likely edge cases for calculations.
- Never assume that your code will be run only on big endian processors.
- Never assume that the size of an instance of a type will never change. Always use sizeof if you need this information.
- Never assume that a pointer will always be the same size as an int or long.

## MACH KERNEL ABSTRACTIONS

Mach provides a small set of abstractions that have been designed to be both simple and powerful.

*These are the main kernel abstractions:*

- *Tasks*: The units of resource ownership; each task consists of a virtual address space, a port right namespace, and one or more threads. (Similar to a process.)
- *Threads*: The units of CPU execution within a task.
- *Address space*: In conjunction with memory managers, Mach implements the notion of a sparse virtual address space and shared memory.
- *Memory objects*: The internal units of memory management. Memory objects include named entries and regions; they are representations of potentially persistent data that may be mapped into address spaces.
- *Ports*: Secure, simplex communication channels, accessible only via send and receive capabilities (known as port rights).
- *IPC*: Message queues, remote procedure calls, notifications, semaphores, and lock sets.
- *Time*: Clocks, timers, and waiting.

At the trap level, the interface to most Mach abstractions consists of messages sent to and from kernel ports representing those objects.

The trap-level interfaces (such as mach_msg_overwrite_trap) and message formats are themselves abstracted in normal usage by the Mach Interface Generator (MIG).

MIG is used to compile procedural interfaces to the message-based APIs, based on descriptions of those APIs.

## TASKS AND THREADS

Mac OS X processes and POSIX threads (pthreads) are implemented on top of Mach tasks and threads, respectively. A thread is a point of control flow in a task. A task exists to provide resources for the threads it contains.

*This split is made to provide for parallelism and resource sharing:*

- *A thread:*
  - Is a point of control flow in a task.
  - has access to all of the elements of the containing task.
  - executes (potentially) in parallel with other threads, even threads within the same task.
  - has minimal state information for low overhead.
- *A task:*
  - Is a collection of system resources. These resources, with the exception of the address space, are referenced by ports. These resources may be shared with other tasks if rights to the ports are so distributed.
  - Provides a large, potentially sparse address space, referenced by virtual address. Portions of this space may be shared through inheritance or external memory management.
  - Contains some number of threads.

Note that a task has no life of its own-only threads execute instructions. When it is said that "task Y does X," what is really meant is that "a thread contained within task Y does X." A task is a fairly expensive entity. It exists to be a collection of resources.

All of the threads in a task share everything. Two tasks share nothing without an explicit action (although the action is often simple) and some resources (such as port receive rights) cannot be shared between two tasks at all. A thread is a fairly lightweight entity.

It is fairly cheap to create and has low overhead to operate. This is true because a thread has little state information (mostly its register state). Its owning task bears the burden of resource management.

On a multiprocessor computer, it is possible for multiple threads in a task to execute in parallel. Even when parallelism is not the goal, multiple threads have an advantage in that each thread can use a synchronous programming style, instead of attempting asynchronous programming with a single thread attempting to provide multiple services.

A thread is the basic computational entity. A thread belongs to one and only one task that defines its virtual address space. To affect the structure of the address space or to reference any resource other than the address space, the thread must execute a special trap instruction that causes the kernel to perform operations on behalf of the thread or to send a message to some agent on behalf of the thread.

In general, these traps manipulate resources associated with the task containing the thread. Requests can be made of the kernel to manipulate these entities: to create them, delete them, and affect their state.

Mach provides a flexible framework for thread-scheduling policies. Early versions of Mac OS X support both time-sharing and fixed-priority policies. A time-sharing thread's priority is raised and lowered to balance its resource consumption against other time-sharing threads.

Fixed-priority threads execute for a certain quantum of time, and then are put at the end of the queue of threads of equal priority. Setting a fixed priority thread's quantum level to infinity allows the thread to run until it blocks, or until it is preempted by a thread of higher priority. High priority real-time threads are usually fixed priority. Mac OS X also provides time constraint scheduling for real-time performance. This scheduling allows you to specify that your thread must get a certain time quantum within a certain period of time.

## PORTS, PORT RIGHTS, PORT SETS, AND PORT NAMESPACES

With the exception of the task's virtual address space, all other Mach resources are accessed through a level of indirection known as a port. A port is an endpoint of a unidirectional communication channel between a client who requests a service and a server who provides the service. If a reply is to be provided to such a service request, a second port must be used. This is comparable to a (unidirectional) pipe in UNIX parlance.

In most cases, the resource that is accessed by the port (that is, named by it) is referred to as an object. Most objects named by a port have a single receiver and (potentially) multiple senders.

That is, there is exactly one receive port, and at least one sending port, for a typical object such as a message queue. The service to be provided by an object is determined by the manager that receives the request sent to the object.

It follows that the kernel is the receiver for ports associated with kernel-provided objects and that the receiver for ports associated with task-provided objects is the task providing those objects.

For ports that name task-provided objects, it is possible to change the receiver of requests for that port to a different task, for example by passing the port to that task in a message. A single task may have multiple ports that refer to resources it supports.

For that matter, any given entity can have multiple ports that represent it, each implying different sets of permissible operations. For example, many objects have a name port and a control port (sometimes called the privileged port). Access to the control port allows the object to be manipulated; access to the name port simply names the object so that you can obtain information about it or perform other non-privileged operations against it.

Tasks have permissions to access ports in certain ways (send, receive, send-once); these are called port rights. A port can be accessed only via a right. Ports are often used to grant clients access to objects within Mach. Having the right to send to the object's IPC port denotes the right to manipulate the object in prescribed ways. As such, port right ownership is the fundamental security mechanism within Mach. Having a right to an object is to have a capability to access or manipulate that object. Port rights can be copied and moved between tasks via IPC. Doing so, in effect, passes capabilities to some object or server.

One type of object referred to by a port is a port set. As the name suggests, a port set is a set of port rights that can be treated as a single unit when receiving a message or event from any of the members of the set. Port sets permit one thread to wait on a number of message and event sources, for example in work loops.

Traditionally in Mach, the communication channel denoted by a port was always a queue of messages. However, Mac OS X supports additional types of communication channels, and these new types of IPC object are also represented by ports and port rights. See the section "Interprocess Communication (IPC)", for more details about messages and other IPC types.

Ports and port rights do not have systemwide names that allow arbitrary ports or rights to be manipulated directly. Ports can be manipulated by a task only if the task has a port right in its port namespace.

A port right is specified by a port name, an integer index into a 32-bit port namespace. Each task has associated with it a single port namespace.

Tasks acquire port rights when another task explicitly inserts them into its namespace, when they receive rights in messages, by creating objects that return a right to the object, and via Mach calls for certain special ports (mach_thread_self, mach_task_self, and mach_reply_port.)

## MEMORY MANAGEMENT

As with most modern operating systems, Mach provides addressing to large, sparse, virtual address spaces. correspond to locations in physical memory at the initial time of the attempted access.

Mach is responsible for taking a requested virtual address and assigning it a corresponding location in physical memory. It does so through demand paging.

A range of a virtual address space is populated with data when a memory object is mapped into that range. All data in an address space is ultimately provided through memory objects. Mach asks the owner of a memory object (a pager) for the contents of a page when establishing it in physical memory and returns the possibly modified data to the pager before reclaiming the page. Mac OS X includes two built-in pagers-the default pager and the vnode pager.

The default pager handles nonpersistent memory, known as anonymous memory. Anonymous memory is zero-initialized, and it exists only during the life of a task. The vnode pager maps files into memory objects.

Mach exports an interface to memory objects to allow their contents to be contributed by user-mode tasks. This interface is known as the External Memory Management Interface, or EMMI.

The memory management subsystem exports virtual memory handles known as named entries or named memory entries.

Like most kernel resources, these are denoted by ports. Having a named memory entry handle allows the owner to map the underlying virtual memory object or to pass the right to map the underlying object to others.

Mapping a named entry in two different tasks results in a shared memory window between the two tasks, thus providing a flexible method for establishing shared memory.

Beginning in Mac OS X 10.1, the EMMI system was enhanced to support "portless" EMMI. In traditional EMMI, two Mach ports were created for each memory region, and likewise two ports for each cached vnode.

Portless EMMI, in its initial implementation, replaces this with direct memory references (basically pointers). In a future release, ports will be used for communication with pagers outside the kernel, while using direct references for communication with pagers that reside in kernel space.

The net result of these changes is that early versions of portless EMMI do not support pagers running outside of kernel space. This support is expected to be reinstated in a future release.

Address ranges of virtual memory space may also be populated through direct allocation (using vm_allocate). The underlying virtual memory object is anonymous and backed by the default pager. Shared ranges of an address space may also be set up via inheritance. When new tasks are created, they are cloned from a parent. This cloning pertains to the underlying memory address space as well.

Mapped portions of objects may be inherited as a copy, or as shared, or not at all, based on attributes associated with the mappings. Mach practices a form of delayed copy known as copy-on-write to optimize the performance of inherited copies on task creation.

Rather than directly copying the range, a copy-on-write optimization is accomplished by protected sharing. The two tasks share the memory to be copied, but with read-only access. When either task attempts to modify a portion of the range, that portion is copied at that time.

This lazy evaluation of memory copies is an important optimization that permits simplifications in several areas, notably the messaging APIs. One other form of sharing is provided by Mach, through the export of named regions. A named region is a form of a named entry, but instead of being backed by a virtual memory object, it is backed by a virtual map fragment.

This fragment may hold mappings to numerous virtual memory objects. It is mappable into other virtual maps, providing a way of inheriting not only a group of virtual memory objects but also their existing mapping relationships. This feature offers significant optimization in task setup, for example when sharing a complex region of the address space used for shared libraries.

## ARCHITECTURE

The foundation layer of Darwin and Mac OS X is composed of several architectural components, as shown in Figure. Taken together, these components form the kernel environment.

"A kernel, in traditional operating-system terminology, is a small nucleus of software that provides only the minimal facilities necessary for implementing additional operating-system services."-from The Design and Implementation of the 4.4 BSD Operating System, McKusick, Bostic, Karels, and Quarterman, 1996.

Similarly, in traditional Mach-based operating systems, the kernel refers to the Mach microkernel and ignores additional low-level code without which Mach does very little.

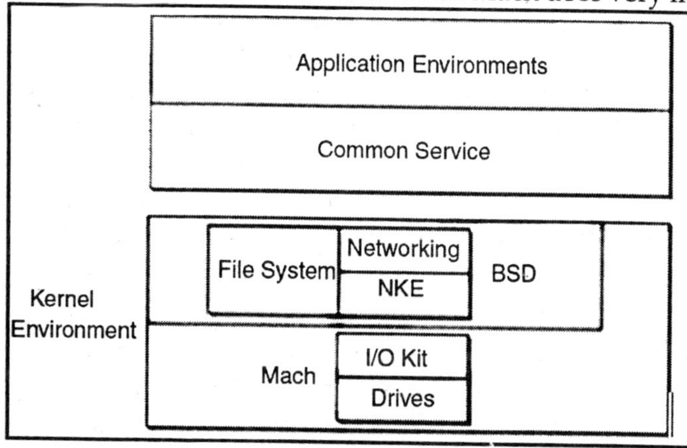


**Fig:** Mac OS X Kernel Architecture

*Important*: Note that Mac OS X uses the term kernel some what differently than you might expect.

In Mac OS X, however, the kernel environment contains much more than the Mach kernel itself. The Mac OS X kernel environment includes the Mach kernel, BSD, the I/O Kit, file systems, and networking components. These are often referred to collectively as the kernel. Each of these components is described briefly in the following sections. For further details, refer to the specific component chapters or to the reference material listed in the bibliography.

Because Mac OS X contains three basic components (Mach, BSD, and the I/O Kit), there are also frequently as many as three APIs for certain key operations. In general, the API chosen should match the part of the kernel where it is being used, which in turn is dictated by what your code is attempting to do. The remainder of this chapter describes Mach, BSD, and the I/O Kit and outlines the functionality that is provided by those components.

## Mach

Mach manages processor resources such as CPU usage

and memory, handles scheduling, provides memory protection, and provides a messaging-centered infrastructure to the rest of the operating-system layers.

*The Mach component provides:*

- Untyped interprocess communication (IPC)
- Remote procedure calls (RPC)
- Scheduler support for symmetric multiprocessing (SMP)
- Support for real-time services
- Virtual memory support
- Support for pagers
- Modular architecture

General information about Mach may be found in the chapter "Mach Overview". Information about scheduling can be found in the chapter "Mach Scheduling and Thread Interfaces".

Information about the VM system can be found in "Memory and Virtual Memory".

## BSD

Above the Mach layer, the BSD layer provides "OS personality" APIs and services. The BSD layer is based on the BSD kernel, primarily FreeBSD.

*The BSD component provides:*

- File systems
- Networking (except for the hardware device level)
- UNIX security model
- Syscall support
- The BSD process model, including process IDs and signals
- FreeBSD kernel APIs
- Many of the POSIX APIs
- Kernel support for pthreads (POSIX threads)

The BSD component is described in more detail in the chapter "BSD Overview".

## NETWORKING

Mac OS X networking takes advantage of BSD's advanced

networking capabilities to provide support for modern features, such as Network Address Translation (NAT) and firewalls.

*The networking component provides:*

- 4.4BSD TCP/IP stack and socket APIs
- Support for both IP and DDP (AppleTalk transport)
- Multihoming
- Routing
- Multicast support
- Server tuning
- Packet filtering
- Mac OS Classic support (through filters)

More information about networking may be found in the chapter "Network Architecture".

## File Systems

Mac OS X provides support for numerous types of file systems, including HFS, HFS+, UFS, NFS, ISO 9660, and others. The default file-system type is HFS+; Mac OS X boots (and "roots") from HFS+, UFS, ISO, NFS, and UDF.

Advanced features of Mac OS X file systems include an enhanced Virtual File System (VFS) design. VFS provides for a layered architecture (file systems are stackable).

*The file system component provides:*

- UTF-8 (Unicode) support
- Increased performance over previous versions of Mac OS.

More information may be found in the chapter "File Systems Overview".

## I/O Kit

The I/O Kit provides a framework for simplified driver development, supporting many categories of devices.The I/O Kit features an object-oriented I/O architecture implemented in a restricted subset of C++. The I/O Kit framework is both modular and extensible.

*The I/O Kit component provides:*

- True plug and play

- Dynamic device management
- Dynamic ("on-demand") loading of drivers
- Power management for desktop systems as well as portables
- Multiprocessor capabilities

The I/O Kit is described in greater detail in the chapter "I/O Kit Overview".

## KERNEL EXTENSIONS

Mac OS X provides a kernel extension mechanism as a means of allowing dynamic loading of pieces of code into kernel space, without the need to recompile. These pieces of code are known generically as plug-ins or, in the Mac OS X kernel environment, as kernel extensions or KEXTs.Because KEXTs provide both modularity and dynamic loadability, they are a natural choice for any relatively self-contained service that requires access to interfaces that are not exported to user space.

Many of the components of the kernel environment support this extension mechanism, though they do so in different ways.

For example, some of the new networking features involve the use of network kernel extensions (NKEs). These are discussed in the chapter "Network Architecture". The ability to dynamically add a new file-system implementation is based on VFS KEXTs.

Device drivers and device families in the I/O Kit are implemented using KEXTs. KEXTs make development much easier for developers writing drivers or those writing code to support a new volume format or networking protocol. KEXTs are discussed in more detail in the chapter "Kernel Extension Overview".

# Bibliography


Brendan, G.: *Component Software: Beyond Object-Oriented Programming*, New York: Columbia University Press, 2007.

Daniel, K.: *On Macintosh Programming: Advanced Techniques*, Philadelphia: Open University Press, 1998.

Donald, E.: *The Art of Computer Programming*, Washington: CQ Press, 2002.

Donald, M.: *The Art of Computer Programming: Fundamental Algorithms*, Ann Arbor: University of Michigan Press. 1999.

Hailperin, M.; *Operating Systems and Middleware: Supporting Controlled Interaction*, MA: Harvard University Press, 2008.

John, M.: *Advanced Programming in the UNIX Environment*, NJ: L. Erlbaum Publications, 2005.

Krogdahl, S.: *From Object-orientation to Formal Methods: Essays in Memory*, N.J: Ablex Publications, 2002.

Krzyszt, R.: *Principles of Constraint Programming*, New York: McGraw-Hill, 1997.

Mark, D.: *Microcomputer Abstracts*, Albany: State University of New York Press, 2004.

Mauro, J.: *Dtrace: Dynamic Tracing in Oracle Solaris, Mac OS X and Freebsd*, Chicago: Nelson-Hall Publishers, 2005.

Pedrozzi, P.: *A Software Tool for the Analysis, Design and Monitoring*, Carbondale: Southern Illinois University Press, 2003.

Randow, R.: *Integer Programming and Related Areas: A Classified*, Chicago: Nelson-Hall Publishers, 2003.

Reed, C.: *Macintosh C Programming Primer: Inside the Toolbox Using Think C*, New York: Teachers College Press, 2007.

Robert, P.: *OpenGL Programming on Mac OS X: Architecture, Performance*, Buckingham: Open University Press, 2006.

Rock, M.: *IEEE Annals of the History of Computing*, Edinburgh: Edinburgh University Press, 2008.

Schrijver, A.: *Theory of Linear and Integer Programming*, New York: Oxford University Press, 1998.

Warden, S.: *Masterminds of Programming*, New York: Holt, Rinehart, and Winston, 1999.

# Index

## A

Algorithm 17, 28, 29, 31, 36, 38, 39, 40, 68, 78, 87, 104, 108, 111, 120, 198, 241
Amiga 20
Anomalies 30
AppleScript 124, 125

## B

Binary 17, 18, 35, 38, 39, 152, 171
Binutils 7
Biochemist 3
Bonjour 128, 131
BootCache 18, 19
Bootloader 8, 9, 14, 15, 146
Bridge 62
Broadband 59, 60, 62, 65

## C

Caller 172, 218
Calloc 158, 166, 173, 175
Catalogs 152
Chronology 47
Cocoa 6, 22, 110, 113, 160, 166, 173, 183, 186, 187, 265
Copland 4, 5, 20

## D

Darwin 5, 6, 7, 8, 142, 148, 152, 262
Debug 9, 13, 55, 78, 146, 159, 163, 173, 174, 175, 177, 178, 179, 180, 181, 182, 183, 184, 185, 186, 187, 188, 190, 204, 214, 216, 220, 244, 245
Decoding 52, 54, 56
Delaying 167
Descriptor 110, 111, 117, 148, 213, 214, 215, 219, 251
Detection 24, 25, 26, 28, 29, 31, 36, 46, 47, 48, 49, 50, 51, 55, 64, 68, 69, 70, 184, 186, 210, 211
Dgraphs 152

Diskutil 136, 137, 138, 139
Divisor 29, 34, 35

E

Explicit 14, 30, 32, 42, 44, 155, 161, 164, 181, 216, 217, 237, 257, 260

F

Fingerprint 27, 28, 30, 33, 34, 37, 40, 41, 42, 46, 47, 48, 49, 50, 51, 52, 53, 54, 55, 56, 57, 58, 59, 60, 61, 62, 66, 67, 68, 70, 71
Firewall 24, 27, 34, 40, 42, 48, 49, 50, 58, 61, 63, 64, 68, 69, 134, 148, 265
Fragile 152, 164

G

Garbage 53, 161, 203

I

Interprocess 198, 199, 260, 264
Inventory 24, 25, 26

K

Kernel 7, 8, 13, 15, 17, 18, 19, 22, 48, 49, 69, 140, 141, 142, 144, 145, 146, 147, 148, 149, 150, 151, 152, 153, 154, 162, 163, 167, 168, 200, 202, 207, 208, 209, 210, 212, 213, 214, 215, 216, 217, 218, 219, 220, 221, 222, 223, 224, 225, 228, 231, 232, 233, 239, 243, 244, 246, 247, 249, 250, 251, 252, 253, 254, 255, 256, 258, 259, 261, 262, 263, 264, 266

L

Laureate 3
Libkern 150, 151, 152, 232, 251, 252
Linux 7, 13, 15, 21, 22, 23, 25, 27, 48, 49, 52, 53, 57, 59, 60, 62, 68, 69, 73, 82, 95, 100, 127

M

MacOSX 19, 141, 142, 144
Malloc 158, 159, 160, 161, 162, 163, 164, 165, 166, 173, 174, 175, 176, 177, 178, 179, 180, 181, 182, 183, 184, 185, 186, 187, 188, 189, 190, 191, 195, 218, 219, 232, 251, 253, 255

N

Navigat 117, 118, 119, 121, 122,

123, 124
Nonzero 42, 43, 44, 46

## O

Origins 1

## P

Partition 2, 13, 14, 15, 134, 135, 137, 138, 139, 152
Polygon 75, 84, 85, 86, 87
Popup 133, 134, 177, 185
Predictability 35, 36
Prediction 29, 53
Premature 201
Priority 223, 224, 225, 226, 227, 229, 230, 236, 258
Probes 14, 24, 30, 31, 32, 34, 35, 36, 37, 38, 39, 40, 46, 47, 54, 61, 62
Proxy 64, 69

## Q

Queue 48, 49, 126, 127, 128, 129, 131, 132, 133, 134, 149, 198, 199, 200, 223, 231, 234, 235, 236, 237, 238, 251, 256, 258, 259, 260

## R

Rhapsody 5, 6, 20
Router 24, 27, 28, 32, 40, 41, 59, 60, 62, 64, 65, 134

## S

Semaphores 198, 200, 234, 236, 256
Setgid 180
Shared 32, 37, 127, 128, 131, 150, 164, 165, 170, 172, 196, 202, 203, 204, 205, 210, 212, 219, 240, 241, 256, 257, 261, 262
Smashing 188, 191

## T

Tailoring exploits 25
TextEdit 123, 193, 195
Threads 146, 147, 158, 159, 200, 223, 224, 225, 226, 227, 229, 231, 232, 233, 236, 237, 240, 241, 243, 256, 257, 258, 264
Toolkit 104, 105
Transistors 80, 81, 82, 85

## U

Uptime 28
Usage 27, 155, 157, 167, 169, 170, 172, 173, 175, 176, 177, 178, 179, 184, 191, 192, 197, 236, 256, 263

## V

Vertex 74, 76, 77, 79, 82, 83, 84, 86, 87, 90, 91, 92, 93, 98, 99, 100, 104, 107

Vulnerability 24, 25

## W

Web Page 2, 130